Genethics

Genethics

Moral Issues in the Creation of People

David Heyd

UNIVERSITY OF CALIFORNIA PRESS
Berkeley · Los Angeles · Oxford

University of California Press
Berkeley and Los Angeles, California

University of California Press
Oxford, England

Copyright © 1992 by The Regents of the University of California

Library of Congress Cataloging-in-Publication Data

Heyd, David.
    Genethics : moral issues in the creation of people / David Heyd.
        p.   cm.
    Includes bibliographical references and index.
    ISBN 0-520-07714-8 (cloth)
    1. Medical ethics.   2. Human reproductive technology—Moral and
ethical aspects.   3. Creation.   4. Bioethics.   I. Title.
R724.H49   1992
174'.2—dc20   91-30300
                                                                                CIP

Printed in the United States of America

1   2   3   4   5   6   7   8   9

The paper used in this publication meets the minimum requirements of American
National Standard for Information Sciences—Permanence of Paper for Printed Library
Materials, ANSI Z39.48-1984 ⊚

To Milly, my other half in genethical choice, and to Uriel, who has proven it our best choice.

Contents

Preface

The relatively short history of the ethics of procreation happens to coincide with the history of my professional work in philosophy. My first assignment as a teaching assistant to Joseph Raz in the late 1960s at the Hebrew University was to mark papers dealing with Jan Narveson's pioneering article on utilitarianism and new generations. My attitude toward the attempt to extend ethical theory to what are now known as "genesis choices" was already then skeptical (though still lacking theoretical foundation). As a graduate student in the 1970s I was attracted to the growing philosophical discussion of the moral standing of future people, both through Rawls's influential sections on intergenerational justice in *A Theory of Justice* and in a seminar in Oxford given jointly by Derek Parfit, Jonathan Glover, and James Griffin. Being intrigued by Parfit's sophisticated analysis of the paradoxes involved in the ethics of creating people, culminating in his book *Reasons and Persons,* I started in the 1980s to investigate the possibility of a consistent person-affecting view that would resolve, or at least obviate, Parfit's paradoxes (Heyd 1988). A person-affecting approach to morality holds (contrary to its impersonal rival) that value is analytically related to the needs and wants, interests and ideals of actual human beings and cannot be ascribed "to the world." The first "wrongful life" suit that reached the Supreme Court of Israel in 1986 provided me with a real-life yet theoretically pure test case.

Any metaphysically tricky issue such as the moral standing of future

generations naturally makes a good conversation piece in nonphilo-
sophical circles as well as a stimulant for intense philosophical debate. I
have gradually become aware that the solution to problems of procreation calls for a systematic approach in which the topic of the creation
of people would be tackled from a wide variety of perspectives. The
issue of population (the number of people to be created) cannot be
isolated from the question of the value of the very existence of human
beings; the creation of people is conceptually connected to decisions
regarding their identity. Consequently, I have defined *genethics* as the
field concerned with the morality of creating people, that is, decisions
regarding their existence, number, and identity. Genethics provides a
common theoretical framework for the analysis of ethical aspects of
population policies, family planning, genetic engineering, education,
environmental ethics, intergenerational justice, "wrongful life" cases,
and even the theology of creation. As the bibliography of this book
indicates, the literature on justice and future generations has prolifer-
ated quickly in the past two decades, but philosophers have been reluc-
tant to take such a broad approach, let alone defend such a radically
person-affecting thesis as the one suggested here.

My primary motivation in studying "genesis problems" has been the
theoretical search for the limits of ethics. The application of ethical
principles to intergenerational relations, especially toward future (potential) people, provides one of the most fruitful ways of examining the
deepest problems of the nature of value and the scope of moral principles. So despite the practical urgency of most of the issues discussed in
this book, my aim is usually more theoretical. The method of treating
the issues of procreation may therefore seem highly abstract and some
of the examples farfetched and fantastical, but this is inevitable in a
work that tries to outline the borderline of ethical theory rather than to
supply specific guidelines for medical ethics, judicial decisions, or population policies.

Any attempt to pay dues to all the people who helped me in forming
the ideas presented in this book is bound to fail. I have engaged throughout the long years of this project in so many conversations, debates, and
colloquia, so much written correspondence, and more formal presenta-
tions, that I can only hope to be able to discharge my duty of gratitude
indirectly, in the book itself. However, I wish to acknowledge my debt
and express my gratitude to Jan Narveson and Partha Dasgupta, who
read the entire manuscript with the most constructive blend of sympathy and incisive criticism; to Eddy Zemach, an indefatigable challenger,

who always appreciated the project though never agreed to the main thesis; and to James Griffin, Christine Korsgaard, Bernard Williams, Onora O'Neill, Joseph Raz, Moshe Halbertal, and Ruth Gavison, who made me believe that the work was worth pursuing while showing where the argument was worth rethinking. My students in two seminars on justice and future generations contributed significantly to the development of my ideas.

Realizing that some readers might be less interested in the polemical aspects of the argument, I decided to relegate most of the critical discussion of other views to the endnotes. It is hoped that the body of the text is self-sufficient in conveying the main thread of the argument. This is presented in the introduction, and in chapters 4, 5, 6, and 8, with chapters 1, 2, 3, and 7 serving as a necessary methodological, "historical," and empirical support. In the absence of any foundationalist or solid intuitive starting point from which the elusive problem of the morality of creating new people can be tackled, I can only hope to prove the force of my thesis through a global picture. There is no knockdown argument to show that the view suggested here is the correct one, but neither is there such an argument for the opposite view. This makes genethics an exciting and fruitful philosophical field: theoretically new, metaphysically perplexing, logically paradoxical, morally pressing, and existentially relevant.

The Hebrew University of Jerusalem
June 1991

Introduction: Playing God

And God said, Let us make man in our image, after our
likeness: and let them have dominion over the fish of the
sea, and over the fowl of the air, and over the cattle, and
over all the earth, and over every creeping thing that
creepeth upon the earth. So God created man in his own
image, in the image of God created he him; male and female
created he them. And God blessed them, and God said unto
them, Be fruitful, and multiply, and replenish the earth, and
subdue it: and have dominion over the fish of the sea, and
over the fowl of the air, and over every living thing that
moveth upon the earth. . . . And God saw every thing that
he had made, and, behold, it was very good.

Genesis I:26–28, 31

Any systematic and well-argued essay should start "in the beginning,"
especially if its very subject is "beginnings." The verses quoted above
are a beginning in more than one sense. They belong to the first chapter
of the first book of the Bible. They also describe the way humanity
started by a divine act of creation. We are not concerned here, however,
with either the literary or the theological significance of these verses.
Rather, I cite them at the outset of this book because they represent one
of the earliest attempts in Western thought to deal with the puzzling
philosophical problem that will be the topic of the following chapters.
But again, we are less interested in the historical beginning of that
philosophical problem than in the logically pure form in which it is
presented by the biblical text. It is this *conceptual* sense of beginning,
that of complete idealization and total abstraction from any further
contingent (human) complications, which makes God's words and
works on the sixth day of creation our starting point.

Playing on biblical connotations, the economist Partha Dasgupta has

1

coined the term "genesis problem" as a name for the idealized context of decision making regarding population policies. Thus he defines a genesis problem as one that concerns *potential* rather than actual human beings. The question it raises is how many people should be created. In pure form it occurs when no actual people exist (Dasgupta 1987, 640; Dasgupta 1988, 110). This is exactly the scene of Genesis I, where God considers the creation *ex nihilo* of the first human being (or rather the first human couple).

However, a close reading of the biblical text will show that God's genesis problem is of a wider scope than the demographic sense suggested by Dasgupta's metaphorical use. Before deciding the number of humans to be created, God has to choose whether to create them at all. Then he has to decide what sort of creatures they are going to be. Only then can the question of number arise. Three questions are thus involved in the original genesis problem: the existence, the identity, and the number of people to be created. In the biblical text they are all (at least implicitly) decided on one and the same ground: the replication and multiplication of God's image in the world. The value of the replication of God's image is the reason given for Man's creation. But it also serves to determine the nature of created Man, his identity; human beings should have the traits that make them "like" God. And their number should be as large as possible so as to permeate the world with God's image.

But the Genesis text also hints at what Dasgupta might have called the "impure" genesis problem, that is to say genesis problems in contexts where there already *are* human beings and the question is whether to create any *more,* of what kind, and how many. From the point of view of the present discussion the important trait that makes human beings resemble God is their power to multiply. The transformation of God's power of creation into the human power of procreation is the means of spreading God's image in the world. Indeed this power is also granted to animals; but by a clear—though linguistically minor—change in wording the blessing "Be fruitful and multiply" becomes in the case of human beings an *injunction* (actually the first one), which in later theological developments places it very high in the order of religious responsibilities and duties. It is a unique commandment, because it is the existential basis for the very possibility of all other commandments. It is conscious procreation rather than simple biological propagation which is the object of the first (moral) duty. Transforming the instinctual sexual drive, which in the case of animals can be only "a blessing," into a matter of rational will and choice, which in the human sphere becomes a prescription, is that which makes procreation an ethical subject.

So after the creation of Adam and Eve populating the earth becomes the business of human beings. God's pure genesis problem is handed on to humans who have to solve it in the light of the guiding principle of the replication and multiplication of God's image in the world. There is a long tradition of interpretations of the idea and nature of God's image, all concentrating on the spiritual similarity of human beings to God as manifested in holiness, rationality or intellect, consciousness, immortality of the soul, the capacity to choose between right and wrong (justice), or in having the divine "breath" of spiritual life (Genesis II:7). However, the only interpretive clue explicitly suggested by the original text is that human beings resemble God in their creative power, expressed primarily by their procreative capacity to replenish the world and secondarily by their power to subdue nature to their own purpose. In other words, God replicates himself and his dominion in the created world by the mediation of human multiplication and dominion, which itself is the image of God's creative power.[1] Human beings take over the sustenance of the divine plan of creation of the first six days, and by thus doing assume a divine image.

This interpretation of the notion of "God's image" as referring to the act of creation of beings resembling the creator is explicitly corroborated by the later version in Genesis V: 1–3:

> This is the book of the generations of Adam. In the day that God created man, in the likeness of God made he him. Male and female created he them. . . . And Adam lived a hundred and thirty years, and begat a son in his own likeness, after his image; and called his name Seth.

Divine creation and human procreation are guided by the same principle and motive. However, as I am going to argue, human creative power should not be understood as merely the biological capacity to create more of the same kind, but in a wider, more abstract sense, as the only source of value in the world. By their very will, human beings *invest* a valueless world with value—admittedly a heterodox interpretation of the idea of *imitatio Dei*. This interpretation will be offered here as a metaphysical model for a secular ethical theory of procreation rather than as an exegetical reading of the biblical text. The reader is again cautioned not to take this book as an essay in natural theology.

Human decisions on matters of procreation are complicated by the fact that these decisions bear on the decision makers and also on their capacity to "subdue the earth." As we shall see later in the book, there is a close connection between the blessing of multiplication and that of domination (of nature), that is, between demography and economics, the quantity of future human beings and the quality of their lives. Unlike God, human beings can be negatively affected by over-multiplication and over-dominion of the world. Furthermore, on what grounds should human beings base their decisions regarding the future of humanity if they happen to be agnostic about the idea or the value of spreading God's image? It is indeed with this secularized version of the "impure" genesis problem that we are concerned.

This is why we take the celestial story of creation only as an abstraction of the very terrestrial dilemmas of the ethics of human procreation. This theoretical idealization of the kind of considerations involved in human reproductive choices is best captured by the metaphor of "playing God," which is so often used in the context of human power to decide the very future of humanity. We are said to play God whenever we make choices concerning abortion, genetic engineering, the basic conditions of future life on the planet, interference with evolutionary processes, or any radical tampering with the allegedly "natural" development of human beings and their environment. Playing God is almost universally condemned as an unauthorized human intervention in a divine plan or in a natural process, an arrogant transgression of legitimate bounds of action in the world. However, if indeed the capacity to invest the world with value *is* God's image, it elevates human beings to a unique (godly) status, which is not shared by any other creature in the world. This is playing God in a creative, "human-specific" way.

Furthermore, the pure genesis problem raises in a trenchant manner the general question of the nature and source of value: if the world as a whole does not exist, how can its creation be considered good? Or, alternatively, if no human beings exist (in the inanimate world created in the first five days), how can their creation be considered of any value? God retrospectively judges his creation as "very good," but what kind of good is it? There are two possible responses to this question. The first is to take the *impersonal* wording of the biblical verse literally, that is to say the state of affairs after Man's creation is better than the one preceding it. It will be a major thesis in the following chapters that such a view of value is problematic or may even lead to paradoxes. Furthermore, it implies that God is serving a certain independent value system rather than constituting it. The second is to view the value of the newly created state of affairs to God, that is to say to see it as good *for him*. This latter reading gains support from the reasoning behind the choice to create human beings, namely the replication of God's image. God wants his image to permeate the world. The theological drawback of this interpretation is that God is usually not considered as having interests or pleasures and that these cannot therefore serve as the basis for the value of his works. God is self-sufficient in his perfect and infinite existence; why should he need (desire) his image to be vicariously augmented by human procreation? Even more difficult is the case of the world being created by a completely nonpersonal force or process: how can the value of its very existence be accounted for? Can coming into existence have value?

It seems that the *im*pure genesis context, that of human beings deciding on the existence of future human beings, is the clue for unraveling the puzzling issue of the value of the creation of humanity. For, as we shall see, in the less pure, more contingent, contexts of human *procreation*, the actual decision makers are the reference point for the source of value. If indeed replication and multiplication are considered by human beings as something good, then these procedures can be easily understood as good *for them*. So the genesis problem that in its pure godly form might look either logically puzzling or metaphysically mysterious can be more easily dealt with in its impure human form. Justifying the view that value is always derived from its effects on valuers is easier and more natural in the human (anthropocentric) sphere than in its metaphysical (theocentric) counterpart. Nevertheless, the pure divine version of Genesis draws for us the conceptual contours of our problem.

Without then claiming any theological insight or linguistic expertise in biblical interpretation, the following reading of the verses from Genesis is suggested as the framework for the nonreligious argument that will be developed in the following chapters: God, the personal creator of the universe, having completed the creation of the inanimate world, the flora and fauna, considers a further creation of a unique creature—one that will resemble God himself in two respects: being able to procreate creatures of the same kind without further divine help, and consequently to rule all the rest of the world in the sense of making it have value. But this unorthodox interpretation holds that the value of the world after the creation of humanity does not arise out of the addition of any precious and valuable furniture to it, but in the creation of subjects *for whom* things (which so far have been valueless) can be of any value! God's deliberation about the prospective creation is conducted in the plural form—understood either as a "pluralis majestatis" ceremonial formula (for instance by Sa'adia Gaon), or as referring to a grand consultation of God with the angels (primarily by Rashi, who regards it as a proof of God's humility), or as an indication of the cooperation of divine and earthly forces in the creation of human beings (Nachmanides). But whatever the meaning of "us," the reasons for creating Adam and Eve have to do with God's wishes, interests, good. God wants his image multiplied and his dominion extended in the world through the mediation of human beings. The success of divine creation is epitomized in the words "behold, it was very good," that is, success in terms of God's satisfaction of the way things have turned out *for him*. But note that the image that God wants to aggrandize in the world according to our reading is the very power of transforming valueless things and states of affairs into things of value through the creation of the necessary condition for the existence of value, namely valuers.

Now, if indeed the existence of valuers (for whom things might be good) is, as we shall claim throughout this book, a necessary condition for anything being of value, then it is either God or human beings (or both) which are the reference points for any assignment of value. The world created stage by stage is said to be good for God (in his eyes), but, as most interpretations of Genesis point out, it is created so as to be good specifically for *man*. It must be "settled" and tilled by human beings, in order for it to become valuable. In that respect human beings must perpetuate themselves so as to secure the ongoing value of the created world. This is the cosmic design (which is of value for God). This way of reading the text can explain the duty we owe to God to be fertile and increase, as indeed is the basic rabbinic understanding.

However, if God's existence is denied, human beings are left as the only reference point or "source" of value in the world. They themselves become God, in the sense that they have full sovereignty over the existence of value. The story of creation becomes a metaphor for the human position in pure genesis context of procreation. Human beings are forced to play God in a God-less world. Although they do not share the omnipotence of God, they have "dominion" over the world in the radical sense that the very continuation of the existence of any value in and of the world is dependent on their begetting valuers. In a God-less world there is no cosmic plan or transcendental design that makes humans the sovereign rulers of the earth; but without their existence as subjects for whom the earth can be of value, the earth will remain valueless. This is the nonstandard understanding of "dominion," and the way human beings "subdue" the nonhuman world.[2]

Human beings, whether they believe in God and the story of their creation, or in biological evolution and gradual development out of lower forms of life, can play God exactly in those two senses: they have control over the existence and number of future people, and they are the source of value of the rest of the natural world. Although the omnipotent creative power of the Word or fiat is transformed into a more limited capacity of sexual procreation, human beings—with their "divine" qualities of rationality, consciousness, and free will—can *choose* whether and how to continue the original celestial design (or alternatively, if they do not believe in such a design, how to devise a human design in a world devoid of any kind of cosmic plan).

If God is believed to exist, then it is this very nature of being able to choose which makes human beings subject to the religious injunctions "be fruitful and multiply" and "subdue the earth." It is their responsibility *to God* which guides both family planning and ecological policies. However, if it is assumed that no God exists and no preceding design in the evolution of humanity can be found, can there be any commandment regarding the use of human (pro)creative power? To whom are people answerable? It is the thesis of this essay that they can have no such duty or responsibility beyond that to their own selves. It is exactly in that respect that they "play God"—a solitary and egocentric game. As it is absurd to ask to whom God owes the creation of Man, so it is absurd in a God-less world to ask to whom does Man owe the perpetuation of the human race.[3] In other words, procreation can only be seen as the necessary condition for all moral virtues and relations, but not itself a moral prescription or duty.

Obviously, an "impersonal" reading of the same text suggests itself as an alternative to this theocentric or anthropocentric interpretation. The goodness of creation is independent of God's wishes. The world with human beings replenishing it and ruling over it is simply better than a world without them. It is a more valuable state of affairs, because there is more of God, or of his image in it.[4] Support for this reading comes from the second biblical version of the story of Man's creation in Genesis II, where Man is said to be created with a *telos,* that of tilling the soil and tending the Garden of Eden. Similarly, on the assumption that no God exists, a world with human beings living in harmony with their environment is better than a barren, human-less universe, or a world of unbalanced ecology. Whereas in the first reading, "playing God" is understood as an *absolute* power of constituting the world in the light of one's goals and interests, the second reading takes "playing

God" in the pejorative-critical sense of overstepping one's designated role, an illegitimate interference with an antecedently given natural design.

These two interpretations have rarely been sharply distinguished and contrasted with each other, and both readings have historically been the source of conflicting approaches to genesis problems as well as to the ethics of environmental concern. The following chapters will contrast the two philosophical views underlying the two interpretations and their ethical implications. The Genesis story provides us with only a first approximation of a profound theoretical issue regarding both the nature of value and the ethics of shaping the future. It serves us as a sort of *Gedankenexperiment,* a model for what is considered playing God in the nonplayful sense of the word. It can be highly illustrative of the unique conceptual difficulties involved in a whole range of issues sometimes referred to as "futurity problems."

Typically the antiquity of the theological inquiry into the pure genesis problem of creation can be matched with the novelty of the ethical examination of the parallel impure version of human procreation. The reason for this is quite simple: only in the past century or so has humanity made rapid progress towards an unprecedented degree of control over the reproductive process, thereby making the compliance with the injunction of propagation a highly complicated and moot issue. Replenishing the earth with people is no longer just a natural practice over which individuals and societies have little discretion. It has become a major ethical dilemma due to a whole new repertory of options out of which people can and have to choose.

For the first time in human history the future *existence* of humanity as such has become a matter of choice. A vast nuclear disaster, either as a result of war or as the outcome of a major accident in a faulty plant could pose a real menace to the very existence of human life (or indeed any life) on the planet. The continuation of the species is, therefore, no longer a natural phenomenon threatened only by natural catastrophes (cosmic or evolutionary), but the responsibility of the existing generation that has the power literally to destroy itself together with all prospects of human life.[5] Environmentalists regularly warn us also about the more gradual forms of collective suicide, such as the accumulation of radioactivity, interference with the protective ozone layers of the atmosphere, or the irreversible pollution of vital resources like water and air.

For those who are less impressed by the doomsday prophecies of gloomy ecologists, simpler indications of the newly acquired power "to play God" can be found in recent developments in human control over reproduction, that is to say over the *number* (although secondarily of course also the existence) of future people. On the individual level, modern techniques of contraception have made the size of one's family a matter of planning, and planning requires decision making and choice. The limited effectiveness of older methods of contraception (and abortion) made the commandment to propagate difficult to violate. But today, at least in developed countries, the primary decision on the number of future members in a family lies fully with the parents.

On the collective level there are also radical changes in the power of societies to regulate the numbers of their members. In the past, societies could to some extent keep desired demographic balances under control by determining the age of marriage or by encouraging (or discouraging) chastity. However, most demographic changes and the formation of demographic balances were in the past a matter of spontaneous social (or biological) adjustment rather than of a conscious political decision. Today, demographic trends in any society have become the responsibility of governments, that is, have become the subject of a policy. To enforce population policies, societies have at their disposal various means, of varying degrees of compulsion: educational, economic, and legal. Most of these rely on medical advances in contraceptive devices and thus have no precedents in social history. The sense of urgency, however, in countering Malthusian trends of overpopulation is, for a variety of reasons, also historically unprecedented. Refraining from exercising restraint may create what is referred to today as a "population bomb."

An even more dramatic illustration of how the discussion of genesis problems is forced on us by scientific and technological developments is genetic engineering. Here we are dealing with another aspect of the godly creative power acquired by human beings, the ability to shape the nature or *identity* of human offspring. By sophisticated screening methods we can for the first time manipulate ("negatively") the human gene pool by eliminating from it certain (undesirable) genes. But by extending our present knowledge of eugenic techniques from plants and lower animals to the human sphere, we will be able in the not-too-distant future to "mold" children by ("positively") deciding at least some of their qualities. Brave New World technology of a similar kind is available in brain surgery and radical chemical intervention in the human nervous system. In all these cases we suspect that the depth of the intervention merits the title of a change in identity, thus raising a genesis problem. Furthermore, medical progress poses a threat over the quality of the gene pool, for example, by the fact that more children with genetic defects are "saved" from natural abortion or from death before the age of fertility. Brainwashing and indeed basic forms of education and upbringing will be discussed in the following chapters under the category of identity-shaping, although they are by no means historically new.

One should note, however, that a much less dramatic means of determining the identity of future persons is deciding the *timing* of their conception. A child conceived now will have an identity completely different to that of a child conceived in two months' time. In the modern age we are not only in control of the timing of conception (as part of family planning), but we are also aware of the dangers of conceiving a child at a certain time rather than waiting a while so as to conceive a healthy child (or for that matter a child with better social or economic prospects) in its stead. By providing us with the knowledge and ability to control the timing of pregnancies, modern science has endowed our generation with an unprecedented power of deciding (at least in a negative way, analogous to genetic screening and amniocentesis) the identity of people in a far from trivial sense.

On a grander scale, the combination of negative and positive genetic manipulation and other techniques of deep personality change could lead to a total transformation of the nature of the human species. Natural selection would give way to artificial preselection, making future generations the product of our creative power, interests, and whims. This (so far sci-fi) scenario would crown us either as gods or as the masters of biological evolution (depending on one's metaphysical beliefs). And it will get us very close to a practical, real-life context of a pure genesis problem (although never absolutely pure, since we, the creators, will always remain actual beings with particular interests and values).

Like previous scientific and technological revolutions that have modified our sensibilities in the past, twentieth-century developments in reproductive control profoundly challenge our long-established modes of thought about future generations: their moral status, their rights, their claims on us. Until not long ago future people were considered as a "given" natural part of the world in which people acted and which morally constrained their conduct. Not only were future people's existence, number, and identity mostly beyond direct human control, but the *quality* of their future life was also only marginally affected by the existing generation's behavior. The modern age has given us the effective tools of long-term economic and technological investments (the benefits of which would be reaped only by our descendants), the power to manage vital but scarce resources in a way that would make future life on earth possible and worthwhile, the knowledge of the means of leaving posterity with an environment free from radioactive waste and with sufficient fresh water and clean air. This puts any generation under a heavy responsibility of a qualitatively new sort: it extends the sphere of moral relations into the *inter*-generational dimension.

It is, however, our primary conceptual concern to distinguish between the first kind of problems (genesis problems) concerning the existence number and identity of future people and the second set of issues regarding the way any generation takes care of the interests and standard of living of future generations (whose existence, number, and identity are "given"). This distinction has sometimes been blurred by recent passionate discussions of environmental ethics, biomedical issues, and the persistent pleas for ecological responsibility. The second category of problems is for ideological reasons much more widely discussed in the philosophical literature of the past decades and illustrates what was called by Peter Singer "the expanding circle" of the subjects of moral concern. Following the gradual introduction into the moral domain of women, people of other races, children, animals, and even plants and inanimate objects, future people have also become candidates for moral consideration.

The main difference between the two kinds of problems is that only the former (genesis problems) raise the unique logical metaphysical and therefore ethical puzzle of the status of *potential* beings, that is to say beings whose existence is not only remote in time but totally dependent on our choice. There is a clear (though sometimes unnoticed) distinction between the question whether we should have another child in the family and the question whether to move out of an asbestos built house so that our future children will not be subject to health hazards. No doubt in the impure context of human genesis problems there is an intimate and intricate relation between the two categories. Thus, unlike God who created humanity *en bloc* with the rest of nature and *ex nihilo*, we plan our families and shape our population policies on the basis of awareness both of the existence of future *un*planned people and of the limited space and resources that will be at their disposal. This complex relationship between principles of genesis and principles of ecology and just savings will require special attention.

So although both types of questions are equally new, owing to their common basis in technological breakthroughs, only the genesis problem is of unique philosophical interest. This can be illustrated by the attempt to apply traditional ethical theories to questions concerning future generations. It seems that with certain adjustments one can devise solutions for economic planning, conservation policies, abortion and care of fetuses, or the maintenance of the historical and artistic heritage in terms of utilitarian, Kantian, or Aristotelian principles. However, when applied to pure genesis problems these principles seem to lead to a conceptual dead end or to yield paradoxes. Accordingly, we seem to be on firm ground in arguing for the prohibition of manufacturing goods now which will prove hazardous to the health of babies in ten years' time. But we lose our moral conviction and philosophical assurance when confronted with a "wrongful life" case in which a child sues his or her parents for having been born. At least part of this philosophical confusion may be ascribed to the growing suspicion, associated with ethical individualism, regarding the validity of impersonal values and eternal moral truths. As we shall see, skeptical trends regarding historicism and impersonalism in ethics undermine consistent solutions to genesis problems.

Genesis problems are therefore unique, not in being new, or in requiring novel adaptation of ethical principles, but in the fact that they resist any kind of ethical treatment. They are novel in the more radical sense of raising the question of the precondition of any meaningful ethical discourse. Here the extension of intragenerational principles of justice to the intergenerational sphere will not suffice, since the question at hand relates not to the borderline of the "moral circle" and the way to deal with those included in it, but to the very creation of its members, to the choice of expanding it. We are here interested in the question of the limits of ethical theory rather than the limits of moral concern.

The question of future generations is of general theoretical interest, since, as we shall see, it touches upon the very limits of ethics, the grounds for the attribution of value, and the logical conditions of moral relations. Pure genesis problems, or their real-life modern impure counterparts, serve as a unique test case for both our moral intuitions and our existing ethical principles. They are of special philosophical interest, for on the one hand they intuitively seem to have a particular moral significance, yet on the other hand the theoretical examination of their nature raises skeptical reflections about their having any ethical meaning. Human choices in genesis contexts will be shown to lie beyond the borders of ethics in the same way as God's celestial consultation (with the angels or with himself) regarding the creation of Man could not have been guided by principles of duty (of the creator) or of right (of the created).

Against this background one should hardly wonder why the theological rendering of the genesis of humanity is difficult to translate into ethical terms, or that the questioning of God's moral motives in this context sounds bizarre.[6] Theoretical interest in genesis problems has emerged only after being forced on us by the new dilemmas of demography, genetic manipulation, "wrongful life" cases, and self-imposed threats to the very future of the human race. Although moral theory has always been interested in the future in the sense of the consequences of human behavior, it is only since the late 1960s that philosophers have become directly concerned with genesis problems. In a pioneering article Jan Narveson (1967) investigated the uniqueness of the moral problem of the duty to procreate in the light of utilitarian theories. Then came John Rawls (1971) in the first systematic discussion of obligations to future generations in terms of a deontological theory of justice. And, of course, Derek Parfit has done more than any other philosopher in the past two decades toward the clarification of the special status of genesis problems. In a series of articles and a whole section of his book (Parfit 1984, pt. 4) Parfit formulated the agenda for the philosophical discussion of the topic and offered a series of imaginative and provocative arguments and examples that have served as the focus for the scores of articles devoted to these problems in recent years.

Do we have an obligation to bring new people into the world? Do we have a duty to have happy children? to avoid having miserable children? Is there a right to be born, or a right not to be born, or a right to be born healthy? Can moral principles guide us in an artificial genetic molding of humans? Is a world with n happy persons morally better than a world with no persons at all? than a world with $\frac{1}{2}n$ equally happy persons? than a world with $2n$ persons who are only mildly happy? Is there a value in the existence (and perpetuation) of the human species as such, regardless of the quality of life of its members? These are some of the questions involved in genesis situations, or at least implied (or presupposed) by them.

In the present discussion we are primarily interested in contrasting two basic approaches to the analysis and solution of these issues. The first, tacitly expressed by the divine conclusion of the act of creation ("and, behold, it was very good"), ascribes value to states of affairs in an impersonal, nonrelative manner. The second, implied by both the reasoning behind the creation of Man and the sense in which humanity is given the dominion over nature, is typically agent-relative, theocentric, or—in Parfit's wording (referring to Narveson)—"person-affecting," or "person-regarding." The great majority of moral philosophers—past and present—hold some form of the former view, in which genesis problems appear (I shall argue only at first sight) to be less troublesome. But those who prefer any version of the latter are confronted with a serious difficulty in genesis situations: whose good is served by procreation? Whose rights are involved? The person-affecting approach raises the logical issue of the attribution of rights and interests of potential people. Some philosophers believe that these can have a moral standing, and thus may on some issues agree with the "impersonal" approach (although for different reasons). Others (though not many) claim that only actual persons can be subjects for moral consideration and hence arrive at skeptical conclusions regarding moral theorization and guidelines for genesis problems.

Although this distinction does not refer to a neat Grand Division of positions, but rather to a spectrum of varying degrees of commitment to "impersonalism," it can safely be said that the tendency of most traditional ethical theory is to the first approach (Aristotle, Bentham, Marx—as typical representatives). Spinoza and Nietzsche might serve as examples for the second approach, insisting on the analysis of goodness in the human-relative terms of good *for*. However, it is in itself a telling fact that such classification of moral theories is a difficult enterprise, and partly a matter of interpretation. The reason is that moral philosophers were hardly confronted by genesis problems and thus were lacking the ultimate test case for their analysis.

This book is an attempt to strengthen the case for the minority approach. But once a human-relative approach to value is adopted, genesis problems raise the question *who* are the human subjects relative to whom value predication is made possible? Most contemporary writers who address the problem of future generations try to include future people in the category of such subjects. But this move will be shown to be logically inappropriate as far as potential people are concerned. Hence, the moral standing of the subjects of genesis problems cannot be accounted for either in terms of impersonal theory of value or in terms of person-affecting theory when the persons affected are those whose existence is deliberated. The only remaining analysis of pure genesis problems is thus an *agent*-relative approach, anchoring all value in the actual decision-making party. This implies the nonstandard interpretation of the biblical story: the creation of Man is not good *tout court*, nor is it good for Man; it is good for God.

This is admittedly a fairly radical view, for which there are not too many advocates. Some of the supporters of the minority person-affecting view shun its meta-ethically skeptical implications and what seems to be the morally repugnant (egoistic) guidelines offered by it for the solution of genesis problems. They try to escape these implications by granting rights to potential people. They present strong objections with which we shall have to deal in detail. Our line of defense would consist of two fronts: first, it will be shown that the alternative views (both impersonalism and attributing moral standing to potential people) lead to conclusions that are even more counterintuitive and hard to live by; secondly, some of the harsh implications of a person-affecting analysis of genesis problems are mitigated by empirical considerations regarding some deeply rooted psychological traits of human beings and the "impurity" of real-life genesis situations due to generational overlap. Not only is there a strong built-in human impulse to have children, our own welfare is to a large extent dependent on theirs because each generation lives for quite a time with its descendants.[7]

It is therefore the purpose of this book not to challenge widespread first-order moral convictions regarding the dilemmas of shaping future people, but rather to use genesis problems as a new, external, standpoint for the theoretical examination of the nature of value, the logical preconditions of moral relations, and the limits of ethics. Many of our basic intuitions regarding the undesirability of conceiving a defective child or the wrongness of overpopulation will remain intact by philosophical argument, but their justification will turn out to be different to that usually assumed. Rather than sermonizing on ecological, biomedical, and demographic issues, the purpose of this work is to offer a systematic and coherent theoretical framework for the discussion of these issues with their implications and ramifications.

The "impurity" of real-life genesis problems is conceptually inevitable. We cannot imagine a completely "selfless" Archimedean point for genesis contexts which will still be *human* in any relevant sense. We human beings can only partly take a godly standpoint. Our choices, even those ungoverned by the moral rights and claims of others, are by necessity guided by those deep-rooted inclinations, interests, instincts, and drives that make us human. In that respect we can never fully extricate ourselves from the human standpoint and thus can never achieve a fully impersonal view of the universe.[8] Even if we are created in God's image, we cannot be of an identical nature: our creative pow-ers, although of a "godly" nature, are necessarily constrained by the other traits with which we were created. The wish to transcend our nature is itself always guided by aspects of our humanity. This is most clearly the case in the genesis choices we make. We want to have chil-dren because thus we achieve vicarious immortality, self-realization, the chance to complete unfinished projects, and most of all a kind of an extension of our own identity.

This not being an essay on the philosophy of religion, we are exempt from the necessity to decide whether such an Archimedean point of view is a theologically coherent idea. The dilemma is the following: if God is a Spinozistic entity "acting" by its own necessity, then the genesis prob-lem has no ethical import. But if God is conceived as a free personal force (as in the Judeo-Christian tradition), then some reference to his "volitions" must be part of the account of the world's creation. This has always been a conceptual problem for theologians trying to reconcile God's freedom of choice and omnipotent creative power with his neces-sary attributes of omniscience, goodness, and universal (nonpartial) point of view. If indeed humans are created in God's image, it must be in the second sense of the above dilemma, that is, having the power to choose. However, human beings are also self-transcending creatures, that is to say they can wish to be different from what they actually are. But despite this essentially human drive of self-transcendence, human beings are always bound by their own nature. Although they may ac-quire (in the future) the ability to change their own human nature, their choice whether to actually exercise this ability will be inevitably con-strained by their given human psychological, biological, and ideological makeup.

The important conclusion of our argument will be that there are no moral constraints (over and above the biological, psychological, and ideological) in that constant human attempt at self-transcendence in genesis decisions. In our reading "be fruitful and multiply" should be understood as a blessing rather than a commandment. In that respect we occupy a godly position with regard to the future of humanity, for God is not in any way morally constrained in his creative act. But unlike God, we can never take a completely impersonal view of the universe and in that sense can only make agent-relative (human) decisions. (And even God, as we have seen, is inevitably bound by "theocentric" mo-tives, like the spreading of his image, in his act of creation.) When later in the book we discuss education as the most common (though impure) example of a genesis problem, we will see that typically the way we shape the personality of our children is partly indicative of our ability to transcend what we actually are but no less indicative of that part of our identity (values, traits of character, interests) from which we cannot and do not want to escape.

If we pursue this line of argument, it seems that the idea of being created in God's image should be understood as a logical limitation even on the divine power of creation *ex nihilo:* whatever is created (either by God or by Man) must necessarily partly reflect the creator's nature. Even the human attempt at transcending the impurity of the human genesis context by idealizing it in a theological form ends up in a theo-relative idea of God creating creatures in *his* own image. From the point of view of this reading it seems that the human impure genesis concern is the source for the extrapolated and idealized pure context of a godly creation of humans rather than the other way round. As a kind of human projection, the creator is portrayed as constrained by agent-relative limitations. "In our own image" turns out to be the only available Archimedean point for resolving genesis problems. In that respect, my reading of the biblical story is indeed highly unorthodox, even heretic.

It is both a historical and a philosophical truth that the more creative (molding) power we have, that is to say the purer the genesis problem is, the fewer value criteria are available for making the relevant decisions. If the number of future people and their basic nature are mostly "given," then the narrow leeway for choice regarding them is governed by moral principles regarding their welfare, rights, and interests. But once a significant measure of control over the number and identity of future humans is achieved (which we are steadily and speedily heading for), we gradually lose the guidelines for making those new and radical decisions demanded by our new powers. This change in genesis powers is therefore both historically interesting (calling for new political, social, and legal measures) and theoretically challenging (calling for new definitions of the limits of ethics). The moral riddles plaguing genetic engineers, population planners, parents and doctors, and even educators, are all based on one and the same philosophical problem that will be the concern of this book: in deciding the existence, number, and identity of future people, can we escape "playing God," and what are the rules of this most creative of games.

PART ONE

Paradoxes

CHAPTER 1

Wrongful Life: A Pure Genesis Problem

ETHICS AND GENETHICS

Morality is basically future-oriented. In saying that it is prescriptive in nature, we mean that it is primarily concerned with guiding human behavior so as to have a certain effect on the agent, other people, and the world at large. Obviously, moral discourse consists also of judgments about past deeds, about hypothetical or counterfactual behavior, and about ideal or tenseless states of affairs or character; yet these are typically derivative, or, one may say, parasitical upon its ultimate interest in shaping the future. Unlike historical appraisals, moral judgments of past actions relate, at least implicitly, to what the agent could have and should have done so as to bring about a certain state of affairs. Unlike metaphysical speculations about ideal forms of existence, the moral discourse of ideal states and of desirable human virtues makes sense only if it refers, at least indirectly, to the way we should strive to mold the world and our own character. In that sense morality always projects to the future.

Not all future states of affairs, however, are subject to moral evaluation. First, there are all those future states that for various reasons have no moral value (either being too petty to carry any value, or having a typically other sort of value—such as aesthetic, gastronomic, or scientific). Secondly, there are those states of affairs that could have had a moral value but do not because they lie beyond human control. They are excluded from the moral sphere because moral judgment is concerned only with the possible ways in which we can affect the future state of the world (and of our own selves). Ethical theory has always tried to delineate the boundary between that future which is under human control and that which is not, but the belief that those future states over which people have no influence are not subject to moral judgment has mostly remained uncontroversial. But then there are those future states that are neither nonmoral in the sense of the first category (i.e., they are important and in a seemingly moral way), nor beyond our control as in the second category (i.e., they are brought about by intentional and deliberate human action), but nevertheless raise serious doubts as to their moral status. These are the subject of our investigation.

The unique status of this third category of future states lies in the fact that they do not refer to the way the future is shaped *for* actual (present or future) human beings, but rather with the very creation *of* those beings. In grander terms, whereas ethics is standardly concerned with world-amelioration, the sphere of action in which we are interested here deals with world-creation. There are various ways of representing the distinction, depending on what one sees as central to the concerns of ethics: making people happy versus making happy people; fighting for a more just world as opposed to creating a (new) just world; respecting people's claims as distinguished from creating new claimants; reforming the vicious so as to make them virtuous as against genetically manipulating the procreation of virtuous people.

No one can deny the theoretical and moral relevance of the distinction represented by these pairs. Even if the second problem in every pair is moral in nature, the principles governing its solution cannot be the same as those deployed in the solution of the first. Even if our ethics is based on the apparently unifying principles of overall promotion of happiness, justice, respect for rights, and virtue, there will still remain an unresolved tension between promoting those values by furthering them in *existing* people and promoting them by creating *new* people manifesting these respective values. The distinction becomes even more crucial if we deny the existence of such unifying principles and relegate ethics to the treatment of existing people alone.

We might want to reserve the term *ethics* for the realm of the first category of actions and decisions and coin the hybrid term *genethics* for the realm of the second.[1] This terminology will serve us in arguing that, strictly speaking, ethics is concerned with the rights, welfare, virtue, and value of actual people, whereas the creation of people is a subject matter that calls for a separate, special scrutiny. Genethics is on the one hand closely related to ethics, as it deals with the deliberate shaping of future states of affairs in a morally significant manner; yet, on the other hand, it cannot be part of ethics, as it does not share with it the most basic presupposition: the existence of actual human beings (or given moral subjects). Ethics is the theory of moral conduct in the world. Genetics is the science of creating new biological worlds. Genethics is the theory of moral worldmaking. It is concerned with "ways of worldmaking" in a sense more literal than Nelson Goodman's.

What happens if the presupposition regarding the existence of moral subjects is dropped? Why does it make the problems of genethics unique and deserving of separate investigation? The simple answer is that both our everyday moral intuitions and our traditional ethical principles seem either to lead us into paradox or to break down altogether when applied to genesis problems. On the one hand these problems cannot simply be swept under the carpet; they are highly important, even critical. On the other hand they do not lend themselves to analysis in terms of existing moral and theoretical tools. In the first part of this book we will examine the puzzling nature of genesis problems, justifying the need for a separate treatment. In the second part we will attempt to provide a framework for the (gen)ethical solution of genesis problems, claiming that genethics can be rationalized only in terms of ethics. This will entail a narrowing down of the relevance of ethics to genesis problems, leaving important aspects of those "future states" beyond the grip of moral discourse. The last part of the book will consider the far-reaching implications of this skeptical view for the limits of ethics as a theoretical enterprise, while showing the relatively marginal effect on our practical moral judgments concerning those dilemmas.

Genesis problems have to do with the bringing of human beings into existence. The question of existence cannot however be separated from the questions of number and identity. If we are given the power to choose the creation of human beings, we are faced not only with a yes-or-no problem, but must also decide how many of them to create, and also of what kind. Genesis problems were thus defined in the introduction as those relating to decisions regarding the existence, number, and identity of future people. These will be the three dimensions of genethics, separately discussed but intricately interrelated.

Although the thrust of our argument is that the distinction between ethics and genethics is of theoretical and moral substance, the two are also interconnected in complicated and varied ways. Modern discussion of our obligations to future generations typically blends aspects of

the two. The question of just savings and investment for future generations, the obligation to bequeath them a clean environment, the value
of passing on to posterity our cultural and scientific heritage—all belong to ethics in the traditional sense (though not easily applied to
modern dilemmas). Population policies and genetic engineering, however, clearly belong to genethics. Yet the distinction is hard to maintain in practice, since, for example, the way we control birthrates is
definitely going to affect the standard of living of future people,
whereas the standard of living of actual people is widely recognized as
a major factor in determining demographic trends. Again and again we
will see that genethics works only in idealized conditions (such as
those of Genesis I) and that empirical circumstances make it heavily
laden with ethical considerations.

THE THREE LEVELS OF MORAL DISCOURSE

The history of science is replete with examples of cases in which the
encounter with completely new experiences or natural phenomena leads
to changes not only in beliefs about the world but also to more radical
revisions in general scientific theory. Furthermore, profound changes in
scientific theory often yield a reassessment of metatheoretical assumptions about the very scope of a discipline or the legitimate application of
certain basic forms of reasoning and validation. Ethics does not usually
provide us with analogous novelties in everyday experience (although
the Holocaust is often presented as exactly such a new challenge calling
for a complete revision of ethical thinking). I believe that the cluster of
dilemmas confronting modern societies regarding population policies,
family planning, decisions concerning fetal research, the status of frozen
eggs fertilized *in vitro,* legal claims for wrongful life, donor selection for
artificial insemination, and the regulation of the selection of recipients
of these donations—all call for what might be justifiably called a revolution in moral thinking.

The paradoxical nature and counterintuitive implications of traditional solutions to these problems can be discussed in terms of the three
conventionally distinguished levels of moral discourse: the intuitive
(sometimes referred to as the "moral"), the theoretical (often called the
"ethical"), and the meta-ethical. In the rest of this chapter we will deal
with the first level, mainly by discussing a real-life case that has caused
confusion in both the legal profession and the general public in recent
years. Chapter 2 will be devoted to the examination of the second level

(mainly by studying some of the major ethical theories of the past). Chapter 3 will discuss the third level, the methodological difficulties involved in addressing genesis problems, especially the relation between theory and intuition and the demarcation of the limits of ethics. Thus the ground will be cleared for an attempted solution to genethical problems (in part 2).

The sense of puzzlement raised by genesis problems on the three levels of moral discourse is equally sharp in the three dimensions of those problems: existence, number, and identity. Take existence first: we are all inclined to believe that, beyond the debate on the morality of abortion, there is a difference between killing a fetus and using contraceptive means as respective methods of family planning. But why is it so? Is the difference due to a belief in the distinction between the moral status of actual human beings and that of merely potential ones? And if so, what is the standing of the latter? Our intuitions are hardly sharp on this matter. We appeal to a more theoretical analysis of the problem by asking whether human existence is in itself a good thing, or whether it is only the underlying condition for anything that can be held as good. If life (human existence) is good, should we treat all nonexistence as bad? And would that mean considering prenatal nonexistence as equally bad as postmortem nonexistence? These highly theoretical speculations might lead to a dead end, implying the meta-ethical conclusion that they lie beyond the valid objects of ethical thinking and moral judgment.

Or consider numbers: if we decide on massive assistance programs to starving people in India, we might save the lives of x people; however, by that very decision we promote the birthrate in an overpopulated country, directly causing *more* starvation in the next generation (and the potential death of let us say $x + n$ people). Is this the morally right choice? Should we sacrifice the lives of a certain number of actual people in order to save the lives of a greater number of potential people (cf. Hardin 1981)? Note that the source of our confused intuitions about this case is not the difficulty of solving moral dilemmas involving the sacrifice of some people for the sake of saving others; it is rather connected with the conceptual problem of the status of potential people: do they have rights at all? Do they have fewer rights than actual people? Or should they be treated on a par with existing people? Again, a typical ascent to a more theoretical level of analysis is called for. Utilitarianism, for instance, might guide us to a policy of sacrifice (based on the maximization of goodness in the world). But then we are baffled by the question *whose* good is to be maximized: that of all actual moral subjects, or that of all possible moral subjects? This immediately leads the discussion to the logical problem of fixing the extension of the group of possible moral subjects, a typical meta-ethical question.

Finally, consider the identity of those affected by our genethical decisions: this is also a source of confusion on the three respective levels of discourse. In premodern moral decision making the identity of the subjects involved in the possible outcomes of our decisions was usually fixed. Basically, comparisons were made between the welfare and rights of one identifiable person (or persons) with those of another equally identifiable person(s). But now we can decide the sex of a future child, and soon many more of "its" deep biological and psychological traits. Is our future child an abstract traitless subject whose welfare we must promote by choosing for "it" the best set of traits? The grammatically neutral language used in the previous sentence attests to the perplexity involved in the very formulation of the question. For we are used to making choices for people only when we know who they are, that is, when they have identity. Intuition again might appeal for a more theoretical analysis of the criteria of personal identity. But unlike the issue of abortion, much of which can be decided after the metaphysical question of the beginning of life is settled, the genesis problem of what kind of person to create cannot be similarly resolved. For whatever the criteria for personal identity and the beginning of a person's life are, there always will remain the question how to decide on the creation of a person of one kind (identity) rather than a person of another kind (identity). Ethical principles do not serve us well in such cases, and the disturbing meta-ethical explanation for this is that they fail not because of any defect in themselves, but rather because of the nature of the cases to which they are being applied.

If this conclusion is indeed true, no revision in ethical principles will suffice to redirect our moral judgments on those unusual cases. What is required is a global reconsideration of the limits of ethics in the light of the confusing implications of traditional ethical principles and a readiness to reeducate our first order moral intuitions so as to make them as coherent as possible.

SUING FOR BEING BORN

Moral problems in the legal sphere are good examples for first-order moral discourse. Lawyers and judges are constantly making moral judgments, which although not "intuitive" in the usual sense, are nevertheless not "theoretical" in the philosophical-ethical sense. One of the most typical genethical issues in recent years has been that of claims for "wrongful life." These are all new cases, involving, as we shall presently see, harsh moral dilemmas. The written law is silent on the matter, judicial precedents were lacking till the 1960s, analogies are hard to come by. Both legal experts and the general public are baffled by the paradoxical nature of these claims.

A few years ago a woman in Israel consulted a doctor about the potential danger of the transmission of a serious genetic disease (known to exist in her family) to her future offspring. Her intention was not to conceive if there indeed was such a danger. The doctor, allegedly out of negligence, concluded after examination that there was no room for concern. Relying on the doctor's opinion, the woman conceived and gave birth to a boy afflicted with the genetic disease, with its grave physical and psychological implications (a short life and one of very low quality).

The parents, both in their own name and in the name of the child, sued the doctor for damages. The district court recognized the parents' standing but not the child's. The doctor appealed to the Supreme Court of Israel against the first decision, and the parents, in the name of their son, against the second. The Supreme Court unanimously overruled and rejected the doctor's appeal and in a majority decision accepted the child's appeal, granted him standing, and returned the case to the district court to decide the substantive case on its merits (i.e., to determine the responsibility for negligence and the amount of damages to be paid if negligence is proved).[2]

Cases of this sort have persistently harassed the judiciary in the United States for over two decades. Contrary to the Israeli Supreme Court decision, the attempts of plaintiffs to recover damages for wrongful life were mostly struck out by the courts in various states. However, the reading of those cases testifies to the serious dilemmas and grave doubts with which the courts were faced. Only very few cases were decided unanimously; most of them were decided only after appeal, and the judges' opinions usually express hesitation and a wish to evade the basic issue of principle by either devising a compromise solution or by deferring the matter to the legislature.[3]

I am presenting the case of wrongful life as a starting point and as a typical example of the complexity and perplexity of genesis problems on the intuitive level (as well, as we shall later see, on the theoretical one), for three reasons. First, it is a *real-life* case, it is morally disturbing, and it can by no means be dismissed as a philosophical *Gedankenexperi-*

ment (we shall have plenty of those later!). Secondly, it is a conceptually *pure* case in the sense that it typically involves a decision regarding a human being who by no means and in no sense yet exists, and whose identity is not biologically or metaphysically given. Thirdly, it illuminates the *negative* aspect of genesis problems, as it highlights the alleged constraints on reproductive behavior (rather than the positive duty to procreate). As often in ethics, the analysis of prohibitions furnishes better insights into the nature of obligations.

If we wish to consider wrongful life cases as pure examples of genesis problems, we should note the difference between three similar categories (often confused in court discussions): the neonatal, the prenatal, and the preconceptive. Many children born with Down's syndrome suffer from an intestinal blockage requiring a lifesaving (though simple) operation. The courts have recurrently faced the dilemma whether to allow the parents to refuse such a treatment (claiming that it would be better for their child to die than to live with the syndrome). This is a tragic choice relating to (involuntary and passive) euthanasia, but hardly a case of wrongful life, for the life of the child is already an uncontested fact. In the prenatal cases, the subject of the majority of the American cases mentioned above, the claim of the child is that due to negligence on the part of a doctor in the course of the mother's pregnancy, the child was born handicapped instead of being aborted. Typically, these cases involve an incorrect diagnosis or the wrong interpretation of the meaning of a diagnosis for the prospective child (e.g., refraining from advising amniocentesis for women in high risk groups). Thus, the handicaps giving rise to such cases in America were usually Down's syndrome, Tay-Sachs disease, or deafness caused by rubella. Only in the preconceptive cases does the claim refer to negligence that led to the very conception of the child and eventually to its birth, like the wrong genetic counseling in the Israeli case.[4]

In the prenatal case we have a human fetus, whose actual life is at stake. One can say that fetuses are full human beings whose life must not be taken for *any* reason; or one can hold that the life of a fetus is not thus protected and can be taken for the sake of avoiding the birth of a miserable human being. But even if we adopt the second approach, the fetus is an identifiable entity that can be characterized as that human entity gradually developing into a full person. Thus, a child born deaf due to the failure of a doctor to warn a rubella afflicted pregnant mother (as in *Gleitman v. Cosgrave*) can be seen as making a retroactive claim for the right to euthanasia. The history of American judicial reasoning in wrongful life cases was therefore much influenced by the *Roe v. Wade* abortion case, which allowed abortions for reasons referred to in wrongful life cases. Once abortions are legal the road is blocked to claims of the sanctity of life of the fetus and the absolute prohibition on taking it.[5] However, in the preconceptive case, like the Israeli one, the counterfactual event of the doctor giving the parents the right medical advice does not refer to any particular individual whose life could be mercifully spared. We are primarily interested in the wrongful conception of this sort as a pure illustration of genesis problems that do not depend on the abortion issue and which are particularly difficult because of the identity problem.[6]

These three categories differ from a fourth one: harm done to individuals whose coming into existence is completely independent of the harm or the wrongful act. Thus, the courts have no analytical problem in determining damages for victims of the thalidomide pill or laying responsibility on a company manufacturing baby food that may poison a child not yet conceived at the time the food is canned. The fact that the individual cannot be identified at the time the alleged negligent or wrongful act is taking place does not pose any special conceptual problem, as long as the coming into being of that individual is itself independent of the wrongful act. The confusion created by wrongful life cases arises precisely from the fact that the wrongful act is the direct cause of the plaintiff's existence.[7]

A RIGHT NOT TO BE BORN VERSUS A RIGHT TO BE BORN HEALTHY

The puzzling effect of wrongful life claims arises obviously from the fact that had the doctor been professionally competent and responsible, the child would never have been born at all. This makes them unique in tort law, for the only alternative to the actual state (handicapped life, or birth with a serious illness) is no life at all. And as it belongs to the context of tort, it is worth noting that

> tort damages serve to compensate a plaintiff for injury caused by a defendant's negligent conduct and are awarded to the extent that a plaintiff can be restored to the position he would have occupied had the tort not occurred. (*Turpin v. Sortini*, 128)

Tort is universally defined as some sort of *worsening* in the condition of a person (damages being an attempt to compensate for exactly that difference between the person's condition before the harm was done and that following it). But in our case, the only condition that can be the subject of such a comparison and a point of reference for the assessment of appropriate compensation is nonexistence.

Does such a comparison make sense? Is there any value to nonexistence (even a negative one) which could serve as a basis for the claim that by being born one was suffering a harm (a worsening of one's condition)? Surprisingly, the courts, which have always been sensitive to this problem of comparability, have regularly brushed aside the question as transcending the sphere of legal discourse. Discussing it has been considered as a retreat "into the meditation on the mysteries of life" (*Curlender v. Bio-Science Laboratories*), unnecessarily indulging in an "inscrutable enigmatic issue" (*Turpin v. Sortini*), or entering into the metaphysical and theological questions of the meaning of death, the nature of nonexistence, and the mysteries of creation "more properly left to the philosophers and theologians" (*Zeitsov v. Katz*). In one of the rare English wrongful life cases Judge Stephenson says that "man, who knows nothing of death or nothingness, cannot possibly know whether that is so," that is, that it would have been better off for the child not to have been born at all (*McKay v. Essex Area Health Authority* 1982 [2] W.L.R., 890–914). And another judge in the same case speaks about "the undiscovered country from whose bourn no traveller returns." The general inclination of the courts has been to avoid these issues, because they are assumed to pertain to a sphere of knowledge to which lawyers, judges, and maybe all human beings (philosophers excepted!) have no access.

What is surprising here is not the systematic avoidance of making such comparisons of defective life with nonlife, but rather the reasoning behind it. Nonexistence is not an unfamiliar or mysterious form of existence that we cannot compare to existence because of the lack of epistemic tools. We do not understand "the unknown," or "the 'essence' of non-existence" (*Zeitsov v. Katz*) simply because there is nothing to understand. Most judges refrain from awarding compensation because they say they do not *know* how to calculate it. Only one judge (in *Becker v. Schwartz*, 903) clearly states that the difficulty is logical rather than epistemological.

The inclination to avoid comparisons in wrongful life cases is not only motivated by the fact that nonexistence is not a state that can be given a value, but also because it is not a state that can be *attributed to* a subject. It is hardly a "state" at all. We find it hard enough to assess the harm involved in death, yet we know at least that even if death means complete annihilation (nonexistence), it occurs *to* someone. We can decide that the extent of harm done to a person by taking his or her life is proportional to the expected net good that could have accrued in the rest of the natural lifespan. All this is of no help in the case of "birth in defect." Had the plaintiff in the Israeli case not been conceived, would it have been a *gain* for anyone, would *this* boy have been better off? Similarly, is being born an injury or harm in his case?

The American courts refer more than once to the nonsymmetry between the so-called "wrongful death" cases (as old as mid-nineteenth century) and the new wrongful life cases. In more philosophical terms we can say that at least from the ethical and legal points of view there is a marked difference between preconceptive nonexistence and postmortem nonexistence. Even if Lucretius is wrong in his attempt to alleviate our fears of death by saying that when we are alive death is not with us and when we are dead we are not there to suffer it, a stoic attitude to the counterfactual possibility of not being born at all is logically required; for only death can be attributed as a loss to a person—not the state of never being conceived.[8] The benefits of suicide or euthanasia are highly controversial, but unlike nonconception they are logically attributable to a subject.

However, an opposite approach to the matter has been simultaneously expressed by the courts, usually by the dissenting minority view. One might say that being born with a congenital defect is worse than being born without it, and that *that* difference should serve as the guiding principle in determining the amount of damages owed to the child.[9] In other words, the question should not be whether there is a right to be born, but whether there is a right to be born in a healthy condition. If this latter right is violated, the injured party can claim compensation for the difference between healthy and defective life. This intuitive way of viewing the case is based on the very appealing idea that there is a certain minimum or cutoff line that makes life worth living, and that bringing a child into the world without guaranteeing this minimum is morally wrong and a legitimate basis for compensation.

Thus, we find in the Israeli case (*Zeitsov v. Katz*) the typical debate between these two conflicting opinions, leading in effect to the mutual invalidation of the ultimate conclusion (shared by *both*) to grant the child legal standing. Judge Barak tries to avoid the absurdity of comparing life with nonlife and that of recognizing a right not to be born by treating *healthy* life as the alternative to the child's present situation. But to his colleague this does not seem to be the real alternative; it is only a hypothetical or fictitious one, since *this* child by definition could not have had a healthy life. If the child wants to sue the doctor for tort he must present the court with a real alternative in which he would allegedly have been better off. This alternative is, as Judge Ben-Porat claims, nonexistence. But in that case, although the real alternative has been identified, no comparison with the present situation can be made because life and nonlife are incommensurable, and even if they were commensurate the child could only prefer his own death (by suicide or euthanasia) to his miserable life, but not "his" nonconception.

So it seems that the mutual critiques of both judges are justified: no healthy existence of the child can be envisaged, as his disease is essential to his identity; and no comparison between life and nonlife can be logically justified, because it is not clear whether there is anything to compare with existence. Therefore, both these lines of argument succeed in undermining their respective alternative view, thus also undermining the logical basis for the recognition of a legal standing for the child. There is neither a right not to be born nor a "fundamental right . . . to be born as a whole, functional human being" (*Becker v. Schwartz*). Put in another way: birth in handicap is in wrongful life cases *necessary,* and hence not a subject for complaint (the child could not have been born healthy); birth as such is not necessary (we can imagine the child not being born at all); but then being born is not the subject of complaint, only being born *in handicap*. Hence, the distinction between the two descriptions of the same event cannot serve as the basis for wrongful life suits.

Still, it is hardly surprising that the courts have not been willing to be led by this purely abstract reasoning into depriving miserable children of the right to recover damages for their handicapped lives brought about by a negligent party. Despite the logical oddity of it, some judges try to attach value to nonexistence. In cases of particularly severe handicap nonexistence can be said to be superior to life. This argument, which since the complaint of Job sounds intuitively plausible, might rest on a logically sound basis as long as one is willing to commit oneself to a certain metaphysic. The metaphysical assumption relates to the ontological status of human beings before birth or conception. It may be tempting in genesis contexts to view the prenatal stage as an *ante-world,* a corridor leading to this world. But once we allow such fantasies to play a role in our reasoning, the question is raised whether there are moral principles governing the passage between this ante-world and the actual world. In some cases one might think that it is the duty (of a doctor or a parent) to block this passage, in other cases that it would be a duty to grant those waiting in that limbo-like state the privilege of entering the world.[10]

An example of such an ontology can be found in the story of Amram, Moses's father, who was convinced by his daughter to continue begetting children despite Pharaoh's threat to kill all newborn male Israelites.[11] The reasoning that convinced Amram was three-fold: that a decision not to beget more children would mean a "death sentence" to female offspring as well; that it would apply to both this world and the next; and that it would absolutely and certainly be irrevocable. This is a metaphysical view that sees the world we know as a passage from a previous mode of existence to a future world and hence as a condition of getting into that future world. It gives special weight to the value of the actualization of human potentialities and rejects the right to interfere with that process by abstaining from procreation even in cases where the passage is painful (in this case involving premature or instant death). This is a coherent metaphysic, yet for many of us it looks awkward and remote from our deeply entrenched views about coming to exist in this world.

The parents' claim for damages in cases such as *Zeitsov v. Katz* was duly recognized by all the courts, as they could easily be shown to have suffered. They clearly viewed parenting a sick child as inferior both to parenting a healthy child *and* to remaining childless (or adopting a child). These three conditions can be unambiguously attributed to them and compared by them. The child, however, could not point to similar comparisons of welfare, first since his very existence as a comparing subject was owed to the alleged harmful act, and secondly the comparison itself was dubious. Nevertheless, we might feel that this logical distinction between the case of the parents and that of the child is morally irrelevant: the case of the child rests on the badness of the state of affairs brought about by the doctor. Even if the child cannot claim that *he* would have been better off not being born, that does not mean that now, having as a matter of fact been born with a defect (a state caused by negligent counseling), he deserves no compensation. Even if we cannot claim damages for having been born, we can claim damages for defects with which we were born.

LEGAL POLICY AND THE SUSPENSION OF LOGIC

Some judges have been willing to concede that although "a cause of action for 'wrongful life' could not be stated" (*Turpin v. Sortini*), and that there is "no way of showing that the 'interests' of the infant suffered" (being born with Down's syndrome as in *Becker v. Schwartz*), considerations of social policy justify a decision even if it runs contrary to strict logical reasoning. The courts often refer to the need to lay responsibility on negligent doctors and to the problem of guaranteeing sufficient funds for the maintenance of a severely impaired life.[12] But social policy reasoning appears to be double edged on this matter, as judges are equally aware of the danger of allowing such claims to stand in court. For example, what would be considered the limits of justifiable claims? Would we allow children to sue their parents for having been born illegitimate (as in *Stills v. Gratton*)? underweight because of the mother's smoking while pregnant? with a low I.Q.? into a polluted world infested with war and insecurity? in 1945 rather than in 1955?

Most judges tend to prohibit claims of children against their parents because of the value of both privacy and reproductive freedom, as well as because of "social impact [that] could be staggering" (*Stills v. Gratton*). However, one of the judges in *Curlender v. Bio-Science Laboratories* would allow such claims, at least in "extreme cases." But why only in extreme cases, and what should be considered extreme? For the courts, much depends on the question whether the alleged wrongful act leading to conception was indeed "an injury" or just a denial of better conditions for the future life of the child. But how are we to decide whether parents eager to have children can be sued for conceiving a child with the knowledge that it has a 50 percent chance of suffering from a handicap?[13] Furthermore, the circumstances of conception (negligence of a doctor, indifference of parents, or coercion of a third party as in rape) do not make a difference in the standing of the child from an analytical point of view, although from a moral point of view they make all the difference in the world.

It is also an interesting theoretical question whether the courts should opt for legal solutions on the grounds of social policy (or moral sympathy) even when they rest on shaky conceptual ground. This question applies not only to the judiciary but also to the legislature, and in that respect it does not seem that passing the buck to the legislature (which is a very popular escape route for many judges in those cases) is a tenable solution. For example, the British Law Commission, in its serious *Report on Injuries to Unborn Children* (CMND 5709, 1974) states:

> [We] have not been unduly influenced by these considerations of logic. Law is an artefact and, if social justice requires that there should be a remedy given for a wrong, then logic should not stand in the way. (sec. 89)

This easy dismissal of the constraints of logic is puzzling, for it seems that lawmakers are no less bound by the logic of tort than the courts. They can of course solve the problem of social justice by enacting laws that would make society financially responsible for the welfare of these unfortunate children. They may even levy special fines on doctors found guilty of creating those burdens to society. But they can hardly amend tort law so as to accommodate wrongful life cases. In other words, they cannot view logical considerations and those of social policy as *alternative* grounds for decision, as the former condition the latter. The willingness to suspend "considerations of logic" may remind lawyers of judicial solutions by way of legal *fiction*. Yet, it is interesting that none of the courts discussed above directly resorted to this means, perhaps because the healthy existence of the plaintiff was not only an empirical falsity but also a logical or metaphysical impossibility, that is, it could not even be *imagined*.[14]

PHILOSOPHICAL SIGNIFICANCE OF WRONGFUL LIFE CASES

We may go a step beyond the history of actual wrongful life cases and predict claims for damages that have not yet arisen. So far, children have tried to recover damages for having been born (claiming that they would have been better off aborted or not conceived). But children might equally try to claim damages for having been born X rather than Y, especially as medical technology enables human control of the determination of the newborns' identity. Imagine a situation in which the genetic counselor in the Israeli case with which we began suggested a treatment that would have guaranteed the conception of a healthy child, but only by changing its sex. Would a child born handicapped due to negligence in *this* case be entitled to damages for not being born healthy though of the other sex? Our intuitions are not clear on these matters that involve identity rather than existence. We shall however see in part 2 why the same objections to granting the child legal standing would apply in this case. Here, on the level of first-order moral intuition, we can only point out the slippery slope leading from the right to be born without defect to the general right we all have to be born better than we actually are—better in genetic makeup, in citizenship, in position in time, in racial or religious identity, even with better parents!

Philosophers too have grappled with the validity of wrongful life claims. Michael Bayles, for instance, is justified in claiming that the unconceived cannot be harmed, and therefore that they cannot be compensated for being born, even when born defective due to negligence. The unconceived lack identity and the harm principle cannot be applied to victimless crimes. However, Bayles attributes the lack of identity of the unconceived to the fact that it is impossible to identify an individual by way of a definite description (as suggested by Hare), such as "the person who will be born if these two people start their coitus in precisely five minutes" (Bayles 1976, 299). However, it seems that the problem is even deeper than that described by Bayles: again it is logical rather than epistemological and has to do with the fact that the identity of an individual in genesis problems is not only beyond human *knowledge,* but also absolutely dependent on human *choice.*

Bayles suggests a positive solution to wrongful life cases in terms that lie beyond the (inapplicable) harm principle. It treats *classes* of people rather than unidentifiable individuals. The law would be used as an instrument for the prevention of the birth of defective children as a group. However, if such a law cannot be justified in terms of the welfare or rights of future individuals, what is its basis? Is it *our* rights—as individuals—or is it an impersonal notion of a better world? This underlying philosophical problem does not concern Bayles, but it is exactly the one we have to address in order better to articulate and theoretically support our intuitive positions on genesis problems.

Wrongful life cases are particularly illuminating for genethics, because of their conceptual purity. They consist of all the elements of a wrong calling for compensation: negligence (an agent responsible for a relevant act), a bad state of affairs or event in the world (a child born with a serious defect), and a causal link between the act and the state of affairs (causally relating the latter to the former). Yet they seem to escape legal judgment because they do not meet certain preconditions of existence and identity. On the one hand, how can we doubt the moral wrongness of the act, the moral responsibility of the agent, the justified complaint of the victim? On the other hand, how can we blame anyone for having brought about a state of affairs (viz., being born in handicap) that by no means can be held bad *for* the subject involved? Wrongful life acts are at most victimless crimes. And in that respect, even if we cannot, for logical reasons, grant legal standing to the child in its claim for compensation, should not the negligent doctor be held responsible for the wrong and be liable to (criminal) punishment? Putting aside the parents' claim, a wrong was done in the world even if no individual can be identified as its victim.

The courts have been baffled by these conflicting moral intuitions, and in their wavering between different and sometimes opposite ways of solving them they reflect the hesitation we all share in our general moral judgments of similar genesis problems. The intricately roundabout argumentation, the use of ambiguous language, the persistent attempt to avoid metaphysics together with an inevitable involvement in metaphysical (or even mystical) rhetoric, the tension between the legal restrictions on justifiable claims for tort and the moral sensitivity to the plight of a defective child, the courageous attempt to square logic and social policy—all characterize the intellectually insecure response elicited by these unprecedented wrongful life claims. This is precisely what makes these cases so interesting as primary examples for the difficulty we face in general genethical problems.

There is however one principal limitation on the relevance of wrongful life cases to our general philosophical discussion of genethics. We noted earlier that the comparison between life and nonexistence is blocked by two considerations: the valuelessness of nonexistence as such and the unattributability of its alleged value to individual subjects. The two considerations are intimately interconnected: one of the reasons for denying value to the nonexistence *of* people is the very fact that it cannot be attached *to* people. This indeed will be the central thesis of the second part of this book. However, it is a substantive ethical claim that is not analytically true, and one should be cautioned not to prejudge the general genethical issue on the basis of the intuitive response to wrongful life cases. This however does not mean that wrongful life claims were not justifiably struck out by most of the courts, for they are solely concerned with tort and claims for damages, which are analytically a matter of attributability to individuals. It remains to be seen whether the incongruity of these attempted claims can be traced also in the wider *impersonal* realm of genesis problems.[15]

The point of this chapter was to emphasize the novelty of genesis problems and how this novelty undermines the attempt to get our intuitions on the matter clear. Our confusion is due to our wavering between a sense of high moral importance on the one hand and of a shaky logical foundation on the other. The case of wrongful life is a major real-life illustration of the uniqueness of these problems, as is well captured by Judge Stephenson's words:

> Here the court is considering not "an ancient law" but a novel cause of action, for or against which there is no authority in any reported case in the courts of the United Kingdom or the Commonwealth. . . . It is tempting to

say that the question . . . is so important that it should be argued out at a trial and on appeal up to the House of Lords. But it may become just as plain and obvious that the novel cause of action is unarguable or unsustainable . . . (*McKay v. Essex Area Health Authority,* 898)

It remains now to be seen whether traditional moral philosophy can provide our discussion with the needed "authority."

CHAPTER 2

The Failure of Traditional Ethical Theories

THE THEORETICAL ASCENT

One of the recurrent themes in the cautious stratagems adopted by the courts dealing with wrongful life cases has been their sincere attempt to assume only partial responsibility for their decisions. This effort, as we have seen in chapter 1, has taken two forms: an institutional deferment of ultimate solutions of these novel cases pending legislative action on the one hand, and an intellectual evasion of the real issue in the name of philosophical ignorance on the other. The courts have indeed been forced to decide concrete cases, at least provisionally. They have done so only reluctantly and with the understanding that such cases should eventually be decided by appropriate new laws and that the basic issue is of a philosophical and metaphysical nature lying beyond judicial arbitration.

Recommendation for legislation on matters that the courts feel ill-equipped to solve is often warranted. The legislature for its part is sometimes slow in responding to such pleas by the judiciary due to political reasons. But in the case of wrongful life it seems that the reason for the lacuna in the law is of a deeper sort, embarrassing lawmakers no less than judges. Wrongful life cases do not merely call for the formal articulation of evolving norms or the legal implementation of new social values, which are typical functions of the legislature. They challenge our very conceptual framework, putting it under a particular logical strain.

Confessions of ignorance concerning problems that should be better left to philosophers and theologians have an honest ring and are in line with the courts' liberal neutrality towards the plurality of metaphysical attitudes regarding the nature of life and death. Yet, I have raised the possibility that the issues that the courts want to avoid are mostly fictitious and that wrongful life cases depend on them, if at all, only if highly dubious metaphysical assumptions are made regarding the world and personal identity. Nevertheless, there is another sense in which it is true that philosophers can contribute to the discussion of the issue of wrongful life, although not directly to its legal resolution. Philosophy can test our moral intuitions in the light of more principled reasoning and in accordance with general ethical theories and the metaphysical assumptions underlying them. A philosophical examination of the peculiar status of unconceived children may lead either to a better understanding of the conditions that could justify such legal claims or to the justification of the courts' inclination to dismiss them altogether.

In any case, both the institutional and the intellectual evasions of responsibility by the courts in wrongful life cases characterize the general tendency of intuitive thinking on genesis problems at large. Unlike other intensely debated ethical issues (such as abortion, euthanasia, or affirmative action), people are inclined to bypass genesis problems by entrusting them to the hands of professional authorities (such as medical experts and demographers) or by dismissing them as abstract theoretical riddles (better left to philosophers). The appeal to philosophical assistance in matters of genethics is much more common than in moral issues on which people have firm intuitive (though controversial) views. Can philosophy lend this highly wanted help? We naturally turn first to traditional ethical theories that have served throughout the ages as the conceptual frameworks for the analysis of moral problems. After showing in this chapter that they disappoint our expectations, we will attempt to draw the proper meta-ethical conclusions (in chapter 3) and reformulate the ethical principles for genethical problems (in part 2).

The object of the following sections is to test a sample of the main *kinds* of ethical theories in their application to genesis problems. For this nonhistorical survey I borrow Ronald Dworkin's tripartite categorization of political theories into right-based, duty-based, and goal-based approaches (Dworkin 1977, 171–172). Although my interest in it is different from Dworkin's, this distinction can be philosophically illuminating rather than just a matter of taxonomic elegance. As we will see in the rest of this chapter, the shortcomings of right-based theories such as Rawls's in dealing with genesis problems are of a different sort than those created by goal-based theories such as utilitarianism and perfectionism. The application of the former involves incoherence, whereas that of the latter leads to coherent though counterintuitive or implausible results. This examination may indirectly undermine Mackie's view that right-based moralities are possible (Mackie 1978). For it is exactly the *individualistic* factor characterizing the right-based view that makes right-based theories logically incapable of dealing with genesis problems. With duty-based theories, such as Kantianism or religious ethics, much depends on the content of the duties involved, that is, whether they relate to individuals or to the promotion of a certain goal. In the first case they resemble right-based theories (the duty being correlative to a right); in the second they are derived from a goal-based view of some sort. In the context of the morality of procreation this goal-based view will become prominent in typically deontological theories.

As a right-based example we choose Rawls, who was also the first philosopher to try to account for "intergenerational" issues in a systematic way. Kant is naturally the representative of a duty-based approach, also because his theory manifests the dual aspect of duty-based theories just mentioned. Finally utilitarianism and historicism serve as cases of goal-based conceptions that play a very important role in the discussion of our moral relation to future generations. Aristotelian ethics of virtue cannot be of much help in the direct analysis of dilemmas of procreation, but we shall see later that it is highly relevant in accounting for some of our deeply entrenched intuitions on these matters.

CONTRACTORS DECIDING ON THEIR EXISTENCE

"The question of justice between generations . . . subjects any ethical theory to severe if not impossible tests" (Rawls 1971, 284). This opening remark of the section on justice between generations is well attested by the serious problems encountered by Rawls himself (and highlighted by some of his critics) in the attempt to apply principles of contract theory to transgenerational issues. It must be noted in the outset, however, that Rawls is solely concerned here with questions of savings, the transmission of culture and knowledge, and (above all) the ongoing historical process of enhancing the institutions of justice. Reference to genesis problems is conspicuous by its absence. This absence is surprising, for population policies are definitely typical cases of intergenerational issues involving specifically distributive dimensions.

One might say that criticizing Rawlsian theory for failing in something it is not trying to do is unfair and beside the point. However, *if* social policies of demographic planning (e.g., the distribution of the rights and incentives to procreate) are matters of distributive justice, the theory must be able to deal with them. And even if they are not, one cannot deny that those problems of distributive justice between generations that *are* of Rawls's concern (like the just savings principle) are directly dependent on genesis decisions. Only twice in the sections devoted to the intergenerational subject (secs. 44 and 45) does Rawls mention this dependence: in both cases in the course of a critical comment on the handling of the savings problem by utilitarian theory (see p. 286 and p. 298). Yet, the population factor is relevant to contractarian accounts of the savings problem no less than to the utilitarian attempts "to mitigate the consequences of wrong principles" (p. 297) by adding a principle of social discount.[1] Utilitarianism indeed takes population size as "a variable" in dealing with the saving issue, and that is problematic due to the indeterminacy that I will examine later in this chapter. But Rawls's opposite fallacy is no less serious from a genethical point of view; he takes population size as given and fixed, instead of taking it as a moral or a political issue that has to be decided. Thus, the dependence relation is deeper than hinted at by Rawls: it is not only that the (expected) numbers of future people should affect our savings policies as some sort of relevant background data; these numbers might very well be a crucial part of, or the very *subject* of these policies. And as population trends have become a matter over which we—the present generation—have gained some control, we cannot avoid articulating normative principles for making those choices.[2]

It is noteworthy that Rawls does refer to the question of population size in an earlier section of the book devoted to average utilitarianism. He even suggests there that it is a subject for institutional arrangements, implying that it is a matter of choice (p. 162). The fact that an increase in the number of people could promote overall happiness by drastically lowering average happiness (the anticipation of Parfit's Repugnant Conclusion) is given as a reason for the contractors' preference for the average version over the classical (total) alternative. Yet, when explaining this preference Rawls fails to notice that the contractors are not just deciding between two alternative societies in which *they* might live but between a large society that, let us assume, will include *them* and a smaller society that, for that very reason, will not include them (or all of them).

I come here to the basic flaw in contract theory in its application to genesis problems (and hence also derivatively to all other intergenerational issues like the just savings principle). In the same way as the choice between average and "classical" utilitarianism is a decision about the number of people who are going to exist, so also is the decision of how much we have to save for posterity (indeed, whether we have to save anything at all). For one of the most efficient ways of fulfilling whatever obligations we may have regarding the level of welfare of future generations is a deliberate limitation of the birthrate. This is an alternative or a supplementary way to that of saving. In an era of efficient birth control methods one cannot ignore the inseparability of savings issues from population policies. This, as we have come to realize in modern times, is not only an abstract theoretical point, but a very practical dilemma faced by both individuals and societies.

With individuals, we all know that modern parents partly decide the number of children they are going to have in the light of their notion of a right amount of savings for their prospective children together with the ratio of their income which they are willing to set aside. With societies, we can say that there is a correlation (though not always an outcome of a deliberate policy) between the awareness of the rights of future people to enjoy a high standard of living and the effort to control birthrates. However, in all these cases the contractarian method of deciding basic social policies seems to break down for the simple reason that the question *who* is to decide the relevant principles remains undetermined.

Let me explain: the idea of an original position is based on ideal universal participation, at least through virtual representation. When applied to transgenerational problems, like the just savings principle, Rawls wavers between two competing interpretations of the participation condition. According to the first, every generation is represented in the original position, thus guaranteeing that no generation is discriminated against in the savings policy. The problem with this interpretation is that it does not satisfy what are known as the "circumstances of justice," as the relations between the bargaining parties are not those of competition and cooperation (thus only the earlier generation can, for example, benefit or cause harm to the later ones, and not vice versa). Therefore, Rawls prefers the second interpretation, called "the present time of entry," according to which all the contractors belong to one generation. They know this condition, but do not know to which particular generation they in fact belong. Thus, the incongruity of transgenerational bargaining is avoided. However, Rawls must add in this interpretation what he calls "a motivational assumption," which guarantees that the contractors will not decide against *any* savings (being assured of whatever was left to them by the previous generations, independently of their putative negative decision). This assumption views the contractors as heads of family lines, having deep interests in the welfare of their descendants of at least the first two generations. This is considered by Rawls to be a natural psychological supplement to the otherwise psychology-free conditions of the original position, and hence a reasonable (though not easy) theoretical price to pay for a contractarian account of the saving principle.

Now, beyond the critique that has been raised by many philosophers against the adequacy of the motivational assumption,[3] I may add that neither of the two interpretations can make sense in genesis contexts.

According to the first, *all* generations have to be represented in the original position in order to decide the issue of how many generations there are going to be, and that is obviously logically impossible. There is no way to visualize a representative of a particular generation agreeing to a policy that would allow the previous generation to declare that humanity should better come to a peaceful end (i.e., stop all procreation). That is to say questions of the *existence* of future generations cannot be decided by contractarian methods.[4]

Furthermore, and more realistically, the question of the *size* of each generation cannot be decided by such a universal conference of generations, because it will put an impossible strain on the idea of representation: why should I let the representative of my generation decide its size, if that decision potentially involves my nonexistence? The very idea of representation presupposes a given number of people—all with the relevantly same interests and status. A wild possibility would be to allow literally *all possible* human beings into the original position, thus avoiding the problem of having to decide in advance who is going to exist. But as the existence of all possible beings would mean a disastrous overpopulation of the world, criteria would be required for limiting the number of actualized possible beings. But again, the conference of all possible beings would not be able to agree on those criteria, because no one would be willing to negotiate "his" or "her" inexistence. And beyond all that, we know that there is no determinate group of all possible human beings, but rather many groups of *com*possible beings. How are the contractors to decide which of those groups is in fact going to be procreated?

And even if the enormous class of all possible gametes (combinations of sperm cells and eggs) can be imagined, it would not include the products of nonsexual reproduction such as cloning, genetic engineering, and divine creation *ex nihilo*. Possible persons cannot be admitted either to a Rawlsian "constructed" original position, or *a fortiori* to a Hobbesian naturalistic state-of-nature bargaining, which in a more marked way takes individuals as given. The grand conference interpretation is viciously circular: we have to decide whom to let into the original situation in order to decide who is going to exist in the world. But only those existing in the world can make the first decision.[5]

The second interpretation, "the present time of entry," fares no better in genesis contexts than its rival. The motivational assumption is indeed a "natural" one, as Rawls claims. But it is natural only as a psychological generalization constituting the background for justifying a certain ratio of savings for future generations that are assumed to come into existence anyway. However, population policies and family planning make this existence the very subject of decision and choice and hence cannot prejudge the issue by pointing to altruistic sentiments as a general human trend. To avoid the possibility of egoistic solutions by contemporaneous contractors, Rawls suggests that

> the parties are thought of as representing continuing lines of claims, as being, so to speak, deputies for a kind of everlasting moral agent or institution. (p. 128)

Again, this view is psychologically sound when we come to deal with intergenerational problems of distribution (e.g., savings). But it hardly helps to guide the decision of an individual whether to *become* a "head of a family" or a link in a continuing generational chain.[6]

It is by this invisible logic of the inherent inapplicability of justice as fairness to genethical problems that Rawls is led to the kind of undeclared goal-based, impersonal, and transindividual propositions alluded to in the lines quoted above. These are hard to reconcile with his right-based approach to ethical theory. It makes individuals the servants not only of transtemporal interests, but also of a transindividual (and metaphysically vague) abstract "everlasting moral agent or institution." When speaking about the natural duty of promoting the institutions of justice it is not always clear whether Rawls is thinking of justice as something good *for* and deserved *by* human beings, or whether he is concerned with a historical process that is valuable *per se*.

The question for Rawls is this: should we decide the number of people in the next generation in the light of the chances of alternative policies to promote the institutions and principles of justice? And if we do so, is it not using procreation (and thus people) as means for the promotion of a certain ideal? Rawls says that "each generation must . . . preserve the gains of culture and civilization . . ." (p. 285). But why? Is it because of distributive considerations of fairness, that is, sharing with our descendants what we inherited from our predecessors? Or because of the inherent value of culture as such? The first interpretation is more Rawlsian in nature, but fails to address genesis problems by presupposing the existence of descendants who have *rights* over these values. The second leaves open the possibility that procreation itself might be required as a means for the preservation of certain human *goals* or values, but that transcends the methodological framework of justice as fairness.

The dilemma might be put in slightly different terms: basically Rawls insists that the duty to further the institutions of justice throughout history is a natural duty agreed upon in the original position, that is as something deserved by individuals (as a right). But, when faced with the problem of applying this natural duty in the intergenerational sphere, Rawls vacillates between two alternative strategies. According to the first, the essentially right-based approach is maintained but the temporal individual agent becomes a transtemporal, "everlasting" individual creature. Logically this is a satisfactory solution, since the concern with future interests becomes similar to the prudential care that any individual takes of his or her future. However, metaphysically it makes for a very difficult conception of a moral agent who is an "individual" but unnaturally extended in historical time. The second possible strategy is to stick to plausible individualistic metaphysics of actual persons agreeing on principles of justice, but supplement the doctrine with goal-based elements such as the ideal of a fully just society. Here the metaphysics is convincing but the methodology clearly stretches beyond the idea of justice as fairness. Contractarian terms cannot explain the duty to further justice "to the last stage of society" in which no more savings are required for the promotion of justice (p. 289), or the duty to bring about "the full realization of just institutions" (p. 290).[7]

It is also not clear why we should both "uphold" and "further" the institutions of justice. If indeed it is rational on our part to want for egoistic reasons to enhance our chances of living in a just society that leads us to agree in the original position on a natural duty to *enhance* justice, then the same would apply to the promotion of wealth from generation to generation. But Rawls explicitly denies the latter (p. 290), which implies that he is treating justice as a particular goal worthy of promotion rather than mere "upholding."

We should keep in mind this difficulty of accounting for genethical questions in purely right-based terms and the natural tendency to slip into some kind of goal-based rhetoric. This tendency is not unique to Rawls, but rather reflects a general problem with right-based as well as duty-based theories (as will be shown in the next section).

The basic issue is the extent to which a contract theorist is willing to go beyond metaphysical or methodological individualism. Rawls interprets the just savings principle as the undertaking of individuals in the original position "to carry their fair share of the burden of realizing and preserving a just society" (p. 289). But clearly, a just society is a value only for individual human beings living in it. Rawls might be challenged with the following dilemma, which may sound a little abstract and remote, yet it could test the limits of contract theory: either double the population in the next thirty-five years (this is roughly the present rate of population growth) and hope at most to maintain the present level of justice, or enforce a zero population growth for that period and significantly enhance the level of social justice. Although the natural inclination definitely favors the second policy, the theory of justice cannot justify it. Or it can justify it only by being extended so as to include transindividual ideals (of the sort characterized by Rawls as "grand projects" for which people are allowed to decide to save, but are not bound to do so by the theory of justice [p. 288]).

It is indeed a plausible assumption that human beings are motivated by love of their offspring (and also of their offspring's offspring); but this can only explain how people ought to share what they have with future people once these are born or at least after it is decided that they will be born. It cannot solve the question whether to conceive children at all and how many. Rawls is aware of the impossibility of "a gathering of all actual or possible persons" as a way to envisage the original position (p. 139), but because he is concerned with distributive problems of savings and conservation, he attributes this impossibility to the overstretching of the fantasy of the original position. Once we focus on genesis problems, we see that the impossibility is logical. It is not only hard for the imagination to visualize a grand conference of all people deciding who is going to be born and who is not; it is a conceptual absurdity. (Note that even had this idea of a grand conference made sense, there would have been no way for me, as a possible person, to forgo actualization, without consulting all my possible descendants, who by my very decision would become "impossible"!).[8]

If we turn our attention to the genethical question of determining the

identity of future people, the conceptual absurdity of contractors deciding their identity becomes no less manifest. For again, the contractors
can agree on the principles that would govern their social life even if
they are ignorant of their individual identities. But the whole idea of the
veil of ignorance is that such an identity is given, that is, not a matter of
choice (otherwise there would be nothing to hide). In the same vein,
Rawls cannot allow the list of primary goods to become a matter of
bargaining in the original position. But could not further progress in
genetic engineering enable us to create individuals with a different set of
primary values? And are any moral limitations on such a manipulation
available to the contract theory? Rawls takes for granted a certain
universal psychological structure of human interests. This is a valid
methodological move as long as the structure itself does not become a
moral issue calling for a decision. The original position is a powerful
and consistent idea up to the point where both human existence and the
identity (in the sense of nature) of the planned existing beings becomes a
matter of choice.

One implication of all this is that the difference between "all actual
persons" and "all possible persons" is crucial. Rawls is concerned with
all actual persons and the way goods are to be distributed among them.
Only by limiting himself to actual beings can Rawls extend his principles of justice to the intergenerational dimension. All persons can be
viewed as if they were contemporaries, and temporal location is neutral-
ized, because the existence, number, and identity of people throughout
time is implicitly assumed as fixed. However when people must by
definition be viewed as possible, as in genesis problems, the contract
theory breaks down, because potential people cannot choose the principles for making themselves actual.[9] Another implication is that the fact
whether an individual exists or not cannot be hidden by the veil of
ignorance in the original position: existence is a fact about an individual, which on the one hand is not a general truth, yet on the other must
be known by the individual in the original position. This might prove to
be the only truth of a *particular* nature which Rawls must allow his
contractors in the original position. But then it also bars him (and them)
from being able to decide genesis problems.

Another typical way of highlighting the difference between genesis
problems and intergenerational problems of just distribution is through
the Rawlsian idea of a "social minimum." The theory of justice is
primarily concerned with that minimum owed to future generations as
the basis for the determination of the right rate of savings (pp. 285–

286). This minimum is determined neither by the average wealth of the present generation, nor by the customary expectations of the future beneficiaries. It is decided rather by the difference principle, that is, *relatively* to what others have. This involves for example a comparison between the worst off in the present generation and the worst off in the next generation as one way of deciding the limit of taxation on present consumption for the sake of future people. However, it seems that the relevant minimum cutoff line in matters of procreation is of an *absolute* nature, related to some notion of a life worth living. In other words, the moral constraints on population growth have to do primarily with a certain view of what makes life worthy, irrespective of the quality of life enjoyed by other people. This difference is natural, since the theory of justice and just savings focuses on distribution, whereas genesis decisions are "existential," with life being on the one hand something that is given to people, yet not exactly distributed, especially not among "them," or between "them" and us.

This leads us to another Rawlsian idea that will require modification before being applied to genesis problems. Rawls is sensitive to the interdependence of intergenerational distributions of wealth and resources and intragenerational distributions of these goods (p. 292). Basically, the present worst off individuals in society have a claim on their contemporaries which puts direct constraints on the level of savings for future generations and vice versa: the responsibility to future people limits the degree of redistribution within a generation for the benefit of its least advantaged members. This sounds plausible. Yet, Rawls admits that it defines only the constraints on the savings ratio but leaves the precise limits of the rate of savings impossible to define (p. 286). My argument is that one of the major reasons for this impossibility lies exactly in the dependence of the rate of savings on the *number* of people we decide to create. Furthermore, this number can be decided in a just way only if certain distributive principles of procreation rights are agreed upon. In other words, genesis problems also manifest a similar, though as we shall see more tricky, interdependence of inter- and intragenerational considerations. Begetting children does not only affect "them"; it primarily affects the contemporaries of the begetters, and in that they must be subject to principles of political justice (what will later be referred to as the problem of licensing parenthood). But as we have shown, the Rawlsian principles fall short of guiding us on these matters.

Of course contract theory can be defended by emphasizing that it is *only* a theory of *justice* and hence should not be expected to be able to

deal with genesis problems, as these lie beyond the scope of the subject
of justice. This in itself would be a significant meta-ethical restriction on
the theory of justice to issues relating to actual people. It will mean that
some important issues of population policy together with those aspects
of savings policies that are dependent on demographic planning cannot
be subjected to the principles of justice and fairness. In fact this is
exactly part of our thesis, as will be elaborated in part 2. What would be
left for a theory of justice to decide in the genesis context would be the
way genethical questions are resolved by a given, actual generation,
including for example the distributive aspects of the burdens of procreation policies on present people. Contract theory, in this case, would be
able to deal with genesis problems only in terms of the justice relations
between actual people, thus depriving potential people (whose very
existence is at issue) of any status (i.e., rights, or participation and
representation in the original position).

The fundamental problem in applying a Rawlsian methodology to
genesis problems (and hence, indirectly also to saving, conservation,
and enhancement of culture and justice) has been shown to lie in the
absence of the circumstances of justice in intergenerational relations.
These are the conditions that make human cooperation both possible
(as people are assumed to be partly altruistic) and necessary (as they can
further their interests only by cooperation). Principles of distributive
justice are required to govern the behavior of cooperating but competing individuals in a world of moderate scarcity. Since Hobbes and
Hume these background conditions making justice a relevant political
ideal have been listed as rough equality in natural powers, vulnerability,
interdependence, limited mutual sympathy, and so on.

Now, the fact that these circumstances are not satisfied in relations
between generations undermines all non-Rawlsian theories of justice as
well.[10] People of different generations cannot cooperate with each
other, they cannot have a Humean sympathy for each other, they are
not symmetrically vulnerable to harm, and even their resources are not
limited in a defined and fixed way. Furthermore, in genesis problems the
question is whether to beget new people and how many. It is as if the
good to be distributed is *life,* human existence. But this is hardly a scarce
good, or at least it is not scarce in the standard sense as are the *conditions* that make life possible and good. So it seems that existence itself is
not a matter of distribution (let alone redistribution), but only the precondition for its maintenance at a certain level or quality. Scarcity presupposes a given number of human beings competing for limited re-

sources. Life itself is not a limited resource, or at least it is biologically so much more abundant than the means of maintaining it on various levels of worthiness.

It is thus also a problem for natural right theories, the historical precursors of Rawlsian contract theory: can the traditional right to life be granted to potential individuals? It seems that no one has the right to be *given* life, as distinguished from the right to *stay* alive once he or she is born or conceived.[11] It is even doubtful whether natural right theories can establish a right to be born with a certain nature (e.g., free), for the same reason that nonactual persons have no rights.[12] This would make the justification of begetting only humans with certain morally relevant features a problem for contract theorists of all sorts. Yet, although possible persons are not subjects of rights, some philosophers want to claim that they have a moral standing, that is to say that they are the object of moral consideration, sympathy, and beneficence. This claim will be examined as part of goal-based ethical views. Although not incoherent in the way that ascribing rights to potential beings is, this view will prove no less baffling.

RESPECT FOR THE UNCONCEIVED?

Duty-based theories of ethics are hardly any easier to adapt to genesis problems than their right-based counterparts. And testing them in the light of issues of procreation also proves to be an ambiguous task, because they can be understood as either referring to *obligations* derived from one person's undertakings to another, or to *duties* derived from a person's position, status, or role. In the first case, the ethics of procreation is understood in terms of undertakings toward either the future people themselves, or to a "third party" (like God, our contemporaries, or our predecessors). This approach is the conceptual mirror image of *right*-based reasoning. It involves an agreement, a tacit promise, or justified expectations, that is, interpersonal relations. In the second case, it seems that duties regarding procreation have to do with such notions as the human potential to beget children or the ordained status of custodians of the universe (two notions used respectively in the two versions of the biblical story of the creation of Adam and Eve). These duties will be shown to be ultimately derived from certain perfectionist *goals* or ideals.

Kant's deontological theory of ethics typically exemplifies these two strands of a duty-based approach: the first, in the doctrine of the categorical imperative; the second, in the doctrine of virtue, in the philosophy of religion, and in the philosophy of history. Although Kant rarely addresses himself directly to genethical issues, a reconstruction of what he might have said about them could serve as an incisive test for duty-based ethics. Would it be closer to a right-based model of a contract and to a common ideal life of rational agents in a Kingdom of Ends, or to a goal-based model of the ideal of moral self-realization attained either by the individual immortal soul or by the historical process of perfection of the species?

The attempt to apply the categorical imperative to the dilemmas of family planning or population policies entangles us in paradoxes similar to those discussed in the previous section. The question is how should maxims of procreation be tested? The uniqueness of the problem lies in the fact that the boundaries of the moral community within which the maxim is supposed to have a universal authority is the very content of the maxim! Who should be included in this community adopting (or willing) the universal law—the existing generation, or the existing generation *plus* those whose very existence is deliberated? The latter option leads to a paradox that is of the same nature as that of a Rawlsian universal conference of all possible beings: it is an indeterminate group. The point is that all options concerning different population sizes, however incompatible and mutually exclusive, can be formulated in universalizable maxims. However, taking into account only actual persons (of the present generation) as the relevant reference group for the universalizability test may seem egoistic or parochial from a universalist Kantian point of view, which, as we shall see, takes the class of all rational beings in its historical, transgenerational sense.

Other formulations of the categorical imperative fare no better when applied to genethical issues. A particularly illustrative case is the prescription of treating human beings as ends and never solely as means. This prescription cannot be extrapolated to genesis problems, because a decision to conceive a child (or for that matter not to conceive it) cannot be guided by respect for it. The idea of respecting a person in creating him or her is logically puzzling. In fact we strongly and intuitively feel that the decision to bring a child into the world is the only one in which the child is taken purely as a means (usually to the parents' satisfaction, wishes, and ideals)![13] Respect for persons might be a moral guide to the way we should treat people once they are born, but it is of hardly any help in deciding whether and how many of them should be born. And to take the argument further to the wilder realm of science fiction, we may raise the question why should we create *rational* humans if we can choose to engineer nonrational robots? We might have perfectly rational grounds for creating nonrational beings; we might equally choose to create rational beings on the ground that we want "them" to become ends in themselves. But we cannot say that being potentially ends in themselves creates a claim on the part of our potential children to be born.

The application of the principle of autonomy to genesis problems seems to be free from these kinds of incoherences. But typically this is so because it refers uniquely to the deliberating agent rather than to the object of the deliberation, that is, to the rationality of the decision-making process rather than to the rationality of the person created by the decision (as in the case of the idea of respect for persons). But even in this case, it is hard to see how any insight into the dilemmas of procreation can be gained by the idea of autonomy or rationality. We often feel that these dilemmas are solved by strong "pathological" motives, biological instincts, irrational hopes of escaping mortality, or a wish to replicate ourselves in the godly manner of Genesis I.[14]

It is therefore not surprising that the scanty reference to genesis issues should be found in that part of the Kantian system dealing with the two ways by which persons *transcend* their lives as actual individuals: religion and history.[15] In these spheres positive perfectionist ideals supplement the negative constraints of the moral law. The highest good cannot be attained in the earthly life of a solitary human being. It requires either an indefinite extension of individual life, that is to say the immortality of the soul (combining, through divine mediation, virtue and happiness), or a collective enterprise of many people over time, that is to say a historical process. These two extrapolations of the life of an actual individual are reminiscent of the two analogous ways by which Rawls attempts to solve intergenerational issues: the everlasting moral agent and the collective enterprise of the promotion of justice. For Kant, the religious way is supported by faith or the introduction of the "postulates" of God and the immortality of the soul. The historical way is partly supported by impersonal forces, like "the cunning of nature," but partly depends on human action. It is here that procreation plays a vital role.

In his essay *Idea for a Universal History from a Cosmopolitan Point of View*, Kant suggests that the way to overcome the natural limitations on the self-realization of rationality is in history:

> In man (as the only rational creature on earth) those natural capacities which are directed to the use of his reason are to be fully developed only in the race, not in the individual. (Kant 1963*a*, 13)

This is because the life of the individual is too short and limited to enhance his natural capacities. Nature requires many generations to achieve enlightenment, and the duty of the individual is to contribute to this process by begetting children and passing on to them the cumulative achievements of civilization. If he does not do so, "his natural capacities would have to be counted as for the most part vain and aimless" (p. 13).[16] "Establishing a perfect civic constitution" (p. 18) becomes the collective goal of the species to which individual life and projects are in a serious sense subservient.

> Moreover, human nature is so constituted that we cannot be indifferent to the most remote epoch our race may come to, if only we may expect it with certainty. (p. 22)

But of course we have no such absolute certainty:

> Since the free will of man has obvious influence upon marriages, births, and deaths, they seem to be subject to no rule by which the number of them could be reckoned in advance. (p. 11)

This passage can be understood as pointing both to a problem for an ideal which is conditioned by the certainty of its realizability, as well as to the absence of criteria for the determination of "the number" of future people. The number of future people is decided by the freedom of choice (Willkür), which unlike moral freedom (Wille), is not itself bound by reason (rationality, moral laws).

The doctrine of the categorical imperative requires the moral agent to imagine himself or herself as living in a Kingdom of Ends, that is in a world *together* with other ideally rational beings. In *Idea* Kant asks the moral agent to contribute to a long-term enterprise whose fruit will be fully reaped only by the last generation.[17] Although the first approach is analogous to an ideal contract view, trying to abstract it from all individual idiosyncracies, the second approach forgoes the Rawlsian effort to guarantee fairness to the intergenerational enterprise by casting a veil of ignorance over the temporal position. For Kant, individuals are bound by a duty to promote the perfect civic constitution even though they know that they are living in an "earlier" generation. And typically, unlike the methodology of justice as fairness, which is right-based in nature, Kant is basing the duty to posterity on a goal-based consideration of a perfectionist nature. This goal is an ideal for humanity as a collective, but at the same time it also is the source of the meaning of life for the individual.

This approach to the question of procreation goes a long way beyond the idea of respect for persons or the notion of taking them as ends. Justifying the validity of the sacrifice of individual interests for the sake of transindividual and transtemporal ends is a task that cannot be achieved by means of the transcendental deduction of the *Critique of Practical Reason*. The doctrine of the categorical imperative would try to solve genesis problems in terms of duties and obligations toward people and in that would get caught in the same paradoxes as a right-based theory. The philosophy of history attempts to give an ethical meaning to the continuation of the species in terms of duties derived from goals and ends and in that requires a new way of moral justification.[18] But this is highly problematic. In section 25 of the second part of the *Critique of Judgment* Kant says that "without man . . . the whole of creation would be a mere wilderness, a thing in vain, and have no final end" (Kant 1928, 108).[19] In that respect, if we read Kant as denying any axiological Archimedean point beyond human agency and freedom, we must conclude that even Kant's later doctrines of both rational religion and moral history will prove futile in the attempt to solve genethical issues; for pure genesis problems ask why create any value-conferring subjects in the first place, and as in right-based theories of justice and in deontological theories of respect for persons, to evaluate the world from a nonhuman perspective is like pulling ourselves up by our own bootstraps. This theme is boldly addressed by Kant in the *Critique of Judgment* (sec. 25), where he shows how dangerously circular (and paradoxical) the attempt to assign value to the very existence of human beings is. Kant's project in this section is to show how Man's existence in the world is of value despite Man's being also the only source of value. I will return to these deep metaphysical problems toward the end of chapter 8, trying to make sense of the idea of self-transcending and value-projecting human beings thrust into a valueless world. Kant's two irreconcilable concerns, for human autonomy and for a transcendent-religious *telos,* set the scene for a better understanding of the procreation issue.

UTILITY AND ITS ASSIGNABILITY

The theoretical advantage of right-based theories of the Rawlsian type and duty-based theories of the Kantian type lies in their formalism, that is to say in their value-free starting point. Ethical principles are derived from assumptions like fairness and rationality rather than from controversial ends and ideals. Yet this may be the very reason why these theories fail to capture the uniqueness of genesis issues and why their deployment for solving those issues leads to paradoxes. By enriching the repertory of ethical tools with nonformal notions we seem to be able to acquire better guidelines for family planning and population policies, genetic engineering, and education. To recapitulate the argument in the introduction regarding the "pure genesis" situation of the creation of Man: how can the divine act of creation *ex nihilo* be morally evaluated? It is definitely not a duty of God to create Man, nor is it Man's right to be created. Rather, it is said to be good (or even "very good"). The world is better, and creation more accomplished, when human life is added to it.

So even if to be fruitful and multiply is a duty of human beings *to* God, this duty must in the final analysis rest on a certain value, that value that makes God himself create them in the first place. The theoretical importance of the *pure* version of genesis problems is in showing that the goal-based justification is more fundamental than the duty- (or right-) based justifications for procreation, which are partly derived from it. This point can be put in the following way: both duty and right are concepts describing normative relations between people (or moral subjects in general). Only human beings have rights and duties. Furthermore, they have rights only against other human beings, and duties only toward human beings (usually others, but arguably also toward themselves, or other moral subjects like God). It is thus hardly surprising that genesis problems—having to deal with the very creation of subjects *for* these normative relations—cannot be analyzed in terms of rights and duties.

It is therefore the axiological way that looks the more promising. But this is so only on condition that the concept of value does not suffer from the same "person dependent" status that makes rights and duties incapable of dealing with genethical issues. The question is whether value itself is attached only to human beings (or another defined group of moral subjects), or if it can also be ascribed to impersonal states of the world. If value can be attached only to moral subjects, then the question of their creation escapes value judgment. For how can the prehuman world be evaluated (as e.g., inferior to the world populated with human subjects) if there is in it no "anchor" to which value can be attached? If the world, however, can be evaluated independently of the way people are "affected," then there might be a way to assess the value of alternative genethical choices, including pure genesis decisions to create humanity *ex nihilo*. But then, it seems that such a notion of value will be harder to articulate and justify. It might prove logically coherent, but at the same time intuitively implausible. In terms of the story of creation, when God sees that everything he had made was "very good," is it very good for him, very good for created humanity, or very good *simpliciter?*

The best example for this dilemma of assignability in axiological theory is utilitarianism. In fact, the first indications of an awareness of genethical problems can be traced to the dispute between the two competing versions of utilitarianism: the average and the total (e.g., Smart 1961, 18). The critics of classical (total) utilitarianism have pointed out that according to its principles there is a positive duty to bring into the world as many children as possible, as long as the marginal utility of the addition of any child (or the net gain) is positive. This duty is directly derived from the duty to promote the *overall* good in the world.[20] But such a duty is not only questionable from the point of view of human (parental) freedom, but also problematic in that the children brought into the world by this principle might turn out to enjoy a very low quality of life. Derek Parfit, who has done more than anyone else to expose the paradoxes of utilitarianism when applied to population problems, has called that option the Repugnant Conclusion (Parfit 1984, particularly 381–390). Although free from logical incoherence, this implication of total utilitarianism is so morally abhorrent so as to cast doubt on the general plausibility of the total version. It sacrifices the utility of individuals to the promotion of the impersonal value of the overall good (welfare, happiness) in the world. What is the good in a world swarming with people having lives barely worth living, even if *overall* the aggregation of the "utility" of its members supersedes that of any alternative, smaller world? The idea of the interpersonal aggregation of utility becomes questionable.

However, as many philosophers have been quick to show, the average version turns out to be vulnerable to the very same critique.[21] If the supreme principle of utility requires the promotion of average utility, two implausible implications become manifest: first, there is a duty to create more and more children, as long as the expected quality of life of the future offspring is at least slightly higher than the average quality of life of existing people; secondly, it is prohibited to bring into the world any individual child whose expected quality of life would be any lower than the actual average (even though it may be fairly high in absolute terms). Average utilitarianism hails an impersonal value (namely, a value to which the "utility" of individuals is subservient) no less than its classical rival. For instance it may require us, x number of existing people, to give birth to another person so that the average happiness of $x + 1$ is higher than that of x, although the average happiness of the x people in the $x + 1$ society will be lower (i.e., *we* lose some of our happiness for the sake of promoting the "impersonal" average). So it seems that both mutual critiques of the two versions of utilitarianism in the genesis context are plausible: neither the sacrifice of average utility for the promotion of overall utility nor the relinquishment of total utility for the sake of furthering the sheer average can be justified.

Total versions of utilitarianism have traditionally been criticized for leaving the supreme value to be promoted undetermined. Thus, the Benthamite notion of "maximum happiness to maximum people" is said to lack a fixed meaning, because there is an indefinite number of different ways to promote a value that is combined of two variables. This case is standardly exemplified by genesis questions, in which the number of people is the one variable that has to be decided by the overall happiness that is the other variable. Putting the following puzzling questions to the total utilitarian exposes this indeterminacy: is a world with human beings (of whatever positive quality of life) better than a totally uninhabited world? Is a world containing 6 billion humans more valuable than a world containing 3 billion equally happy people (Smart 1961, 18)? Is a world populated by 6 billion people overall better than a world of 3 billion people whose average utility is higher but not to the extent that their total utility exceeds that of its larger counterpart?[22]

But again, average utilitarianism suffers from equally perplexing problems. Unlike transtemporal total utilitarianism, which tries to avoid it, the average version cannot escape the question—*whose* average: is it the average utility of only presently living people, or rather that of past and present people, or that of past, present, and future people? The problem is that the past seems irrelevant and the future indeterminate, so we remain with present people's average utility as the only guide for genethical choices. But as some philosophers have pointed out, this temporal parochialism should be rejected as discriminatory, that is, an unjustifiable favoring of the present generation and its standards of life as the basis for the assessment of the value of possible future states of affairs.

R. I. Sikora takes the example of a group of survivors of a nuclear disaster, living in difficult conditions (Sikora 1978, 145–146). Should they bring new children into the world, knowing that by doing so they will have to lower their standard of living (though prepare a better world for their offspring)? This is an instance of what Parfit has called the Paradox of Mere Addition (Parfit 1984, 419–441). Total versions of utilitarianism naturally give a positive answer. But average utilitarianism is ambiguous: it depends whether "average" includes only the actual, existing generation, or whether it includes also the future one(s). In the first case the answer will be negative (they should do everything—their reproductive behavior included—to further *their own* happiness); in the second—the answer will be positive (a sacrifice of our happiness is justified for the sake of an overall net gain in the average happiness of future people). The first option sounds egoistic and discriminatory, favoring one group over another on allegedly arbitrary grounds of temporal position. The second policy appears to be repugnant in its demand for sacrifices of actual people's happiness for the promotion of the *im*personal goal of a "higher average of happiness." The present generation is asked to create people as a means for establishing a new, higher average utility. Moreover, the average version might also yield a Repugnant Conclusion, because it lays a duty on a suffering generation to beget suffering children (as long as the children are slightly better off than their parents) and the same duty again on the next generation (Sikora 1978, 128–129).

The field of the morality of procreation has also provided ethical theorists with a test for the usefulness of the Popperian distinction between positive and negative utilitarianism. The classical principle of utility has persistently been challenged by the universal intuition regarding the asymmetry between promoting happiness and preventing misery. The latter is assigned moral priority of various kinds: obligatoriness (versus a supererogatory status of the former), lexical priority (always having to be discharged before any positive contribution to happiness is attempted), extra weight (in the Benthamite calculus of overall utility). Much of the literature on the morality of procreation revolves around the issue whether there is a difference between the duty to bring a happy child into the world and the duty to avoid conceiving a miserable child. Most people feel that the latter is a more stringent duty than the former, which might not be a moral duty at all. But the theoretical tools for justifying this intuition are hard to come by. Considerations of both total and average nature do not support the distinction.

Some writers believe that the asymmetry can be argued for in terms of the existence of an object for the respective benefit and harm: although a happy child is not harmed if its parents decide not to bring it into the world, a suffering child is a subject of harm if its parents make a positive decision to beget it (Warren 1977, 285–286; Parfit 1982, 150). Analogously, in the first case there is no one to complain for having been born, whereas in the second—malpractice or wrongful life charges can be made (Narveson 1973, 68, 75). However, things are not really so easy for the theory of asymmetry. For, as we have seen in chapter 1, it is logically problematic whether one can be harmed by being born (even in misery); and secondly, the existence of a subject reacting to our behavior toward it is a double-edged argument: one can equally say that although there is no subject who can be grateful to us for not being begotten (in misery), there is a subject who can thank us for being born (happy).[23] Thus, the asymmetry argument can be turned around to serve the opposite conclusion, which points to its doubtful cogency.

Negative utilitarianism, which seems promising in guiding us in genethics, also urges (at least in its impersonal versions) paradoxical (and to some, morally abhorrent) solutions to the miseries of humanity. Primarily it recommends the painless annihilation of all humanity— either by the collective suicide of all actual beings, or by total abstention from procreation by one generation (Smart 1958, 542–543). Furthermore, an epistemological version of the asymmetry of promoting good and preventing pain introduces another paradox: as the decisions about procreation are always taken under conditions of uncertainty, the dominant strategy (in game-theoretic terms) should be never to conceive; for if the child turns out to be miserable, then there is a stringent duty not to conceive it, and if the child turns out to enjoy a happy life, then there is only a less stringent duty (or no duty at all) to conceive it (Vetter 1971, 301–302). Thus humanity will be led to gradual self-annihilation, justified by the negative utilitarian ideal of the elimination of suffering even at the cost of the disappearance of happy human beings.[24]

Nor does the more sophisticated Pareto version of utilitarianism lend much help in the analysis of genesis problems. It is indeed plausible to support any action that betters the life of existing people without making any individual worse off. But how can this be applied to the unconceived? It is true that begetting a child with the intention of using one of its kidneys for transplantation is Pareto-efficient in that no one involved can be said to be worse off, including the child (who otherwise would not have been born at all). But such a decision appears to be morally repugnant. And beyond that, grounding it in the fact that the child cannot be said to be "worse off" is conceptually problematic; for it is doubtful whether there is any sense in the first place in applying comparative judgments of increase or decrease in welfare to the process of coming into existence.[25] In any case, such a use of Pareto principle leads directly to the Repugnant Conclusion.

And again, the metaphysical problem of personal identity is a major stumbling block in the application of utilitarian principles to genesis problems. Parfit, whose general ethical orientation is utilitarian (adhering to a "maximizing principle" as a legitimate impersonal goal), has been particularly sensitive to this dimension. Parfit insists on strict constraints of personal identity in the utilitarian assessment of alternative population policies. Thus, we have duties and obligations only toward actual individuals, and actual individuals have by necessity a fixed identity. The paradoxical nature of genesis decisions arises out of the incomparability of a policy x, which affects an individual A, and a policy y, which affects an individual B, living in a different world.[26] Parfit accordingly distinguishes between Same People Choices, which are not plagued by the problem of indeterminate identity, and Different People Choices (either of the Same Number variety or of the Different Number variety), which challenge the validity of utilitarian principles in the genesis context (Parfit 1984, 356).

Parfit's whole work on the morality of procreation is a desperate (and in his own opinion unsuccessful) attempt to reconcile the two mutually exclusive principles: the classical utilitarian impersonal ideal of promoting good in the world (or decreasing suffering) and the logical constraint of personal identity (or the idea that utility must always be attached to an independently identifiable individual).[27] In his later work, Parfit offers a solution in perfectionist terms: the reason for preferring our smaller world to a much larger one with greater overall happiness but a much lower average happiness is of a *qualitative* nature. The Z-world is devoid of those higher type experiences, and no amount of lower type experiences can compensate for this loss. No quantity of Ravel can outweigh a Mozart (Parfit 1986, 145–164)! However, Parfit's argument rests heavily on the analogy between the choice between *worlds* and the choice between one *life* and another for an individual. Parfit might be right in claiming that a person would prefer a life of a hundred years with Mozart-quality experiences to eternal life of potatoes and Muzak (p. 160); but this, although difficult, is a meaningful choice, because utilities can be assigned to a subject. In comparisons between worlds, however, no such condition of assignability obtains, and hence supplementing utilitarianism with a qualitative dimension is of no avail.

It should be noted that the problem of assignability does not haunt utilitarianism alone, but all other consequentialist theories, as well as the theory of value in general. It is therefore a problem also for historicistic ideals regarding the progress of humanity toward a specified goal (be it Kantian, Hegelian, Marxist, or Christian; the establishment of social justice on earth, the perfection of humanity, the preservation of nature, the achievement of scientific truth, eugenic progress, or the universal rule of a church). These are all conceptually coherent as goals for given human beings, but using them as a justification for producing human beings is problematic.

Rational choice theory can serve as an illuminating way to highlight these difficulties. Using Jon Elster's terminology of adaptive preferences, we may ask how should our power to fix the identity of future people in the sense of molding their basic preferences be exercised? As utilitarians, we may *either* strive to guarantee for our descendants the best environmental and cultural conditions on the assumption that we want them to have (and that indeed they will have) the same preferences as ourselves; *or* we may equally (and maybe more efficiently from a utilitarian point of view of the costs to us and the net gain for their total happiness) manipulate their preferences (by genetic engineering or radical educational means) so that a depleted environment and culturally lacking world would best suit their interests![28] This is the same old problem of Mill's satisfied pig, or its modern Orwellian versions. One might always say that brainwashed people are harmed in that they cannot express their *real* interests and potential. But if a new species of completely nonhuman creatures is somehow brought about, its interests and potential would be radically different from ours. Can any of our moral values decide the desirability of a creation of such a species?

This brings us to the ultimate question, which because of its fantastic nature has not usually been addressed: is not the notion of utility itself a matter of choice? Future people might turn out to have a completely different concept of utility, different parameters for quantifying and comparing utility, due either to different Millean judgments as to which pleasure is of a higher quality or to a different psychological makeup. Evolution can serve as the testing field for such a stretching of the imagination. Human history can hardly be subject to an overall assessment in terms of any unified Benthamite concept of utility and may contain phases of radically incommensurable notions of utility, satisfaction, or pleasure. This hypothesis casts another doubt on the plausibility of an impersonal notion of total utility. It follows that incomparability is due not only to the difference in identity of the subjects of utility but also to the difference in the parameters constituting utility itself. This is an argument parallel to the above mentioned doubt regarding Kant's conviction that human beings will always be rational. It also casts doubt on the coherence of the idea of eugenics, which again presupposes a common set of parameters by which the genetic betterment of the human species is judged. The products of our eugenic procedures might have *genes* that make them take issue with us regarding the *eugenic* value of these procedures!

We have tried in this section only to sketch some of the conceptual difficulties involved in the application of utilitarianism and value theory in general to the genethical sphere. This is by no means an exhaustive list of problems. We will see for example how the issue of the definition of a minimum quality of life (life that is worth living, or subsistence level) evades a utilitarian account, because it involves standards requiring comparisons that are metaphysically impossible. For instance, can a life of zero quality (viz., neither below, nor above the line of a life worth living) be said to be of a value equal to the nonexistence of its subject? We will have to examine the challenge to standard utilitarian calculus of the idea of the discount of utility in time, which intuitively is a principle of weighting the interests of future people as against ours. Some might defend utilitarianism's applicability to genesis problems by substituting ideals and interests for happiness and pleasure, thus attempting to disentangle utility from its "person-affecting" basis in actual human conscious states (this will be shown to be an illusory improvement, as interests and even ideals are by necessity *of* actual human beings). Then there is the question whether the existence of human subjects (who invest the world with value) is itself valuable. This is a metaphysically elusive question and may prove meaningless; yet it seems to lie at the core of genethics. The intention of the present section has only been to point out some principal shortcomings of utilitarianism. The fuller discussion of the paradoxes listed above will be undertaken in chapters 4, 5, and 6, in which an attempt will be made to outline a coherent and, it is hoped, plausible framework for the solution of genethical problems.

To summarize the common lesson of the various sections of this chapter, we may say that traditional ethical theories have failed to delineate the relevant reference group for genethical decision making. Unlike liberal and humanistic expansions of the reference groups (to women, children, other races, animals), sensitivity to the lot of future people cannot be expressed simply by embracing "them" into the moral community. For it is exactly the indeterminacy of "them" which makes it impossible to apply contractarian, Kantian, or utilitarian principles to decide "their" lot. It is not the assumption of the timelessness of the moral community which makes theories of ethics incapable of handling genesis problems, but rather the paradox of being expected to provide ethical principles for membership in the community which is the basis of all ethical principles. Right-based theories could not supply any such principles, because potential people cannot be said to have a right to be born. Duty-based theories looked a little more promising, but again only on the assumption that either there is some moral being to whom such a duty is somehow owed (mainly God) or that the duty to procreate is derived from a certain goal. In the first case *pure* genesis problems remain unresolved; in the second, we are led to goal-based theories. But with goal-based theories we have to choose between a person-affecting concept of value, which traps us in the same problems as right- and duty-based theories, or settle for an impersonal concept of value which is difficult to justify and leads to uneasy implications. Basically two alternatives seem to suggest themselves as a way out of this logical catch: either do away altogether with the constraint of justifying moral judgment in terms of deontic relations between individuals and the assignment of value to identifiable persons, or limit the boundaries of the relevant reference group (the individuals who have rights and are the subject of duties and value) to actual, existing people.

The Meta-ethical Deadlock

THE METHODOLOGICAL ASCENT

Genethical issues, we may recall, have been raised in modern discussions in the course of attempts to compare the relative merits of the total and average versions of utilitarianism. Thus when trying to decide which world is morally superior—that with 1 million people or that with 2 million equally happy people (on average), Smart comments: "I cannot help feeling preference for the second universe. But if someone feels the other way I do not know how to argue with him" (Smart 1961, 18). This is a typical admission of methodological agnosticism, which for many philosophers (though not for Smart) is coupled with lack of conviction regarding the substantive genethical issue at hand. Not to know the answer to an important question is bad enough. Not to know how to go about solving it is even worse. Genesis problems have been shown in the last two chapters to strain our intuitions and challenge our established ethical theories. But it seems that they also prompt a sense of methodological uneasiness, raising doubts concerning the definition and scope of basic ethical concepts, the validity of certain methods of justification in ethical argumentation, and indeed the very limits of ethics.

In chapter 1 I pointed out the confusion that characterizes our intuitions concerning the moral status of the unconceived, especially through presentation of the real-life cases of legal suits for wrongful life. I attributed this confusion to the novelty of the choices involved in modern techniques of birth (and conception) control, population regulation, and

genetic screening and engineering. A typical way to deal with such conflicting and vague intuitions is to resort to theoretical principles, which
derive their force from more general considerations and are less dependent on the circumstantial factors that mold our first-order beliefs and
gut reactions. However, as I took pains to show in chapter 2, the retreat
to the level of principled ethical discourse hardly serves the purpose of
clarifying the scene. Instead, it adds to the sense of paradox inherent in
questions regarding procreation. Unlike newly debated topics such as
feminism, affirmative action, even abortion—which though controversial still lend themselves to discussion in terms of justice and rights,
welfare and satisfaction, ideals and duties—genesis problems turn out to
resist analysis in these terms. The conclusion of chapter 2 led us to realize
that something was basically lacking in all traditional ethical theories,
something that goes beyond the internal debate on their comparative
merits, let alone beyond the differences in "intuitions" we might have
regarding procreation.

The puzzling and conflicting implications of all ethical theories
would seem to call for a second "ascent": from ethical discourse to a
methodological examination of the reasons for the failure of this discourse. Such an analysis might suggest either where ethical theory can
be revised so as to enable it to account for the unresolved genesis problems, or how to redraw the borderlines of ethics in a way which would
leave genesis issues outside the realm of ethics. In other words, the
methodological turn would be necessary to decide whether genethics is
part of ethics, or whether it belongs to a nonmoral sphere of deliberation and evaluation. Following the general argument of this book, the
significance of this methodological discussion, if it yields results, would
not be confined only to the attempt to account for awkward genesis
problems; the method of genethics might then serve as a radical test-
case for the methods of ethics in general, a test that might teach us
lessons far beyond those relevant to genethics.

However, this appeal to a higher level of discourse in order to solve
the problems infesting discourse of a lower level proves a hopeless
strategy. The three-tier distinction of morality, ethics, and meta-ethics
has become discredited because of the interdependence of our moral
principles and first-order beliefs on the one hand, and the definitions
and methods of argumentation in ethics and our deeply rooted substantive ethical views on the other. This interdependence is particularly
relevant in the analysis of decisions on procreation. There are neither
purely empirical considerations, nor *a priori* constraints that in them-

selves commit us to any general solution of genesis issues. No morally neutral methodological or formal procedure can decide on its own whether children can sue their parents for being born with inferior genetic chances, or whether it is our duty to postpone a planned pregnancy in order to avoid the conception of a defective child.

Consider population regulation in China: are the measures confining the size of a family to one child morally justifiable? Our judgments, even in a more reflective mood, are confused. We believe that such measures go against the basic right of individuals to procreate. But then we are told that such a limitation is the only way to avoid future demographic catastrophe, involving mass suffering, starvation, and death. If that is so, we ask, what is the right balance between parental freedom and future people's welfare? Or, how far should the population control policy go, or how strictly should it be applied? We are pushed to a more theoretical level of principled discourse. But however we look at the problem—as a conflict of (present) rights versus (future) welfare, or (present) rights versus (future) rights, or (present) welfare versus (future) welfare—we get stuck in unresolved dilemmas: can the very language of rights, duties, and welfare deal with these conflicts? Unlike other moral dilemmas involving a conflict of rights and duties, in which we are hard pressed to decide between opposing though equally relevant principles, in genesis issues the very relevance of the principles is questioned. The unborn Chinese individuals cannot be said to have rights, hence it is hard to say that we have duties toward them. And if the welfare of the Chinese people in the future is the guiding principle, what is this "people"? Whom exactly does it include? If we cannot answer this question we will have to redefine either the concept of "a people," or the conditions of applying the concept of welfare in this context.

So genesis issues call for a deeper kind of meta-ethical reconsideration than do other hard moral cases. If we again take Singer's idea of the "expanding moral circle" (Singer 1981), we realize that the addition of moral subjects into this privileged circle does not usually require the formation of completely new moral concepts. Once a society or a culture realizes that women are no less rational than men, or (as the early Christian conquerors of America "discovered") that Native Americans have souls, or that animals feel pain, we apply the relevant respective moral principles to these newcomers into the moral circle. Of course, the interdependence of the first two levels of morality may be reflected by denying the adequacy of a certain theoretical principle because of its failure to account for the moral status of the "newcomer." But we can usually resort to another, competing principle, which does the job (e.g., animal liberationists substitute Benthamite sentience for Kantian rationality). The appeal to such a principle is usually supported by empirical facts or discoveries. However, with future people these procedures of liberal expansion are of no avail. No competing principles offer themselves, and newly discovered empirical data are often the source of theoretical confusion rather than evidence for any particular principle.

Genesis problems raise doubts regarding methods of ethical argumentation as well as regarding the relevance of moral concepts. The critique of the universalism of Kant's categorical imperative applies to Hare's meta-ethical test of universal prescriptivism. Hare argues that abortion is *prima facie* wrong because it violates the Golden Rule (which is derived from the meta-ethical principle of universal prescriptivism and the definition of a moral argument) (Hare 1974/1975). But applying the universalizing principle to genesis problems prejudges the normative issue whether future people have a moral standing, ignoring the paradox of "the potentiality principle," which confers a moral status on potential people (Warren 1977, 17–21). Although all meta-ethical principles (such as that of universal prescriptivism) are circularly supported by normative considerations (e.g., the universal right to equal concern, or the essential equality of human beings as rational or sentient beings), the genesis case is more troublesome for the validation of the meta-ethical principle: it is dependent on highly controversial normative views regarding the appropriate way of treating potential individuals. Circularity in this case becomes vicious and methodologically unacceptable.

Naturalism also faces obstacles in supplying a methodological framework for the validation of ethical arguments in the genesis sphere. The issue here is not whether *ought* can be derived from *is*, but whether there is any *is* from which the *ought* can be derived. For it is the way we want the world and future people to be which is the subject of genethical choices, and hence no recourse to their essential (as well as nonessential) nature is of any use. Even if we believe that human nature is the ultimate source of our moral principles, it can serve us at most to derive what we should do so as to express *our* human nature, but not what we should do so as to respect the nature of future people, which stands to be molded by us.

The Is-Ought issue lies at the core of the methodology of genethics in another sense. There is a close relationship between metaphysical truths about the nature of the self (or conditions of personal identity) and the moral status of future individuals. For example, an essentialist view, taking human identity as a function of the existence of a fixed property or an unchanging element (soul, genetic makeup), would support different ethical principles regarding the procreation of human beings than a Humean or a Parfitian view, which suggests weaker identity criteria. Thus, as we will see below, impersonalism, as a meta-ethical analysis of the nature of value, tallies with the theory of psychological continuity of personal identity. For both prudence (taking care of one's own future interests) and moral altruism (taking care of another person's interests) are based on the same principle of concern for a person who is psychologically close to the agent's present self. Differences between "my" future self and "another" person are only a matter of (contingent) degree (Zemach 1987, 227–228; Parfit 1984, chap. 15). The basic duty derived from (or compatible with) such a metaphysical conception of personal identity is the promotion of overall goodness in the world, the maximization of happiness and satisfaction; the assignability of welfare to subjects with "fixed" identity becomes less important. The attitude toward future individuals is naturally based on the same lines of impersonal maximization. However, a strict essentialist view of personal identity (Cartesian, Lockean, or Kripkean) is confronted with the question of the assignability of value, the need to identify the subject of value, beneficence, interests, satisfaction, rights. It is obviously closer to a "person-affecting" concept of value and more troubled by the paradoxes of including potential people in the moral circle. Moral concepts are attached to well-defined individuals rather than to an abstract overall lump. Right-based theories must assume a concept of a person as a separate, strictly defined and continuous subject, to whom rights, interests, and life plans can be ascribed. A social contract, for example, can only occur between individuals who on the one hand are separate from each other and on the other hand are essentially connected with their future selves. Otherwise no sense can be made of the ideas of bargaining, promising, and planning on the basis of long-term expectations (Daniels 1979a, 263).

Now it seems that there is no methodological reason to give priority to metaphysics over ethics, in the sense of deciding meta-ethical issues on the basis of metaphysical considerations. Some of our metaphysical beliefs may be influenced by deeply held ethical commitments. In other words, the concept of personal identity is at least partly a function of our moral views (as is typically illustrated by Locke's theory). The interdependence of morality and metaphysics points to the methodological difficulty inherent in both ethics and genethics: in the same way as the issues of brain death and euthanasia, abortion and *in vitro* fertilization force on us a reconsideration of the metaphysical criteria of "life," so do the issues of genetic engineering and wrongful life urge us to reformulate the metaphysics of personal identity. And the plausibility of ethical principles would lend support for a given view of personal identity no less than such a view could uphold ethical principles.

The interdependence of ethics and metaphysics is most typically illustrated by what might turn out to be the ultimate question in genethics: what is good in the very existence of human beings? (Or, to borrow Jonathan Glover's title, what sort of people should there be?) Any attempt to answer this question on the two first levels of moral discourse leads to the realization that there is something unique in it, since it asks about the very framework *within* which moral relations and evaluations occur. This realization stresses the meta-ethical or methodological doubt whether the question has any *meaning*. If it has, then a metaphysical theory of the nature of being and value is called for (see, for instance, Jonas 1984, 45ff.). If it does not, how does this fact affect the feasibility of any kind of ethical meaning and value? Are Kant and Aristotle correct in claiming that treating the metaphysical question of the value of the very existence of valuers (human individuals) as meaningless would make all the rest of our moral life meaningless as well? Or can we hope to save the meaningfulness of morality (including that of procreation) by *limiting* its scope. The last option is the one to which this essay is tending. But the method of establishing its plausibility cannot be purely "analytical." The only way out of the meta-ethical deadlock is through the reintroduction of normative considerations as a test for newly suggested theoretical solutions for genesis problems. A natural candidate for such a methodological approach combining moral views and theoretical principles is that of reflective equilibrium proposed by John Rawls.

TWO LEVELS OF REFLECTIVE EQUILIBRIUM

Reflective equilibrium is a method in ethics which characterizes the attempt to avoid both intuitionism and *a priorism*. Its major advantage is its dynamic nature, allowing for the constant revision of both our first-order moral beliefs as well as the theoretical principles that unify and justify them. Moral beliefs ("intuitions") are never immune to scrutiny by newly articulated principles; and ethical principles are constantly reviewed in the light of deeply held (often new) moral judgments. As in grammar, moral theory is expected to yield normative rules whose validity is partly constrained by "considered judgments" (regarding right and wrong, correct and incorrect). Having raised doubts concerning the suitability of naturalism and universal prescriptivism as methods for dealing with genethical problems, can reflective equilibrium serve as a methodological alternative?

The main obstacle in applying this method to genethics lies in the relative shakiness of our moral intuitions regarding typical genesis problems. Unlike the principles of justice and the idea of justice as fairness which can be tested in the light of deeply held convictions regarding liberty, equality, opportunity, and self-respect, most people feel systematically confused in their beliefs about the right not to be born in defect, the optimal population size of their society, and the desirable guidelines for deciding the essential nature and identity of future people. At the other pole of the equilibrium, traditional ethical principles that have proved "effective" in dealing with ethical problems fail in application to genethical topics. This means that the dynamics of creating a reflective equilibrium has no firm Archimedean point from which mutual testing and revision can start.

Proponents of reflective equilibrium are aware that by its very antifoundationalist nature this method cannot rely on Archimedean points and must leave *all* beliefs and principles susceptible to revision. However, the fruitfulness of reflective equilibrium lies in assuming (at least provisionally) a relative stability of *some* set of beliefs (or principles) against whose background the disputable ones are examined and revised. By having independent grounds for holding these beliefs, we can use them without fear of circularity to corroborate (or undermine) the disputed ones. Now, this logical condition of the (relative) independence of the evidentiary grounds of the beliefs justified by reflective equilibrium is much harder to satisfy in genesis cases. For these, by their very nature, challenge the usually uncontroversial notions of personhood, essential human character, and legitimate interests. In ethics, at least the existence, number, and identity of moral subjects are taken as *given* and thus can serve as some sort of a starting point for the dynamic process of creating a "fit" between principles and beliefs. In genethics these constitute the subject of the equilibrium. In abortion and involuntary euthanasia, we try to establish an equilibrium by asking whether the fetus and the "human vegetable" are persons, or whether they can be said to have rights. Certainly, these are hard cases because of their fuzzy contours (when does the life of a person begin and end, what are the conditions for ascribing rights); but they are subject to the traditional ethical discourse. In genesis problems, however, the very relevance of the language of personhood and rights is to be questioned.

This fact may lead to the search for a reflective equilibrium of a higher level. In a series of articles, Norman Daniels has developed Rawls's own distinction between narrow and wide reflective equilibria and examined in detail the methodological implications and limitations of the two (Daniels 1979a; Daniels 1979b; Daniels 1980). The narrow form is concerned with the "fit" between intuitions and moral principles and can thus be expected at most to provide consistency (coherence) to our ethical views rather than plausibility (justification) (see also Raz 1982, 311, 329). This may be sufficient for grammar as a theory of syntax, but not for ethics. For in ethics our considered judgments are deeply dependent on scientific beliefs (e.g., the genetic basis of personal identity), on metaphysical beliefs (e.g., a Platonic view of souls existing prior to birth), or on methodological assumptions (e.g., methodological individualism). In contrast, the sense of the grammaticality of a given sentence hardly ever depends on extra-linguistic beliefs. We can add that the narrow version is particularly unhelpful (even as a unifying mechanism) for resolving genesis issues because of the relatively unstructured nature of our first-order beliefs. The wide notion is added as a defense of the idea of reflective equilibrium by viewing both intuitions and principles in the light of general background theories (of human nature, the place of an individual in society, the role of moral theory) to which we adhere for independent reasons.

However, the relationship between background theories and particular ethical principles in the wide equilibrium is itself marred by the threat of circularity. Rawls himself views the theory of mind as underdetermining moral theory and claims that the concept of a person is largely a function of our moral ideas and ideals (such as the well-ordered society or the just institutions of the society in which people live). And although Parfit is correct in aligning an essentialist ("simple") view of personal identity with the morality of justice as fairness and the continuity ("complex") theory of persons with utilitarian approaches— the way we decide between the two options of metaphysical theory is partly dictated by our moral views. Now it is true that the wide view is not completely and unfruitfully circular because it appeals to metaphysical and other background theories for which we have independent (e.g., scientific, sociological, psychological) grounds. This makes Daniels's defense of the Rawlsian idea of reflective equilibrium convincing. But, when we come to genesis problems we again see that this defense is mostly beside the point. For the background theories underdetermine genethical principles in a deeper sense: not only are they compatible with conflicting moral theories; they are the very subject of the moral theory.

This point can be illustrated in the following way. Rawls says that theories of human nature do not fully determine the theory of morals and are partly decided by the latter. Daniels refers to this idea as the "plasticity thesis":

> ... different social institutions, which we may assume reflect different, at least implicit, moral conceptions, can *shape* persons to have different "actual continuities." (Daniels 1979b, 273)

This means that within an independently grounded background theory of human nature there are various ways of fixing the exact concept of a person through the mediation of moral and social ideas and ideals. My point is that in genesis issues the ethical choices we are forced to make run even beyond the borderlines of such a "plastic" conception of a person, since they open up possibilities of creating radically different "human"(?) creatures. Daniels believes that the basis for the "provisionally fixed points" for a wide reflective equilibrium lies in the fact that if we decide to question them "we might imagine persons quite unlike the persons we know" (Daniels 1979a, 267). But the morality of procreation forces us to *choose* whether we want to have exactly such kinds of persons.[1]

The same point also applies to social constraints, too. Rawls's later writings particularly emphasize the social nature of the concept of the person, namely the political ideal of a well-ordered society as the basis for the ideal portrayal of the contractors as agents having certain moral powers and lacking certain kinds of knowledge. But genethic possibilities (either in the form of *revolutionary* social ideas, such as in Marxism, or in the form of *imaginary* science-fiction Brave New Worlds) challenge the validity of the deeper sociological assumptions and normative preferences inherent in the notion of a well-ordered society. Why not, for example, *create* a society that prefers the average utility principle to justice as fairness? Or take the right-based views, such as justice as fairness or other liberal ideologies of a Millean or Dworkinian type: are they not all based on the acute sense of the idiosyncrasies of the values of individuals, the deep differences in personal conceptions of the good life? It is true that a morality of rights (or equal concern) makes good sense in this pluralistic context. But if we can create future individuals in a much more uniform manner, namely with similar preferences and scale of values, would not a totally different ethics be appropriate? An ethics of efficiency in achieving common goals rather than respecting individual life plans? And would not the very method of reflective equilibrium or the meta-ethical idea of a social contract (with the requirement of veto power and unanimity in the original position) as a method of derivation become obsolete in such new circumstances? If we cannot take either the nature of society or the nature of persons as *a priori* given (because they are interdependent), then we have to decide on both simultaneously. The threat of circularity is more ominous in such cases and cannot be brushed aside by merely denigrating their fictional nature.

Although Rawls was aware of the difficulties of intergenerational extension of the principles of justice, he did not see these as stumbling blocks on the methodological level. His doctrine of reflective equilibrium assumes that we are engaged in planning *our* society and *our* future. This is a perfectly natural assumption for a social contract (right-based) theory, but planning future society and future people shifts the discourse necessarily to an impersonal (goal-based) level and involves the tricky issues of identity (namely, the criteria for "our"). We cannot appeal to the method of reflective equilibrium in this sphere, because any balance we might strike between principles and beliefs might not be shared by the subjects of our decision (future people).[2] The idea of reaching a consensus or convergence of moral judgments through the method of reflective equilibrium is unattainable in the genesis context.[3] Similarly, the right-based requirement of unanimity in the original position (justified also by Dworkin 1973, 531, in terms of the right to equal concern) cannot be applied to principles regarding future generations.

It is important to note that genesis problems are methodologically confusing because on the one hand we feel that in contrast to many other ethical issues we have too little control over the outcome of our choices (due to ignorance and sheer distance in time); and on the other hand we have too much control (in the sense that the nature of the future is "up to us"). In epistemological terms, knowledge of future states cannot serve as a basis for present decision making, either because it is not at hand and is difficult to predict, or because it is itself dependent on our decision. The first obstacle is sometimes exaggerated by critics of futurology, but it still calls for caution. The expected consequences of our decisions regarding the future are not just like any other future-oriented moral choices in being based on probabilities; they are partly mediated by the free choice of future people over which we have no control. Yet the second obstacle seems to be of a logically deeper nature and hence insurmountable. Future human conditions cannot serve as background data for moral choice once they become the subject of the choice.

So it seems that we are deprived in the case of genethics of firm moral beliefs and intuitions (of the kind most people have in the abortion issue for example); we cannot appeal to traditional ethical principles, which have been shown to lead to paradoxes when applied to genesis problems; and we can also expect little help from general background independent theories, of the sort suggested by Daniels, because their content is sometimes the ethical issue itself. What in this situation is left of the idea of a reflective equilibrium? I suggest a version that is even wider than the Rawlsian wide one. It amounts to a reexamination not only of ethical principles and background theories of the nature of the individual and society, but of the nature of value and the limits of moral duty and rights. Furthermore, it turns *onto itself* by questioning the kind of insight we can gain from any balancing of "intuitions" and principled reasoning. The common objection against the idea of reflective equilibrium asks whose considered judgment should be balanced against moral principles, which raises the threat of relativism. But in genesis issues this point carries a particular logical meaning, as the balance struck by *us* may seem completely unfounded by *them,* the "products" of decisions based on the allegedly well-reasoned genethical principles! In positive terms, the method of reflective equilibrium may offer a *systemic* approach to the articulation of genethical principles, that is to say a global review of principles, psychological and sociological theories of human nature and society, some first-order beliefs and convictions, in other words, a *holistic* method of reasoning and validation.

The combination of the denial of foundationalism and the awareness of the interdependence of normative principles and meta-ethical methods and concepts means that no method of acceptance in ethics is itself immune from reconsideration in terms of newly formulated principles and beliefs. This is particularly true of radically novel moral challenges posed by futurity problems. However, there is no guide in the task of global consideration of theory and norms other than the existing variety of beliefs and methods. The metaphor of a Neurath-ship, repaired and remodeled in high seas, is very pertinent for our purposes and should be taken as including a possible change also in the *methods* of changing the decaying planks.[4]

A systemic approach to theory acceptance starts, of course, with the conditions of coherence and consistency, which constrain the acceptability of theories. This requires an attempt to derive as many relevant implications as possible, draw analogies, inquire into presuppositions and background data, and constantly inspect the way a proposed solution to the new issue is embedded in the wider system of beliefs, principles, and methods. But of course, as critics of reflective equilibrium have pointed out, consistency is never a sufficient condition. We may for instance, be able to formulate a consistent set of beliefs and principles by "trimming off" all those troublesome elements that have proved not to "cohere" with each other. This leads us to the much harder condition of plausibility or reasonableness. Like consistency, plausibility is also a systemic notion; it cannot be atomistically applied to particular judgments or principles. Using an economic metaphor, we may put it as the question of the cost involved in the adoption of a system of beliefs and principles. Costs and prices are relative; everything has a cost; and the ultimate aim is to reduce it as much as possible. This means that the method of testing the adequacy of genethical theory must consist of the juxtaposition of alternative sets or systems of overall views (including beliefs, implications, underlying assumptions, etc.) and assessing the relative costs of the acceptance of each. These costs are varied: they may relate to the intuitive appeal of the beliefs forced upon us by the theory; they may involve the need to abandon long-cherished principles; they may require us to restrict the very scope of moral discourse.

Remaining faithful to the Neurath metaphor, we should note that unlike the economic sphere, there is no *a priori* method of cost accounting in moral theory. This is due to the fact that human preferences are not just taken as given (in their existence and degree), but rather are approached by a normative scale that is independently formed.[5] In genesis issues this means that the way we assess the "profitability" of theoretical principles is itself liable to change with the constantly evolving balances between theoretical gains and losses. This may raise the accusation of philosophical gerrymandering, that is, the manipulation of the borderlines of ethical theory so as to accommodate a particular moral outcome. But the contours of ethical theory, unlike those of election districts, cannot and should not be defined independently of the outcome, and the idea of fairness, which in politics is a procedural ideal, is not a methodological principle in the formation of theories. A "revolution" in ethical approach to traditional problems (similar to the Kuhnian concept in science) is characterized precisely by the demand (and readiness) to abandon old criteria of theory evaluation. Thus, the medical capacity of artificially prolonging life challenges the well-entrenched value of the sanctity of life (and the right to life). But in a much more radical way, the medical capacity to create life and mold its character forces us to reconsider the superiority of life to "no-life," and even that of a happy life over a miserable life (of *another*, potential person).

So being deprived of any *a priori* starting point—methodological, normative, or intuitive—we are left with a fairly shaky systemic approach whose only advantage over its foundationalist rivals is that it explicitly attempts to view the controversial issues in the *widest* context. Once the alternative options are presented holistically, the selection of the preferred one can at least be said to be intellectually responsible, even if no objective rules of theoretical cost effectiveness can ever be articulated. This calls for particular patience, especially in the case of genethics (where the costs of each theoretical alternative are naturally high both because of the counterintuitive nature of any general solution and the difficulties encountered in applying traditional ethical principles). Intuition and common sense will not be of much help, since they do not side with any particular theory (and many people admit having no intuition on many of the issues). Ultimate judgment on the proposed positive approach to genesis questions should therefore be passed only after examining its "systemic" implications in a whole spectrum of issues: metaphysical, psychological, ethical, and methodological. The technique of rebuilding a ship in mid-sea can be appreciated only on the basis of speed, efficiency, beauty, material costs, ingenuity, and safety considered *en bloc*. And even then, there is no guarantee of consensus, because of the differences in weight given to each of these parameters by different evaluators. Indeed, equilibrium might turn out to be for the time being impossible to achieve, since only further developments in our moral experience and attitudes to new genethical phenomena in the future will afford us with a relatively stable balance of thought and sentiment.

Therefore, it is both historical and theoretical patience that are called for. Furthermore, we can safely deny that such a wide and "open-ended" method of reflective equilibrium enhances ethical conservatism, as some of the doctrine's foes have objected. It advocates conservatism only in the trivial sense that the building blocks of a moral theory must consist of *some* given judgments, beliefs, scientific theories, and methods. All the rest remains open to the formation of new "balances."

The peculiar problem in genethics is that even on that global, holistic level the choice between competing theories and explanations requires an exceptional measure of idealization. In contract theory we are asked to imagine an idealized state of nature or an "unreal" original position; but the issues that are to be solved by such theoretical devices are very real and concrete. In genethics, however, the issues are themselves (still) partly imaginary, remote, and unconnected to everyday experience. Accordingly, we can hope to gain better insight into their resolution only through "fantastic" analogies and thought-experiments that artificially highlight their uniqueness.

Abstraction and idealization have always been illuminating methodical devices in ethics. But they have also often been suspected of being able to yield (at most) irrelevant results. For, it was argued, ethics deals with real-life problems, whose solution is of any practical interest only if it is couched in a relevant empirical context. And as ethics is concerned with guiding human action in the world (unlike metaphysics or logic which are concerned with truth, which lies beyond the empirical), it must be bound to empirical reality. Accordingly, "desert-island examples" were dismissed in the 1950s as having no force in the debates over utilitarian accounts of the wrongness of breaking promises, or of punishing the innocent. Unlike the discussion of personal identity and survival, in which science-fiction examples serve as legitimate test cases for metaphysical principles and criteria, the question of our obligations to future generations may seem to be only further confused by highly contrived stories about five human survivors of a nuclear holocaust having to decide whether to bring children into the world at the price of lowering their own standard of living!

Yet, such exercises in stretching the imagination turn out to be inescapable in cases where the very control of the empirical conditions (including the "deep" ones, concerning the existence and essential identity of the subjects of moral discourse) calls for guidance. It would be paradoxical to constrain the discourse by considerations of social, genetic, or demographic "reality." It is therefore not surprising that much of the literature on the morality of procreation is conducted through extremely artificial and fictitious examples (see, above all, Parfit's plethora of imaginary cases, distinguished from each other by properties of only "theoretical" interest). The problem is that despite its inevitability such a reliance on *Gedankenexperimenten* has its limits; for it is aimed in the last analysis at testing our judgments and beliefs, or at winning sympathy for a certain principle and eliciting revulsion toward certain implications; and this can be achieved only if the examples retain enough relation and similarity to real-life cases.[6]

In the subject of genethics we can safely argue that although the method of abstraction and idealization is fruitful and unavoidable, it yields theoretical results that should not be taken as threatening as they may seem at first sight. In chapter 7 we will show why deep empirical data make much of the theoretical solution offered in chapters 4–6 of little practical consequence. Methodologically it is important to be aware of the way empirical facts about the nature of human beings as we know them constrain theory: these facts do not in themselves determine the validity of the theory (especially, as we noted, in genethics), but they may mitigate the apparently counterintuitive nature of some of its implications. In that respect, they have a negative contribution to theoretical constructions in restraining the force of opposing intuitions. Theoretical arguments can then serve to uncover the sources of justification for genethical choices without coming into direct conflict with first-order beliefs.

From the point of view of everyday moral choice, *pure* genesis problems are the most farfetched. And indeed it is empirically inconceivable that human beings be situated in circumstances of solitary existence in which procreative decisions have no effect on any actual person (including themselves). It is not surprising that the only realm in which such a situation might make any sense is the theological account of the creation of human beings by God. But this story shares relevantly important elements with everyday *impure* decisions of family planning to make it philosophically illuminating beyond its theological assumptions. It marks out the absurdity of grounding free acts of total creation in the interests or rights of the created. Decisions concerning the size of a family are *relatively* pure because parents, for ethical reasons, are usually given an extensive liberty to make these choices, unconstrained by the interests of other people. A lesser degree of purity of genesis applies to education, in which, as we shall see, the freedom of parents is (to a gradually growing extent) limited by the child's developing identity. In demographic planning we shall see the least pure case of genesis: decisions highly conditioned by the concern for actual people and by empirical facts about world resources and the actual procreative wishes of individuals. But beyond the differences in degrees of purity and the independence from contingent circumstances, all these kinds of genesis decisions have the same conceptual structure and call for the same theory of justification.

IMPERSONALISM IN ETHICS VERSUS PERSON-AFFECTING AXIOLOGY

> First of all, it appears that such words ["good," "obligation"] can have no application or relevancy in a world in which no sentient life exists. Imagine an absolutely material world, containing only physical and chemical facts, and existing from eternity without a God, without even an interested specta-tor: would there be any sense in saying of that world that one of its states is better than another? (William James 1949, 189)

The lesson drawn from the examination of the major kinds of ethical theories in chapter 2 was the superiority of a goal-based approach to genethical issues over the duty-based and right-based alternatives. And indeed, although right-based wrongful life suits have been shown to be highly problematical, the more interesting attempts to deal with ethics for future generations have been conducted in terms of the conse-quences of our decisions, future welfare (or utility), ideals of a better humanity, the value of maintaining and developing a certain grand human project or enterprise. But before discussing those attempts in detail, it would be worthwhile to look into the meta-ethical dimension involved in a goal-based approach to genesis problems. Essentially I am going to suggest that the crux of the current philosophical debate on the moral status of future generations lies in the analysis of the most general concept of goal-based theories, namely value.

The nature of value is the philosophically deepest way to examine the roots of the debate between different solutions to the genethical prob-lem, because it is the focus of the general way in which ethics is "con-nected" to the world. There are two mutually exclusive and exhaustive alternatives of viewing this connection. According to the first, value is attached to the *world,* that is to say it characterizes states of affairs in the widest global meaning of the term. According to the second, value is attached only to human beings (or other relevantly similar creatures), that is, through the way it *affects* (human) subjects. The difference between the two approaches consists in the sort of conditions that must be satisfied for a value judgment to be applicable: certain absolute characteristics of the world as against certain person-relative states of the world. Unlike right- and duty-based approaches, both presupposing a person-relative connection between ethics and the world, the goal-based approach does not prejudge the issue of the possibility of an ethical dimension to the world *as such,* namely unmediated by person-affecting changes or states of affairs. Hence it is a notable test for the relation of genethics and ethics.

This debate over the nature of value is surprisingly new. There is little explicit reference to this crucial issue in the tradition of ethical theory. One hypothesis why this important question has eluded closer examination in the past is that one of the main theoretical motivations to tackle it has been the increasing consciousness of genesis problems, which as we have seen is a fairly recent phenomenon. In other words, as long as moral value had, as a matter of contingent fact, been ascribed to a world of existing human beings, the remote possibility of a world judged as having or lacking value independently of the existence of human beings was of little theoretical interest.

But recently the debate over this issue, conducted under the title of *impersonalism,* has been intensified. Especially in the context of the morality of procreation, the controversy has been whether value (in general, but also moral value in particular) is an "impersonal" attribute of the universe, or whether it is (in Parfit's terms) "person-affecting," that is, an attribute that necessarily relates to human beings. As we shall see, this dilemma cannot be easily classified as either meta-ethical (analytical, semantic) or moral (normative, evaluative), which again marks out the interdependence of the two levels of moral discourse. For paradoxically, the nature of value cannot be decided "neutrally," that is with no evaluative assessment of what is important or valuable! But of course, it is equally true that a question such as the value of the existence of human beings cannot be settled without first defining the concept of value and the "formal" conditions of its applicability. Nevertheless, in the remainder of this section we shall try to separate the two levels of discussion and address the conceptual analysis of value rather than the normative argument for what is valuable.[7]

Following the general line of argument in this chapter, my contention is that although the issue of impersonalism versus person-affecting axiology lies at the heart of the genethics debate, *part* of the evidence for either of these approaches would turn out to be drawn from the genethical solutions found most convincing. This obvious circularity is again inevitable and forces upon us a strategy of a second-order reflective equilibrium (a version of wide equilibrium).[8] The rest of this book will be an attempt to provide a *global* argument for a person-affecting approach to value (and ethics) together with a particular genethical theory. By claiming that the issue of impersonalism in value theory is the crux of genethics, I do not argue for the truth or falsity of imper- sonalism. I only claim that we are confronted by a choice that cannot be avoided: either to adopt an impersonal view of value and pave the way to the inclusion of potential people in the moral community, or adhere to a person-affecting view and treat all genethical choices either as a matter related only to actual existing people or consider them as lying beyond the scope of ethics altogether. Only a theoretical cost-benefit analysis will settle this global dilemma, carefully weighting the pros and cons of each overall solution.

An elegant introduction to the issue of impersonalism can be found in the famous Moore-Sidgwick debate over the moral and aesthetic value of a world unpopulated by human beings, existing beyond the reach of any possible human perception. Can such a most beautiful world be said to be better than an ugly, equally inaccessible one, independently of human awareness and appreciation? Sidgwick emphatically claims that all good—be it happiness, perfection, or excellence—must be *of* "Human Existence." And he does not consider his view to undermine the possibil- ity of objective value judgments. For objectivity of value (beauty, good- ness) is not existence independently of "any mind whatsoever," but the existence of a common standard "valid for all minds." Moore, no less passionately, argues for the comparability and hence superiority of the unpopulated beautiful world over the ugly one. Moore concedes that his thought-experiment is highly hypothetical and that as a matter of fact choices relating to the creation of valuable states of affairs are guided by their impact on human beings. Nevertheless, in the hypothetical case, we are told, "impersonal" preferences are perfectly rational.[9]

Now, this debate cuts across the deepest controversy regarding the nature of value. It is a crossroads of metaphysical, logical, ethical, and methodological issues. It is not confined to the status of moral value, but applies to any kind of value. The tendency of so many philosophers since Plato toward impersonalism can often be attributed to their com- mitment to realism and objectivism. Eager to ascribe to value judgments an absolute and objective status (usually claimed for truth), these phi- losophers, at least implicitly, treat value as some kind of a property of the world. However, it is extremely important at this point to dissociate the issue of axiological impersonalism both from objectivism and from realism. For the person-affecting approach is fully compatible with both ethical realism and the objectivity of moral values (or judgments).

One should not be misled by Thomas Nagel's use of the term "impersonal" to describe detachment from the individual's subjective and paro-chial perspective. Nagel's view of the incessant pursuit of objectivity by transcending the "personal" point of view is concerned with the *basis* of value judgments rather than with the *nature* of value or the conditions of value attribution. In that respect it is compatible with a person-affecting analysis of the nature of value. Accordingly, pain is objectively bad, that is, a disvalue irrespective of a person believing in its badness; yet we can add that it is person-affecting in the sense that it is only bad because it relates to people in a certain way, and not because of any person-independent property of it. So when Nagel says "that headaches are bad, and not just unwelcome to the people who have them" (Nagel 1986, 146), it is the distinction between appearance and reality, subjec-tivity and objectivity, with which he is concerned—not with the (obvi-ous) person-affecting nature of pain. Nagel explicitly says that seeking objectivity by a complete detachment "from all interests" is not necessar-ily the only way and that objectivity is compatible with the idea that "things can be said to matter at all only to individuals" (1986, 146). However, later in the chapter, Nagel is unnecessarily driven to an imper-sonal concept of value, a value that is not "*for*" anyone" (such as the Frick collection surviving a total destruction of sentient life [p. 153]). Nagel admits that he does not know how to establish whether there are such values, and again like many others he is attracted by the controver-sial analogy to aesthetic value, whose impersonality is easier to grasp.

The general lesson from these propositions is that it is of utmost importance for the method of genethics to distinguish between the na-ture or content-conditions of value, that is, value as a *relational* prop-erty, and the way value judgments and attributions are grounded or validated, that is, from which perspective they are justified. The person-affecting thesis applies only to the first, and confounding it with the second, as Nagel sometimes seems to do, leads to the fallacy that objec-tivism requires impersonalism. The first distinction applies to the evaluator's point of view; the second, to the carrier of the attributed value, the "object" of the evaluation.[10]

In that respect Sidgwick is absolutely right in insisting on the possibil-ity of objectivity of a person-affecting concept of value. In other words, the fact that the beautiful world is epistemically (or perceptually) inac-cessible to us is not the reason for denying it any aesthetic or moral value. It is the lack of any *effect* on human beings (or other possible evaluators) which makes it valueless. In the same vein, and from the opposite pole, one can be an "impersonalist" in ethics (à la Moore) while believing in the subjectivity of value judgments. For instance, one could say that the world destroyed by a nuclear holocaust, sparing no forms of life, would be a bad world, a less valuable world than the present one, yet still hold (for meta-ethical reasons) that this very evaluation is based merely on subjective grounds or personal preferences.

For lack of a better term, I shall refer to the basis for the person-affecting approach as "volitionism." A volitional conception of value analyzes value in terms of any of the wide spectrum of human attitudes and states: desires, wishes, ideals, interests, rights, expectations, satisfactions, and so forth. Which elements in this list are relevant to *moral* evaluation is a matter on which perfectionists, eudaimonists, hedonists, right-theorists, welfare economists, and idealists passionately disagree. But none of them is necessarily committed to an impersonal view, which regards value as an attribute of the world existing apart from any of these human "pro-attitudes." The volitional concept of value holds that value is always *for* human beings; it has to do with what they—in the broad sense—want or need.[11] In that respect, volitionism draws an un-Platonic distinction between truth and goodness: truth is an attribute of the world, which is independent of any knowing subject (although knowing it obviously presupposes the existence of such subjects); value (the good) is dependent on the existence of human beings not just for its being known but for its very existence, since it is *constituted* by the human "will." Unlike truth, the concept of value always requires an answer to the question "for whom."[12]

To avoid a possible misunderstanding, let us note that the person for whom something is of value, the person affected by the valuable state of affairs, is not necessarily the evaluator, the person actually judging the state of affairs to be good. It can be, and often is, another person. So something can be valuable even if no one actually values it, as long as it is valuable for someone, that is, affects the welfare or interests of a human being. Not only does volitionism not entail subjectivism, it is by no means a mentalistic view, treating value as a mental state in the evaluator's psyche. This is why value according to the volitional conception can be a state of affairs of which people are not necessarily aware.[13] Furthermore, volitionism is not necessarily committed to individualism; the "carrier" of value, the entity for whom something is good, can be a group of people, a collective. Nor does it entail any particular view about the identity of the evaluators: these can be human or superhuman (God, the angels), or subhuman (animals). In that respect, volitionism is not necessarily anthropocentric or "humanistic." It is only "evaluator-centric." More important for our discussion, the carriers of value can be past and future individuals as well as present ones.

However, the essence of volitionism is that value must be ascribable to individuals who are themselves evaluators, that is, have volitions. To the volitionist "for the river" is not an acceptable answer to the question "for whom are the antipollution policies good?" Unfortunately, so much of the environmental rhetoric of the recent past[14] has fallen victim to the confusion between the question whether rivers, rare species, and clean atmosphere are values (and surely they are in the most elementary person-affecting sense) and the question whether they have intrinsic value in the sense of being possible bearers of value (which obviously they are not, as nothing can be good *for them*).[15]

The person-affecting framework serves to separate the whole question of environmental ethics from genethics. For no value is accorded to nature as such. We will see the implications of this view in chapters 4 and 7. At this stage we should only note that "anthropocentrism," so much derided by the more radical versions of ecological ethics, is indeed characteristic of the person-regarding thesis in that only what satisfies (human) volitions can be of value. However, the fact that value is always person-relative does not mean that only valuers (human or nonhuman) have value. On the contrary, our main person-affecting contention here is that the very existence of valuers can *not* be a value. And in that sense, our view is not anthropocentric. Human beings are like the meter-rod in Paris: they are the measure of all value; but as such they cannot be measured in value terms![16]

Nevertheless, the identity of "carriers" of value, or rather those who are affected by valuable things, is a difficult question, which we cannot discuss in the present essay. For if indeed person-affecting theory is not committed to individualism, then value can be "attached" to human groups or collectives, classes or nations. But even if the person-affecting conception takes an individualistic form, it remains to be decided whether what is meant is the individual throughout his biological life or only the individual in certain phases of his life, namely those defined by certain continuities of character and identity-fixing features. In other words, the carrier of value can in principle be an individual in time t, an individual in a particular period of his or her biography, an individual in the legal sense (from birth to death), a human community at a certain place and time, the whole of humanity at time t, or even the human species as a continuous body of actual beings from the past through the present into the future. As long as the existence of these alternative carriers of value is presupposed, that is, nothing of value can be attributed without their existence, they satisfy the logical conditions of a "person-affecting" view. My own inclination is toward a more individualistic definition of "person," taking it in a relative sense, that is, as requiring in some context of value attribution a segmentation of human life into relevantly defined phases. This will become a necessary aspect of my solution for genesis problems in the context of education (as will be elaborated in chapter 6). I find the attribution of volitions to groups and communities implausible, although some kinds of interests and rights might be ascribed collectively. But the notion of "person-affecting" is not in itself confined to any particular metaphysics of persons or personal identity.

The volitional concept of value should also be seen as neutral between different theories of what is valuable. Volitions must be understood in a very wide (linguistically overstretched) sense. Thus, justice, autonomy, and authenticity derive their desirability from the positive way they affect human beings—be it by satisfying certain interests, fulfilling certain ideals, according with certain expectations, relating to certain forms of self-image, actualizing certain essential potentials. Volition should be understood as referring to the whole spectrum of human *conative* stance. The objects of this stance can be "ideal," that is, unrealistic and utopian (like eternal peace), as long as they relate to people's welfare or interests. There is no logical problem in assuming hypothetical states of affairs as ideals or values (for human beings); the problem is with assuming hypothetical human beings as the subject for whom these ideals are good.

Christine Korsgaard has offered a very forceful case for a person-affecting concept of value. It is primarily based on an argument against the conflation of the intrinsic-extrinsic distinction with the final-instrumental distinction. Essentially keeping the two distinctions apart allows us to value something as being good "for its own sake" (in the sense of not being instrumental) without having to assume that it is good in an unconditional absolute or intrinsic sense (that is irrespective of human needs, interests, or ideals). And indeed such exactly is the Kantian line that Korsgaard wishes to follow (against Moore and Ross). Value—even if "final"—is always " 'conferred' by choice," that is, it never lies in the world regardless of human practical attitudes. In this respect, value is *constituted* by human beings.[17] The fact that goodness is always in some sense "for us" also has the advantage of connecting value with the will to attain it (Korsgaard 1983). Following the Sidgwick-Moore debate, beauty is again taken as an example of a noninstrumental (objective) value, which nevertheless is agent-relative (although not in the mentalistic sense). Analogously, moral goodness can be good for its own sake and still be person-affecting (although again not necessarily in the hedonistic sense).

The thesis that value is person-affecting should not be confused with the claim that something is good only if it is good for someone in particular. Things can be good in an agent-neutral way, that is, from no particular point of view, though still person-affecting in our sense. This distinction is important because impersonalism is used to characterize both the alternative to person-affecting views as well as the alternative to subjectivistic views. Unfortunately some philosophers try to suppress the use of "good for" altogether because of this confusion (e.g., Hurka 1987). Good from a universal point of view can be analyzed in person-regarding terms no less than good from an individual point of view (see Bond 1988). For the person-affecting view "good for" is a wider notion than that used in the debate between subjectivism and objectivism (or between deontology and teleology); it only requires that there be actual volitional beings to whom the good can be ascribed.

Some support for this volitional perspective can be traced back in the tradition of ethical theory. Without sharing its epistemological dimension, we can take Protagoras's dictum "Man is the measure of all things" as a concise formulation of axiological volitionism. Spinoza was eager to treat the sources of value and of truth as sharply distinct: truth is a matter that is anchored in ontology, in the way the world is; value is a function of human volition ("conatus" is his term for the repletion of human "pro-attitudes"). Kant's practical philosophy is also dominated by a volitional analysis of value, grounding morality in the Will, rather than in any set of natural properties of the world. And, of course, the Nietzschean conception of value is typically volitional, attributing all value of human will to power and portraying the world as such as "cold" and valueless.[18] It is not clear however how these philosophers would have reacted to modern genethical dilemmas, and we have reason to suspect that some of them would have backed off a little from their volitional views (as is the case with Kant). Utilitarianism is, as we have seen, equally open to volitional and nonvolitional interpretations of value. It seems that it is closer to volitionism, because it takes as its chief value typically volition-dependent states—happiness, want satisfaction, fulfillment of interests. Yet, an impersonal reading of Bentham and Mill is incompatible with volitionism and may require a redefinition of the nature and sources of utilitarian value. Finally, William James is noted for his staunch person-affecting view, although some of his expressions emphasize the "subjectivity" of values (antirealism) rather than their person-regarding content, that is, their being dependent on the evaluator's perception rather than on their "effect" on persons in general (see, for example, his claim that the *esse* of value is *percipi*, in James 1949, 193).

The merits of a volitional theory of value will be further elaborated in chapter 4. For the present methodological purposes it is sufficient to note its centrality to a person-affecting view of ethics and its incompatibility with ethical impersonalism. Much of the debate in genethics relates to the tension between intuitions regarding the personal aspect of ethical judgment and intuitions which allow for value attributions to the world as such. The work of Derek Parfit is particularly sensitive to this tension: on the one hand it exposes the paradoxes of comparing utilities of different possible persons as a guide to choices regarding their procreation; on the other hand it insists on the validity of some form of a "maximizing" (impersonal) principle as a constraint on all genesis decisions.

Jan Narveson was among the first to deal systematically with the morality of procreation and to notice the unique challenge to impersonalism involved in any rational attempt to articulate moral (and specifically utilitarian) principles for deciding whether to bring children into the world.

> [T]he principle of utility requires that before we have a moral reason for doing something, it must be because of a change in the happiness of some of the affected persons. (Narveson 1967, 67)

> Morality has to do with how we treat whatever people there are. . . . On this view, moral questions *presuppose* the existence of people. (Narveson 1973, 73)

> [I]f no person is affected by an action, then that action (or inaction) cannot be a violation or fulfillment of a duty. This we may call, adopting Derek Parfit's useful terminology, the "person-regarding" view. (Narveson 1978, 43)

In part 2 I am going to follow Narveson's general person-regarding meta-ethical approach, but will show that a consistent person-regarding view entails conclusions that Narveson stops short of accepting due to normative (partly "intuitive") reasons.

Parfit, as we noted, is fully aware of the person-dependent nature of value attributions in ethics, yet is not prepared to abandon the impersonal view completely. On the one hand it is *prima facie* reasonable to surmise that "our choice cannot be wrong if we know that it will be worse for no one" (Parfit 1983, 169); on the other hand Parfit adheres to the view that "it is bad if those who live are worse off than those who might have lived" (1983, 175). His conclusion is accordingly an expression of the need of "a new theory of beneficence" (Parfit 1984, 443), which would reconcile personalistic constraints of personal identity on value attributions with the basic impersonal preference most people have for a good world over a less good world (or no world at all). Although predictions as to possible future theoretical achievements are obviously a risky enterprise, I cannot see how such a middle ground between impersonalism and person-affecting theory can be found. One cannot eat the cake of attributing utility only to those who can be said to better or worsen *their* lives and have the cake of a *global* preference for a world with more happiness for certain people over a world with less happiness for different people.

On the basis of this section's discussion, the general structure of my argument will be the following: there is no direct refutation of impersonalism. The only way to support the person-affecting rival is through eliciting whatever unacceptable implications impersonalism has, primarily in the genesis context; then to show that person-affecting approaches do better in accounting for genethical issues. This is the method of wide equilibrium in the holistic sense outlined in the previous section. But even those who adopt the person-affecting thesis are left with the following dilemma: as its application to genesis issues leads to paradoxes (mainly due to the lack of identity of possible individuals), one can either be drawn back to some form of impersonalism (as Parfit and many of his followers are), or (as I propose to do) stick to the person-affecting thesis and accept the conclusion that genesis problems can be solved only by reference to actual people. This is a conclusion that strictly limits the scope of ethical arguments in genesis contexts and in that respect can be seen as a mixture of what I shall call "generocentrism" and ethical skepticism.

The upshot of this chapter is that even the appeal to the "higher" meta-ethical, analytical level of moral discourse does not give us an independent and sufficient clue to the solution of genesis problems. It only suggests the two main options (impersonal versus person-affecting conceptions) and explains why the ultimate choice must be made on the basis of the success of the alternative methods, success being partly a normative term. Thus, only "systemic" considerations, a wide reflective equilibrium balancing normative, methodological, and metaphysical costs and benefits can serve as an heuristic guide. The second part of this book is a suggestion of one such "package deal," which should be judged globally, namely by examining its theoretical coherence as well as its intuitive appeal in comparison with those of its impersonal rival.

PART TWO

Generocentrism

CHAPTER 4

Existence

Not to be born, by all acclaim,
Were best; but once that gate be passed,
To hasten thither whence he came
Is man's next prize—and fast, Oh fast!

Sophocles, *Oedipus at Colonus*, 1224–1228

THE AGENDA FOR GENETHICAL THEORY

The conclusion of the first part of this essay was twofold: common intuitions are too confused to serve as a firm ground for genethical judgment, and traditional ethical principles mostly lead to further confusion or even paradox. The methodological strategy suggested as a possible lead out of this deadlock was the adoption of a person-affecting concept of value, trying both to put it to work in genethical analysis and to test its general adequacy by examining its usefulness in genethics. But if the person-affecting approach is indeed the most effective framework for genethical theory, two fundamental questions must be answered: (1) *who* are the persons affected by genethical decisions; (2) *what kind* of considerations can guide these decisions.

The first question involves difficult metaphysical issues, such as the nature of persons and the boundaries of personal identity, as well as conceptual issues relating to the general criteria for being a subject of moral concern (or indeed any concern). The second question is of a more normative nature and relates to the substantive nature of the reasons for which genethical choices are made. Part 2 of this essay is devoted to an attempt to outline a positive theory of genethics by discussing these two questions. The answer to the first will be formulated in terms of the distinction between *actual* and *potential* persons. This distinction relates to the conceptual or logical problem of the conditions of being "morally considerable" in general, that is with the least commitment possible to any particular metaphysical view of personhood and personal identity. The answer to the second question will consist of the normative thesis of *generocentrism* with its skeptical implications regarding the limits of ethics.

The elaboration of a theory of creating future people comes under the three principal headings of genethics as defined in chapter 1: existence, number, and identity. The distinction between the three is more a matter of convenience than a reflection of a neat or conceptually sharp distinction. For the three are intricately and closely interdependent. Choices regarding the existence of people are by necessity related to the number of people to be created. Furthermore, in analogy to Quine's dictum "no entity without identity," it makes sense to speak of human existence only under the description of human nature or identity. So, any decision regarding the creation of new people is at least implicitly a choice of the number of people and the sort of people who are going to be created. And there are also some possible interesting relations between the number of future (planned) people and their nature or their identity.

Let us take some examples for such forms of interdependence. One can say that if the nature of future people is necessarily such that they will be to some extent evil (or alternatively that they will suffer pain), then it might be better (or even morally obligatory) not to bring any more children into the world. Or, if eugenic processes are dependent on a large genetic pool, this might create an imperative to take care that humanity is not depleted in number. However, if overpopulation is a cause of the deterioration of the basic quality of life of human beings, then an attempt to create a certain sort of people must involve control of the birthrate. Finally, if the very existence of humanity is considered valuable, then there are both lower and upper limits to the number of people that can guarantee the continuation of the species: too few people may be vulnerable to natural disasters; too many may be the victims of self-induced catastrophes. In the realm of family planning this interdependence is even more conspicuous: we decide whether to have children only on the basis of the prospects of their being "of a certain nature"; and we usually constrain the choice of the number of children we want to raise by a certain notion of what sort of life we want them to have and the standard of living we want them to enjoy.

Yet, the separation of the three headings of genethics is not just a matter of pedagogical convenience or expository elegance. The three involve philosophically distinct problems, which must be dealt with

separately, especially as some forms of their interdependence are controversial. (For example, is it indeed impossible to refer to future people
despite their having no identity, i.e., being merely the grammatical subject of a definite description?) Existence is in a way the conceptually
purest case of genethics, for it involves the direct choice between being
and nonbeing, creating human life or abstaining from such creation. It
relates to the problem of comparing the value of a human world with
that of a world devoid of *any* human existence; or the primary decision
whether to have children or to remain childless. Pure genesis problems
are best discussed under the title of "existence," for they relate to purely
potential beings who allegedly stand to be affected by the choice. Under
the title of "existence," the genethical problem involves *solely* the created, that is, it is a pure genesis problem both in the sense of creating an
individual *ex nihilo* (in contrast to the shaping of the identity of an
existing person) and in the sense of being independent of the effect such
a creation may have on other individuals (as in demographic planning).

Number is conceptually more muddy. As will be shown in chapter 5
it is never a pure genesis problem, since the number of people created by
a particular decision is of tremendous significance in the welfare, rights,
interests, and quality of life of *other* persons. Now if these other persons
are already existing, that is, new people are created in (added to) a
populated world, then genethical issues become mixed with ethical issues of the rights and interests of existing people. And as we shall claim
that actual people can also be future people, that is, not yet existing, the
very distinction between actual and potential will be shown to be relative and controversial. However, if the other persons affected by the
number of people created in the light of a genethical choice are themselves potential, that is, part of that very choice, then again serious
questions arise: is there any sense in trying to determine an "optimal"
number of future people at all? If there is, what is the status of those not
born because they are in the group of the unwanted? And how is the
"right to be born" distributed or allotted? Furthermore, under the title
of number, questions of aggregation press upon genethical theory. Even
if we believe that human existence is of value, is it a value that can be
"piled up," added to? Is "the more, the better" a meaningful principle
of genethics (as it is, for example, in utilitarian ethics)?

Identity adds further complications. Unlike genethical problems of
number, which have to do with matters of coordination, distribution,
and dependence of the value of the creation of one individual on that of
the creation of another, the genethical problems of the molding of the

identity and nature of people turn out to depend on the way personal identity is developed and formed. In other words, even once a person is created, only part of the person's identity is given. What about those aspects of identity which are gradually shaped only later? Especially such that are a matter of choice (be it of the people themselves or others, with the power and responsibility to "enrich" their identities)? Here genethical principles will be shown to call for relativization to ethical principles regarding actual people in a way different to that called for by population policies (i.e., number). For the genethical choice in this case is constrained not by the interests and rights of *other* people (existing or not-yet-existing), but by the nature of the very same person whose life and character are gradually being formed. The basic thesis of chapter 6 will be that genethics must take personal identity as a relative concept—relative in the sense of the multi-layered, hierarchical, or concentric facets of a person's identity-fixing properties, which are gradually cast in the light of those facets that already exist (or those that are closer to "a core").

The fundamental principle of the genethical theory outlined in this essay may be called "generocentrism." It is essentially the thesis that genesis choices can and should be guided exclusively by reference to the interests, welfare, ideals, rights, and duties of those making the choice, the "generators," the creators, or the procreators. In collective in-tergenerational choices, like population policies, the generator is the present generation; in family planning it is the parents; in the creation of human beings *ex nihilo* (if indeed it is by an intentional act of creation rather than evolution that humanity came to be), it might be a god or a "demiurgus"; in the case of a cloning technique it can be a scientist in a laboratory; and so forth. The term "generocentric" should not be taken too literally: in its etymological sense the thesis of generocentrism ap-plies only to *pure* genesis problems, that is, those in which there is no third (human, volitional) party involved in the act of creation beyond the creator and the created. This is typically the case in the ideal theologi-cal context with which we opened our discussion, and partly the case in the context of parenting (which though taking place within a world inhabited by other human beings, is *normatively* considered as almost the unique business of the (pro)creators (the parents). But, of course, most genesis problems as a matter of fact involve third parties. That is to say they must take into account people other than the "generators," those who actually make the genesis decisions. These others, as we shall see, can be both existing people *and* future people. So in the *impure* contexts, the generocentric principle should be understood as referring to a wider class of people than the direct creators. This is the class of *actual* beings.[1]

ACTUAL VERSUS POTENTIAL PERSONS

The subjects of genesis choices are, by definition, persons who do not exist. For it is their existence that is the subject matter of these choices. It is also true to say that the subjects of genesis choices are persons who are possible, that is, whose future existence is neither inevitable nor impossible. They might exist but they might equally well not come into existence. Their being possible is expressed by the physical and biological conditions that obtain in the background of the genesis decision; their being *merely* possible is manifest in their existence being dependent on other elements beyond the physical and biological conditions, primarily a *choice.* Now, it is natural to refer to such a kind of possible existence as *potentiality,* but only as long as we take heed to interpret this in a specific way. There is, for instance, the Aristotelian idea of potentiality which is based on a distinction between two sets of factors, the essential and the contingent. Under this notion of potentiality, a being may become actual only if some essential properties are given the opportunity to develop, and it is the contingent circumstances that create the opportunity. Another concept of potentiality may draw the distinction between the logically possible course of events and the empirical way the world actually evolves. Thus, an event can be seen as potentially harmful in the sense that it is not self-contradictory to think that harm will come out of it; but only the actual course of events determines whether a particular event was indeed harmful or not.[2]

In the context of genesis problems we are interested in a concept of potentiality which contrasts the actual empirical course of events with that governed or guided specifically by human choice (intervention). It is therefore potentiality in a moral rather than a metaphysical (biological) or modal (logical) sense. The definition of "potential people" in genethics is accordingly *people whose existence is dependent on human choice.* Of course, their existence can also depend on other, "natural," factors or contingencies, but it is in being dependent on a human decision that they are regarded as potential.[3]

The first implication of such a moral definition of potentiality relates to the slightly deviant sense of the correlative concept of actuality. Actuality is the status of people who do not owe their existence to a human choice. This means that actual people do not necessarily actually exist! That is to say, actual people may be either those who exist now, actual living people, or those who will exist in the future, who are not yet living but are going to live anyway. Those who are already living cannot be potential in our technical sense because their existence is not dependent (now) on our choice. Those who will be living independently of any human choice are no less actual from that moral point of view. One can think of fairly clear examples for the distinction between potential and (future) actual: when a couple deliberates conceiving a child, the subject of their deliberation, the child, is a potential being; when long-term economic and ecological polices are decided in the United States today, the future existence of 120 million Mexicans in the twenty-first century is taken as a given fact; these are actual people, although they do not yet exist. Many of them are typically the product of unintended, accidental, or unplanned intercourse. Note too that being actual does not mean being known to have a certain identity or nature. Most future actual people are not "known" to us; nevertheless they enjoy a moral status and may have a claim upon us despite their anonymity. Thus an obstetrician has a moral duty (e.g., to keep himself professionally up to date) toward those neonatals of the future who might need his help, no less than an emergency room doctor has a duty to stay alert in tonight's shift so as to be able to treat whichever patient might visit the hospital.

Although this definition of the "actual-potential" distinction deviates from common linguistic usage, the moral problem of drawing the lines of moral considerability lends it theoretical support. For it is exactly the insistence on avoiding discrimination against future people (just because they are not around yet) which from the moral point of view makes them actual, that is, actually present in the class of people whose interests, welfare, and rights we have to consider in making decisions and changing the world.

The importance of the distinction between potential persons and future persons cannot be overstated. Essentially it separates the issues of intergenerational justice from the issues of the ethics of procreation (genethics). The moral status of future people is a serious problem, involving the question of the just savings principle. This principle, widely understood, refers to the amount of capital, technology, natural resources, clean environment, aesthetic value, scientific knowledge, cultural heritage, historical records, and so forth that we should pass on to future generations. It is basically a problem of distribution, of fairness, of varying degrees of responsibility to people of varying degrees of proximity to us. There is a big debate whether temporal proximity is a relevant moral parameter at all. This is usually discussed by economic theorists as the problem of social discount. Some insist that any discrimination on the basis of remoteness in time is repulsive; others claim that there is an analogy between the relevance of personal or communal distance in determining the extent of responsibility on the intragenerational axis and the relevance of temporal proximity on the intergenerational axis. In both cases, it is argued, there are pragmatic, epistemological, and moral reasons for preferring the closer to the more remote. But in any case, this whole debate is conducted on the assumption that future people are *actual* in the moral sense suggested here, that is, that even if their existence and character is obscure, and the strength of their claim on us debatable, they deserve *some* sort of concern, as does any existing human being.

Potential people, however, are not just beings whose features are vague, whose character is hard to predict, with whom we can hardly sympathize because of their remoteness. On the contrary, some potential people, *if* they are actualized, will be very close to us (in time and in relationship), and in many cases (like parenthood) we know much more about "them" than about any one of the million children who are going to be born in the next ten months in Egypt. The issue of their moral status cannot be a matter of degree, proximity, or strength of claims; for we might decide not to make them the subject of any kind of moral status whatsoever. Their problematic status in moral reasoning is not due to lack of sharpness in the contours of their existence and identity, but to the logical dependence of their existence on our decision. In contrast to the *social discount* of actual future people that characterizes intergenerational problems of distributive justice, it is the *conceptual noncount* of potential people that defines genethical decisions. My argument is that the question of discrimination against potential people cannot even arise as they have no moral status of any kind, not even a weak one.[4]

It is again important to note that potentiality applies not only to existence as such, but also to number and identity. When a population policy is deliberated, it is the existence of potential people *in a certain number* which is the issue. If a genetic intervention in the process of conception and pregnancy is considered, it is the existence of a potential person *under a certain identity* which is referred to. As we have already made clear, no decision about existence can be absolutely severed from that of number (even if it is just one) or identity (even if this is left to the natural genetic process to decide by default). But of course abstract theoretical distinctions can be made between existence on the one hand and number and identity on the other. Population planners are concerned mainly with numbers and less with identity. Family planners are concerned with the existence of another child. Parents, educators, and some religious missionaries and revolutionary ideologues are concerned with the formation of a certain identity and character in biologically actual people. But in all these cases, there is a sense in which some future outcome—in one of the three parameters—is potential, that is dependent on a choice.

Furthermore, the existence of a child may be potential for its planners (parents), but its identity and even number may be actual. For what stands to be decided (in normal situations of family planning) is whether to conceive or not. The identity of the child (determined by which particular sperm cell would fertilize the egg) usually remains beyond our control and hence beyond the decision-making process. So is number, because outside the context of artificial *in vitro* fertilization we do not normally have control over the number of embryos resulting from a conception. This again makes the distinction between potentiality and actuality relative to the specific dimension of reproductive decision and justifies the methodical distinction between existence, number, and identity.

The distinction between actual and potential is by no means committed to metaphysical individualism. What the actual "entity" is, is a matter for independent philosophical scrutiny. It might be individuals at a certain time or stage in their lives. It might be individuals throughout their whole biological lives, raising the issue of personal identity and involving questions of the degree of control we have over certain features of our evolving identity in the course of our biographies (see chapter 6). It might be collectives, either as "organic" entities or as aggregations of individuals who are all actual (see chapter 5). It might be—as a limiting case—the human species as a transtemporal entity evolving in historical time (see part 3).

Unfortunately, the actual-potential distinction is beset by conceptual difficulties. It is in a profound way relative, that is, contingent upon the identity of the subjects making the decision, the scope of their knowledge, and their willingness to interfere in those decisions. Thus, a future person X may be potential *for me* (having to decide whether to create him) but actual *for you* (having no control over the matter). A future actual person Y may become potential *for me* at the moment I gain knowledge about the way I can control the process leading to conception. And a person Z might be actual for me as long as I, for instance, for moral reasons, refrain from interfering in the parents' decision to conceive, but potential once I take the liberty (and have the power) to interfere. These are epistemic, moral, and political factors that relativize the distinction.

The moral factor (best exemplified in the defense of the parents' privacy in most procreative decisions) is of particular interest, since it again illustrates the dependence of conceptual distinctions on ethical values. Thus, whether a planned child to parents carrying a genetic disease is potential or actual from the point of view of society (having, let us assume, the *capacity* to force the parents to refrain from begetting it) can be decided only on the basis of a normative view regarding the limits of the parents' right to privacy in this case (or the point at which society may have a say regarding its future members). In the same vein, in today's China future children are considered potential by the state, because the social interests of actual people are considered more important than the procreative rights of individuals, making the decision of family size a legitimate matter for state intervention.

This relativization of the actual-potential distinction has *prima facie* strange consequences. If indeed (as we are trying to argue) potential persons have no moral status or rights, a person may have a claim for moral consideration on the part of one person but not on that of another. Take for example a desert island with you and me and our spouses considering begetting children. Now, assuming that we do not have either the power or the right to interfere in each other's reproductive decisions, it appears to be the case that your (future) child is for me an actual person, whose interests I have to take into account (among other things in my own decision whether to beget a child of my own). But for you, of course, that very same child is typically potential. And the same applies in reversed symmetry to the double status of my (future) child. It is not too difficult to draw analogies to real-life situations of demographic planning in a modern liberal society. Thus, as we shall see in chapter 5, special problems of coordination in the allocation of the right to parenthood may arise in a future society that will have extensive control over procreation. The idea of relativization of the actual-potential distinction will be elaborated and illustrated there.

Nevertheless, within the relativized boundaries, the distinction between actual and potential seems to be theoretically productive in the formulation of a generocentric solution to genesis problems. The fact that individuals can be potential for certain people and actual for other people is not as embarrassing as it first appears. Many ethical relations are relativized in a similar manner. Responsibility is dependent on knowledge; duty (ought), on power (can); rights, on the existence of persons against whom these rights can be claimed; and so forth. The fact that an individual can be potential from one point of view and at the same time actual from another, or at one moment actual and later (as a result of learning how to avoid conception!) potential, raises intuitive uneasiness. But this uneasiness is probably caused by a fantasy of future people waiting in some imaginary limbo to be actualized and brought into this world, as if they have to cross a boundary between mere potentiality and (future) actuality. We must get rid of the misconception of the actual-potential distinction as an ontological distinction in the degree or mode of existence of (future) persons and treat it as purely relating to the dependence of the existence of one person on the choice of another. Once we succeed in doing so, the possibility of being at once potential and actual (for different people), or first actual and later potential (for the same person), will not appear paradoxical.

Another problem for our distinction relates to the moment at which a person becomes actual. Here again we do not stand on firm ground. As long as you have not decided whether to bring a child into the world, I too cannot relate to it as actual. Once you decide to have it (and assuming that I have no right to interfere in your procreative choices), I cannot but take its future interests into account (e.g., in my own reproductive or economic behavior). This does not mean that for *you* the child has at the same moment become actual. For you can still change your mind and decide not to bring it about. For you the child becomes actual some time between conception and birth, when it is actually created, and changing your mind might be considered as killing it. But personhood and the moment of its creation is a metaphysical issue that we do not have to enter upon in order to claim that the actual-potential distinction is relative to *any* of its proposed solutions. Whatever metaphysical view of the beginning of a person's life and identity is adopted, the formal actual-potential distinction can be based on it.[5]

It is also important to note that actual future human beings are not only those whose individual identity is, or even can be, known by us. It is just their existence that is considered as given. Thus, we may say that the 15 million people who are predicted to live in Cairo in the year 2010 are (for us) actual, as is the even vaguer class of Americans who are going to live in the twenty-first century (or take even the class of people referred to as "humanity in the foreseeable future"). Their moral claim on us is derived from their existence being for us a *given* fact, that is, beyond our control.[6] The strength of their claim is, of course, dependent on the degree to which we are sure that they are indeed going to exist and the nature of our knowledge about their character, interests, preferences, conditions of life, needs, and ideals. Such knowledge might be scanty and hence imply a lesser degree of moral obligation to those people; but in principle it would not deny them the right to be "morally considerable." The fact that there will be human beings on the planet or in our society in the future lays certain duties on us now: for instance, taking care to pass on knowledge necessary to human survival. But knowing *also* the number and identity (nature) of these future people may add further duties. For example, if we know that they are going to be more numerous we have to save more, or knowing that they will live in a highly technological environment makes it our responsibility to invest more in technological education, and so forth.[7]

Not being committed to individualism, one might want to include in the class of actual future people not only unidentified individuals but also collectives, like nations, races, ethnic groups, families, even "the moral community"—as long as their existence is not dependent on our genesis choice. When it is so dependent, the collective entity, as in the case of individuals, is defined as potential. This point will be of particular importance in the discussion of genesis choices regarding numbers.

THE PARADOX OF FUTURE INDIVIDUALS

Parfit and Kavka formulate the paradox of future individuals as that involved in the thesis that moral duties are owed only to individuals having full (strong) identity, that is to say that all the properties determining their identity are fixed. This notion of identity is typically represented as the combinations of a particular sperm cell with a particular egg. From this strong claim they both derive a paradox, namely that we have no duty toward any future individual, because as a matter of empirical fact policies of energy consumption (over which we have control and which are subject to our choice) indirectly affect the moment of conception and hence the identity of all those future individuals. In other words, modern human capacity to manipulate the environment ecologically and economically makes practically all future people potential in the sense of the distinction made in the previous section, and hence lacking moral standing.[8] But this counterintuitive, paradoxical conclusion is not inescapable. We can avoid it by taking the actual-potential distinction in a more subtle way, namely by separating the existence and identity dimensions under which the distinction is drawn. This might be achieved by saying that insofar as the *identity* of future individuals is dependent on our choice (even the indirect kind of dependence to which Parfit is referring), they are (for us) potential and hence do not have any moral rights against us. But as future *existing* individuals of *whatever* nature, they are actual in our sense, and hence have claims on us.[9]

There are obviously limits to the interpretation of "whatever." As we have already noted, existence can be referred to only under some sort of identity, primarily (for the context of ethics) as *human*. That is to say, our obligations to future generations are not just derived from the assumption that they will actually exist (irrespective of our decision now), but that they will consist of creatures of a certain kind. They will need clean air for breathing, they will need food and water for biological survival, they will probably have a preference for aesthetic beauty over ugliness, and so forth. It is *qua* having these properties that our moral relations to them as actual people are articulated.[10] Existence can be referred to only under some sort of identity, but there are various dimensions of identity, and various levels of identity-fixing properties, and hence the actual-potential distinction must be also relativized to these dimensions or levels.

R. I. Sikora maintains a distinction between actual and possible people that is very similar to the one suggested here. He introduces as a relativizing device the useful concept of an "inevitable slot," that is, the notion of *some* child who is inevitably going to be born although its particular identity is not yet determined, especially when he argues that a person can be inevitable for me but not for you (Sikora 1978, 125–126). However, I draw a conclusion diametrically opposite to Sikora's unexplained sweeping inference that there must be obligations to possible (potential) people. Even if we allow inevitable slots to have moral standing no less than actual future individuals, purely possible persons (i.e., occupying a slot that is not inevitable) should not count *at all* (let alone as "tie-breakers"). In other words, the question regarding the creation of new individuals (e.g., their number) can similarly be raised regarding such "place-holders" (how many slots should be created). This is typically the problem of demographic planning.

In other words, "person-slots" can also be either actual or potential according to our definition. A description such as "your third child" does not refer to an individual who has moral standing if you are still hesitating whether to beget it at all! Similarly we cannot *harm* "the first person born in London in January 2015" if it is we who are going to decide whether any such individual is going to exist at all and whether he or she will have properties that would make him or her susceptible to such harm. Only if the individual denoted by this description is someone whose existence and identity lie beyond our control, can such an assignment of harm be coherently made.[11] It would thus be absurd to compare the welfare of *two* different potential individuals just because they are denoted by the same description. Allowing such comparisons leads directly to impersonalism. In that respect I strongly disagree with the idea that "who the members of a future generation turn out to be should not matter to the moral assessment of our actions that determine their environment" (MacLean 1983, 196), for we may have the power to create persons whose properties would make them indifferent or less concerned with the effects of our environmental policies.

It seems that the concept of a placeholder, a slot, or a description serves as an attempt to reconcile person-affecting intuitions with impersonal ones. But if the actual-potential distinction applies to this concept in the same way as it applies to individuated persons, it will fail in solving the paradox of future individuals in genethics. MacLean himself is aware of the difficulty in finding a nonarbitrary principle for applying the concept of a wrong to placeholders. Furthermore, a slot is like the frame of a picture: although it can be filled by various different individual entities, it determines many important properties of these entities, that is, it has a particular identity too, which has to be decided and chosen. In that respect, the device of slots only defers the identity problem one level, but leaves the basic genethical problem as it is. It is still useful as a tool, however, for the relativization of identity-dependent decisions.[12]

The context of energy policy allows (indeed requires) such a relativization, because the affected beings are going to be affected as biological creatures who have certain needs irrespective of their particular (strong) identity. But there are typical contexts that do not allow such a relativization. These are the subject of many of Parfit's examples. Take the choice whether to conceive a child now, who would suffer deafness because of its mother's present rubella, or to conceive a child in three months' time (after the mother recovers from her illness), who will not have this handicap. Here the choice is between two *particular* individuals, whose existence, *as* particular individuals, depends on a human choice. In this case they are both potential and have no moral standing. It is only a parentocentric reasoning that can support a decision to postpone conception. At most it can be a generocentric reasoning (i.e., relating to the extra burden of the existence of a deaf person on the parents, on society, or on existing siblings in the family) which can make it a moral duty to wait. The potential deaf child has no right not to be born; nor does the healthy child have a right to be born. As we shall see in the next section, this may give rise to counterintuitive implications that cannot be circumvented by the Govier-like presentation of future individuals under an "unspecific" identity (Sikora's "slots"), or by any relativizing procedure. The idea of relaxing the strict criteria of individuation through the relativizing device of defining existence under various kinds of identity was so far discussed in the context of *future* people, that is, as a tool in deciding whether future people are actual or potential. In chapter 6 a parallel mechanism will be used in the context of education to decide whether an identity-fixing feature of an already existing individual is actual or potential.

THE SLAVE CHILD: THE ISSUE OF ASYMMETRY

On the basis of the general distinction between actual and potential people, we can now put in general terms the following proposition: only actual people have moral standing, that is, rights, claims to being morally considerable, a status of belonging to the moral community, or to the class of those whose welfare or utility is to be taken into account. Potential persons have no such standing. In genesis contexts (viz., when decisions regarding their creation are taken) this essentially means that they have neither a right to be born nor a right not to be born. Derivatively, it means that they do not have a right to be born with a certain nature or in a certain number. And since they—as potential persons— have no moral standing, the only ethical considerations relevant to decisions regarding their creation are those that refer to actual people, either present or future. This is the generocentric (or parentocentric) thesis.[13]

There are two fundamental objections to this controversial thesis, and the attempt to deal with them will allow us to elaborate and support it. The first objection accepts the general actual-potential distinction but rejects some of its moral implications by claiming that the (alleged) right to be born and the right not to be born (in certain circumstances) are not logically and morally symmetrical, and hence the issue of the standing of potential persons must be decided relatively to the life prospects of the potential person in question. The second objection is more radical: it denies the moral significance of the actual-potential distinction altogether. On the basis of an impersonalist conception of ethics the question of the status of the person(s) affected by genesis choices appears to be irrelevant. We shall deal with the first objection in this section and defer the discussion of the second to the following section.

Since the beginning of the debate over obligations to future genera-tions, philosophers have been troubled by the conflicting intuitions most of us hold. On the one hand it seems that there is indeed no positive moral duty to bring children into the world, even if they are expected to be happy. On the other hand, it seems equally obvious that there is a duty not to beget children who are going to be miserable, defective, or severely handicapped. This conflict of intuitions leads some philosophers (notably Parfit and many of his followers) to abandon the pure person-affecting conception and look for explanations within an impersonal "maximizing" (utilitarian) principle. Within this impersonal context, one may either explain the asymmetry of intuition as a function of some version of negative utilitarianism (giving priority to the preven-tion of evil and suffering over the creation of good and happiness), or deny the asymmetry as philosophically groundless (thus making it a *prima facie* duty to promote overall happiness by creating new well-off people). The denial of asymmetry is also the line of this essay, but my conclusion is the opposite one: there is no duty to avoid the birth of a less happy child when a happier one can be conceived in "its" stead. However in this section we are concerned with the attempts to deal with the problem of asymmetry within the framework of a person-affecting approach.

The slave child example proposed by Kavka has become a classical challenge to person-affecting views, that is, to all genethical principles that maintain a strong logical constraint of personal identity. Should a couple who have decided to remain childless accept an offer of $50,000 to produce a child and hand it over to a slaveholder (in a society where slavery is legal) (Kavka 1982, 100)? If the person-affecting principle is indeed valid and properly understood as constrained by the particular identity of the person affected, then it seems that there should be no barrier to such a deal: for no one seems to lose anything by it. The parents get their money, the slaveholder gets the child, and the child— even if it cannot be said to have gained anything (by being born), cannot

complain of having lost anything; for not striking the deal would not
have meant a better life for it, but no life at all. However, as Kavka
remarks, we find such a deal morally outrageous.[14]

A possible way to reconcile the enormity of the case with person-
affectingness is to claim that the wrongness of the parents' conduct is
related to the act of handing the child over to the slaveowner *after* it is
born, that is, in the treatment of an *actual* (rather than a potential)
person. Kavka believes this will not do, because the story can be told so
that the parents know in advance that they will have no choice but to
give up the child (or as in wrongful life cases, that the child will inevitably be born with a genetic defect). But it seems to me that if indeed the
story is told in such deterministic terms, and brought closer to the
wrongful life cases of the type discussed in chapter 1, then our sense of
outrage will be somewhat mitigated. But even if it is not so mitigated, it
seems that the aversion is to the moral character of the parents, their
scale of values, their indirect support of the immoral institution of
slavery, and the fact that they can see such a deal as not standing in
conflict with *their* interests. It is not the wrong done to the child which
is the source of the iniquity of the deal. Also note that unlike the conceptually pure case of wrongful conception, discussed in chapter 1, the
condition of being sold into slavery—even if "deterministically" set in
advance—is not a constituent of the child's *identity*. After being born,
the child might easily imagine the possibility of not being sold to slavery
but rather living as a free person.

Kavka, who himself suggests this second way of explaining the
wrongness of the act in terms of the character of the agents, says that
this too will not solve the counterintuitive implications of person-
affecting conceptions, because negative reactions would be prompted
even by cases in which producing a child is chosen for a morally
legitimate purpose. Here, I believe, lies the crucial fallacy of the whole
project of undermining person-affectingness through the idea that any
manner of using conception as a means is morally repugnant. For
generocentrism (or parentocentrism) reminds us that genesis choices
are *always* "egocentric" in some sense, that is, "use" procreation as a
means. People produce children for a variety of reasons: emotional
satisfaction, to provide extra work force in the family, to have someone to transmit the family name (estate, business, reputation, political
power, noble lineage) into the future, to guarantee support in old age,
to obey God's commandments, to gain self-esteem or reputation for
virility, and so forth. None of these reasons or motives refers to the

welfare of the child; none of these takes the child as an end in itself. Some of these motives are regarded as morally superior by some people; others are regarded as less respectable (by the same or by other people). But all this is beside the point. Kavka cannot show what *kind* of motives are in principle morally legitimate in terms of a Kantian imperative of respect for persons.

Now, I fully agree with Kavka's denial of the possibility of a "beneficent motive" (Kavka 1982, 102), that is, to do good to the future child, because—by definition—as a potential being, the child cannot be the object of beneficence. The parents cannot say (either as a justification for procreation as such or as an excuse for selling the child into slavery after birth) that the child is benefited in any way by being brought into life. But *equally*, and for the same reasons, we cannot hold the child to be an object of maleficence. That is to say, it is not done wrong by being brought to life (although, having been born, the child has the right not to be sold into slavery). Here precisely the question of asymmetry emerges. Is the status of potential people symmetrical with regard to being born miserable (defective) and being born happy (healthy)? My contention is that as the moral status of potential beings is denied on *logical* grounds, the prospects of the *value* of the potential being cannot be of any relevance. There is a full symmetry in generocentrism between reasons for producing happy children and those for not creating unhappy ones.

Symmetry not only implies denying a moral status to the potential child in procreative choices. It means that it is equally meaningless to resent our parents for having been born unhappy as it is to be grateful for having been born happy. Coming to life is neither a harm nor a gift. Furthermore, symmetry means that generocentric considerations apply equally to the abstention from procreating healthy children and to the procreation of handicapped children. For instance, society may view the increase in population as vital for its welfare and thus penalize those who remain childless by imposing higher taxes on them and encourage those with large families by giving them special privileges. Or alternatively, it may view population decrease as a major social goal (of actual people) and hence legally restrict or economically discourage large families. This may also be the place to suggest a possible solution to wrongful life cases: although children cannot claim damages for having been born handicapped, once they are born, their interests must be taken care of by society. And society, being in the sense of our definition actual, is definitely in a position to claim that *its* interests have been harmed by the negligent act leading to the conception of the child. Consequently, it makes perfect logical sense for *society* to sue the negligent party for damages, which would be used for the support of the child (although pragmatically and legally such a proposal may turn out to be difficult to implement). If the negligent parties are the parents, there is a case for society withholding its charge-free services to them, forcing them to bear the costs of raising the child.

There is a further noteworthy challenge to the symmetry argument that we are trying to uphold. Kavka himself, in his attempt to substantiate the *a*symmetry argument through the slave child example, suggests one version of it. There is a moral duty to refrain from creating "a *restricted* life, a life that is significantly deficient in one or more of the major respects that generally make human lives valuable and worth living" (Kavka 1982, 105). The notion of a restricted life, or—as Parfit usually refers to it—life that is not worth living, distinguishes between the case of the conception of a "normal" child in circumstances in which there *could* have been an even happier one (e.g., if conception was delayed) and that of the conception of a slave child or a genetically defective child. This sounds plausible, as it supports our everyday intuitions. Thus, we feel that parents do nothing morally wrong in conceiving a normal child now, even if it can be expected that if they delay parenthood by five years their economic situation would make the child conceived then even better off. However, we share Parfit's objection to a fourteen-year-old girl refusing to postpone conception (Parfit 1984, 358–359).

Yet, it is doubtful whether the distinction can do the work it is expected to do. For again, if we take the person-affecting approach seriously, the quality of life of the prospective subject cannot play any role in the decision whether to bring him or her to life. The idea of a life having meaning or worth living is itself person-affecting, that is, it can be worth living only *for* its subject. Unlike Kavka, I maintain that the existence of people with "restricted lives" can no more be considered "intrinsically undesirable" than the existence of happy people can be considered intrinsically good (desirable). This is exactly the idea of symmetry: logical reasons make the quality of potential lives (both negative and positive) irrelevant to decisions about procreation.[15]

If procreation, according to our view, always "uses" the future child as a means for the promotion of some interest, ideal, or good of actual people (usually the parents), we are still left with the possibility of judging the *parents'* motives or reasons. This allows us to criticize the genesis choice of the fourteen-year-old girl as immature, irrational, contrary to *her* interests. It leaves room for a feeling of moral repugnance at the parents of the slave child, whose very indifference to *their* prospective lot (as partners to a contract leading to the selling of their child) reflects badly on their character. Similarly, the woman suffering from rubella and still refusing to postpone pregnancy is in some sense masochistic. Furthermore, one might propose a moral principle that prohibits the intentional creation of promises or commitments that are known in advance to be impossible or wrong to fulfill (e.g., Narveson 1973, 76). Thus it would be wrong (toward the partner to the contract) to make a slave-child contract with the knowledge that it would be struck out by the courts when expected to materialize. Similarly, it is wrong for the young girl to decide on motherhood when she knows that she will not be able to fulfill her duties as a mother—not a wrong to the child, but to her own moral integrity.[16] Similarly, it could make person-affecting sense to argue that conceiving a slave child is morally wrong because the institution of slavery has a corrupting effect on *existing* people, that is, stands in conflict with what we think is good for them as human beings dealing with other actual human beings. However, distinguishing between various kinds of "using" from the perspective of the prospective child, such as by identifying those cases in which the using is a form of extortion or exploitation, makes no sense according to the person-affecting principle.[17]

We may sum up this section by arguing that to a significant extent an account of the negative feelings we have in slave-child cases can be given within the generocentric terms of the person-affecting view. This conclusion is important as, unlike Kavka, I believe that the paradox of future individuals can be disentangled only by either adopting generocentrism or by accepting an impersonal concept of morality. And beyond the general problems inherent in it, impersonalism (e.g., in the form of classical utilitarianism) implies symmetry of the creation of happy people and the avoidance of creating miserable children, a symmetry that Kavka himself seems not to accept.

PERSONALISM AND ASYMMETRY

The problem of asymmetry is at once the severest intuitive challenge to the person-affecting view adopted in this essay and the tallest theoretical obstacle on which person-affecting theories as such often stumble. It is very typical of many person-affecting theories of genethics to stop short of the full conclusion to be drawn from the person-affecting thesis by desperately clinging to some form of asymmetry. Jan Narveson, who was the first to articulate the person-affecting view, tried to avoid both its counterintuitive implications and the impersonalist critique by arguing for such asymmetry. Narveson says there is no duty to beget a happy child, because the child cannot be said to be happier in being born than in not being born; but there *is*, he says, a duty not to beget a miserable child, because we can say that the child would be less happy than the child we *could* have brought into the world had we (as Parfit suggests) waited with conception (Narveson 1978, 49). I find this argument for asymmetry unconvincing. For it is by no means clear why in the second case a person-affecting view allows for a comparison of two potential lives, whereas in the former it does not. Narveson's attempt to answer this charge of inconsistency in terms of an analogy to setting up a business when another firm could have been more successful (p. 55), misses the uniqueness of genesis problems. For firms are successful or unsuccessful only in terms of their benefit to us, whereas with new people this is the very issue on which the whole debate rests.[18] Asymmetry pays dues to our moral intuitions at the price of overstepping the boundaries of the person-affecting framework. By allowing comparisons between the quality of life of different potential children ("once we decide to produce one") Narveson must realize that he is willy-nilly led to impersonalism.

In another essay Narveson tries to support asymmetry in a slightly different way: "true affirmative existential statements are not necessary to fulfil duties, but *are* necessary to *infringe* them" (Narveson 1967, 70). Accordingly, we have no duty to beget a happy child because such a duty cannot be derived from the duty to make everyone as happy as possible ("everyone" meaning *actual* people). But we have a duty to avoid producing a miserable child because there are two ways by which we can fulfill the duty to reduce suffering: one, by there not being anyone who suffers, the other, by reducing the suffering of an existing sufferer. However, Narveson falls into the same trap as in the previous formulation of the asymmetry argument: by producing the miserable child, we do not inflict or cause any harm *to* him, and thus only within an impersonal view (unacceptable to Narveson) can this act of conception be in this case considered a wrongful infliction of suffering. A person-regarding view cannot take the impersonally described situation or fact of "there being no suffering subject" as a way of fulfilling the duty of reducing pain! On the one hand Narveson correctly insists that by giving birth to a child we cannot be said to inflict any pain on it (p. 70). On the other hand he contends that we do actually inflict pain if we know that child is going to suffer malnutrition or disease (p. 71). This is hardly consistent. Narveson is indeed right in suggesting elsewhere (Narveson 1973, 68), that a potential miserable child who is brought to life is "all too real"; but he is wrong in treating it as "a victim" (of its parents' reproductive decision), since his becoming real is not in itself an infliction of pain, as it is not a beneficent act in the case of a happy child.[19]

A different kind of attempt to support asymmetry involves denying the very relevance of Parfit's concerns about the Non-Identity Problem, though without abandoning the person-affecting conception. Hanser considers Parfit's case of the Risky Policy, which on the one hand would change the identity of future people and on the other would subject them to a terrible catastrophe. Unlike Parfit, he does not see any difficulty in considering these people as *harmed* by us, despite the fact that they would not have existed had we not chosen the particular policy. He even claims that these people are harmed more than they would have been had the policy not been adopted (by us), since in that case they would not have existed at all (Hanser 1990, 56). I find this argument typically fallacious. First, there is no way to compare the *amount* of suffering of states of actual people and the state of nonexistence of these people. We should resist the temptation of assigning a zero-value to nonexistence, thus making it quantitatively commensurable with either the positive or the negative net value of the lives of actual people. Secondly, there is a characteristic equivocation in Hanser's argument, as he simultaneously contends that "had the radiation not leaked, they would have gone on living happy lives" (Hanser 1990, 56). But this is obviously not the case, since the leaking of radiation is tied up to their very existence. The counterfactual runs contrary to the terms of the example (as Hanser himself admits a few lines later). The equivocation is in the *description* of the event: should the ethically relevant event in Parfit's example be described as the act of adopting a risky policy (leading both to the existence of certain people and to the radioactive catastrophe), or only as the leak of radioactive material causing the death of actual (existing) people. Hanser's attempt to brush aside Parfit's concerns regarding the Non-Identity Problem can be successful only if the latter description, which is a misleading one, is admitted. This description is also incompatible with the former, which serves Hanser himself in comparing the amount of suffering of existing people to that of the state of "their" nonexistence. Hanser's attempt to give a " 'person-affecting' explanation why the act [adopting the risky policy] is objectionable" (p. 59) is unsuccessful: we must either go along with Parfit in the search for a more impersonal theory (consisting of a maximizing principle) or stick to pure personalism and accept the generocentric approach, as suggested here.[20]

On the other side there are those who view the creation of happy children and the avoidance of conceiving miserable ones as fully symmetrical. However, both their motives and their conclusions vary. Sterba, for example, draws an analogy between the status of future generations and that of fetuses, treating on a par the right of healthy fetuses (or future people) to be born and the right of defective fetuses (or future people) not to be born. To avoid the problems of personal identity, in characterizing the status of fetuses, he is even willing (like Hare) to apply the symmetry argument to conception and contraception. Consequently, he argues, liberals—so much concerned with the rights of future generations—should restrict the right to abortion on demand (Sterba 1980, 424–440). Now, although the symmetry argument is in itself convincing, the conclusion drawn could equally well be the opposite one, namely a "liberal" or permissive principle regarding *both* contraception and population policies. This indeed seems to be a more adequate conclusion from the symmetry argument, because Sterba does not justify his underlying assumption that by causing a happy child to exist one *benefits* it and by causing an unhappy child to exist one *harms* it (p. 438). Sterba, like many others, fails to see that whatever its status as a person, the fetus is an identifiable, actual being, whereas the unconceived child is purely potential, an abstract, unidentifiable possibility. This is not enough to decide the abortion issue, but it undermines the analogy to contraception.[21]

Utilitarians, like Sikora, naturally tend to the symmetry thesis. One of their arguments is that if we want to justify the procreation of *some* wretched persons (whose existence is inevitable in the course of the procreation of a large number of people), then we must treat the addition of happy people to the world as good and *prima facie* obligatory (Sikora 1978, 114).[22] Again, what is controversial from our point of view is not the symmetry between letting happy people be born and avoiding the birth of unhappy ones, but the very assumption regarding the obligatoriness of the latter. This can be established only on impersonalist grounds of there being "at least some intrinsic moral worth in adding happy people to the world" (p. 136). In other words, a person-affecting view does not need a justification for the fact that among the many people we bring to life there are some whose life is miserable; it does not need a positive addition of net value into the world (by counting the happiness of new people) as a means to offset the misery added by reproduction. It does not require the justification of the procreation of individuals who are expected to suffer some pain in their lives in terms of the expected larger amount of happiness they will enjoy. Such weightings could be relevant, but only as long as they relate to the welfare and interests of actual people. Generocentrism means that we have to calculate the worthwhileness for us of the risks involved in procreation—for example, as older parents or as couples having certain potentially transmittable genetic diseases. But such calculations are independent of what would be the optimal (or minimal) balance of happiness and suffering for the future child, since its very existence and identity are partly constituted by this balance.

Trying to reconcile our asymmetrical intuitions with the symmetrical requirements of utilitarian theory, one might be tempted to apply the distinction between obligation and supererogation. Thus, although it would be *prima facie* (and "theoretically") equally wrong to prevent the existence of happy people as it would be to create miserable children, the latter would be said to create an obligation whereas the former might be seen as a supererogatory act (commendable, but not obligatory). From the point of view of the person-affecting conception of value, there is however no sense in assigning value to the creation of new people, and hence it cannot be commendable.[23] Even if the strict symmetry maintained by classical utilitarianism is wrong, that is, that there is a difference in the deontic status of the requirement of benevolence and that of nonmaleficence, this difference is grounded in reasons that have nothing to do with the status of potential (versus actual) persons. For genethics, potential people have equal standing regarding our beneficence and our nonmaleficence.

THE VALUE OF LIFE

The paradox of future individuals and problems of the slave-child kind are disconcerting only to believers in person-affecting theories of moral value. Impersonal versions of utilitarianism, perfectionism, eugenics, or historicism do not have to resort to a distinction between actual and potential persons. Nor do they have to grapple with the hopeless attempt to establish an asymmetry between the need to restrain procreation and the full liberty to pursue any contraceptive choice or policy. For they do not judge the morality of genethical decisions in terms of their effects on individual or specific people. They can conveniently adhere to a principle that symmetrically prescribes the creation of new (happy) people and proscribes the creation of miserable ones, because they have no difficulty in maintaining that there is an intrinsic value in (good) human life as well as an intrinsic disvalue in the existence of suffering and pain in the world. Impersonalism is theoretically attractive in its coherence and in bypassing the difficult issues of the identity and moral considerability of nonactual people. It is attractive in its being able to avoid the uniqueness of genesis problems, which according to our definition calls for a separate genethical discussion.

But is the existence of life in the world itself a value? And if it is, is it only the good life that has value, or the worthwhile life? And if it is the latter, how should we characterize that which makes life worthwhile? It seems that an impersonalist should look for a universal, objective criterion for the cutoff line between a life worth living and a life that is not. We should immediately note that by saying that the value of life is *intrinsic* we do not necessarily mean that it is good "impersonally." Even if life is considered only good *for* its subject, it can be (as it indeed often seems to be) intrinsically good for that subject. Most of us value our lives not in any instrumental sense, and we fear death as such, namely over and above whatever would be lost with it in terms of other values we wish to realize. Life is more than the opportunity to have certain specific goals and wishes satisfied. It is the existence of any goals and wishes that is of value for us. Yet it is only *for us*, the living subjects of that life.[24]

So the impersonal value of the existence of human life does not lie just in its being "intrinsic" in nature, but in its being independent of the way it affects its subject. Otherwise there is no reason to wish that the world remain populated with human beings, or that the biological species should multiply. Whatever the merits of impersonalism, the argument that justifies the continuation of the human race may also justify the *prima facie* superiority of more happy people over fewer (equally happy) people.[25] But justifying the proposition that there is good in the existence of life *per se* is far from easy. Ironically, it is as symmetrically problematic for the impersonalist to hold that there is a moral obligation to add happy people to the world as it is problematic for the personalist to argue that there is no obligation to avoid the procreation of miserable people. The two are more or less equally counterintuitive. Hence, intuition alone cannot decide the choice between person-affecting theory and impersonalism. We feel equally uneasy about a moral duty to procreate as many happy children as possible (for the promotion of overall or average good in the world) and about moral indifference toward the creation of expectedly handicapped children (who cannot complain for having been born).

Let me declare at the outset that I have no direct argument against *vitalism,* against an Albert Schweitzer concept of the sanctity of human life (or indeed any biological life) as such. Such metaphysical (or maybe semantical?) issues can only be "resolved" by comparing alternative positions and trying to articulate their respective implications and difficulties (including, in our case, in genesis choices). Two distinct conceptions of value underlie the debate, and it seems that no compromise or dilution of the two in an integrated conception can be hoped for.[26]

The view offered here can be put in the slogan "existence is not a moral predicate." This implies two claims: first, the existence of *anything* in the world is of (moral) value only if it somehow volitionally affects human beings (or other subjects with volitions); secondly, the existence of human beings is itself included in the category of "anything in the world," that is, their existence is of value only if it satisfies the volitions of someone. Now, impersonalists in genethics would gladly embrace the second proposition, since they would claim that the value of human life is indeed conditioned by its being valuable for the living subject. It is therefore an almost universal rhetoric (especially since Parfit) to refer to genesis problems in terms of the worthiness of life, that is, whether it is worth living or not. The impersonalist would thus say that it is indeed not life as such which is valuable, but only life that is worth living, that is, life that affects its subject in a net positive way. Is this a possible reconciliation between person-regardingness and impersonalism?

Not really. For the second proposition suggested in the previous paragraph is logically connected to the first. And it is doubtful whether the impersonalist could accept the way the second must be interpreted in the light of the first. When it is said that the world as such has no value, that is independently of valuers, the value of the valuers becomes a problem. For indeed, if nothing can be of value independently of valuers, then valuers have a unique status as the *condition* of there being any value. But in this we are not committed to the conclusion that the existence of valuers is itself a value. On the contrary, being part of the world ("anything in the world"), valuers can have value only if they satisfy some volitions, that is, their value is necessarily *reflexive:* they must be valuable to themselves. Once they exist, they have value only in relation to what they value in themselves. But being a condition for having any value does not in itself make the condition valuable.

To illustrate this point we must turn our attention again to the purest of genesis contexts: the creation of valuers, that is, the transition from a valueless world (due to there being no valuer) to the existence of volitional life (and hence—value). It is the thesis of this essay that this transition cannot itself be judged in value terms, that is, the coming into being of Man is devoid of any axiological dimension. A world with no human beings is neither more nor less valuable than a world with human beings, because the existence of value is itself of no value. It is typically a volitional account of the biblical story of the coming into being of humanity, namely its *creation,* which succeeds in giving it both meaning and value. God is a volitional agent, a valuer, and that is how the act is explained: "and God saw . . . it was very good." However, a more impersonal and nonvolitional account of the Ascent of Man, like that of Darwinian evolution, leaves this transition from the nonhuman to the human world hardly susceptible to value judgment. Similarly, the coming into being of children is considered such an important value because it is the result of an act of procreation, rather than an impersonal process. It is the investment of the world with value which gives meaning to *our* life, to ourselves—valuing subjects and agents. The fact that someone is born into the world does not add any moral worth to it. It is good only if it is desired by actual people—the parents or other actual beneficiaries (present or future) of the existence of this extra person. The fact that there is good in satisfying human wants does not imply that it is good that there *be* human beings whose wants can be satisfied.

Robert Nozick seems to follow a volitional theory of value when he says that valuing is itself a value, as are "value-seekers," because they "have a cosmic role: to aid in the realization of value, in the infusion of value into the material and human realm" (Nozick 1981, 519). Nozick speaks in explicitly person-affecting terms when he says that "[v]alue is not merely something that exists out there (or in us); it also is something to which we are to have, when possible, a certain relationship" (p. 429). Nozick, however, declares that "it is valuable that there be values" (p. 446). This implies that a populated world is superior to an unpopulated one, since only in the former is there an activity of valuing. But it is tautological to say that valuing is of value whereas the absence of valuing is a state of valuelessness. The question that must be asked is *for whom?* Valuing is itself valuable only *to* value seekers! And there is no transcendent, nonhuman perspective from which valuing can be preferred to nonvaluing. Even if we, together with Nozick, value the activity of valuing independently of its objects (i.e., the values), that is, derive its value from the volitional basis of the pro-attitude of the valuer or the affected person, valuing is valuable only in relation to our essential nature as volitional beings. This interpretation seems to agree with a later comment in Nozick's book: "the choice that there be value is ungoverned by preexisting value standards" (p. 565). However, the former, "cosmic" and impersonal conception of value is not wholly consistent with the volitional sense of this latter quotation.[27]

The crux of our argument about the nature of value and what it implies for genethics lies in its reflexive character: if things have value only in relation to the way they affect valuers, we must conclude that the subject and the object of valuing ultimately converge in the same "entity," namely, volitional subjects, who are standardly human beings. The same sort of entity (though by no means the same particular entity) which is doing the valuing is also the object on which it is projected or by which it is recognized and measured. As we have already said, this is a version of the Protagorean dictum that "man is the measure of all things," although restricted to the axiological domain (the case of truth might prove to be totally different, supporting an impersonal conception, according to which the truth-*seeker* is not necessarily the "measure" of *truth*).

This reflexive nature of value explains why human life can be considered so important *by* human beings *for* human beings. Valuing is indeed, as Nozick rightly claims, the basic human activity, encapsulating the whole range of affective life: ideals, interests, wishes, hopes, needs, want-satisfaction, happiness, self-fulfillment—"volitions." But there is no *external*, prevolitional point of view, from which this "closed," reflexive (most serious) game of valuing can itself be valued, and hence no Archimedean anchor for a pure genesis context. As in any game, the rules start to apply only after certain non-gamelike circumstances have occurred, in our case the existence of human valuers and value-affected subjects. The presuppositions of a game are not governed by the rules of the game. The Moral Law applies within the Kingdom of Ends; it does not rule over the creation of the Kingdom, or the procreation of its citizens.

The reflexive property of value is also significant for the issue of the notion of life worth living widely debated in genethical literature. It is often said by both person-affecting and impersonal theorists that there is value (hence obligation, permission, and so forth) in bringing new people into the world only if their predicted or expected life is going to be of a certain minimal quality. This cutoff line is sometimes referred to as subsistence level or life that is worth living. Thus, the impersonalist argues, the promotion of total or average happiness in the world is constrained by the condition that the means of attaining this promotion would not involve the creation of people whose life is below this minimal level. This minimal level can be defined in terms of an overall positive balance of positive and negative experiences or satisfaction within a given life. And the person-regarding theorist argues that even though it is logically fallacious to maintain a right not to be born, one may enjoy a right not to be born miserable, handicapped, below the standard that makes life worth living. The reasoning behind this adherence to the notion of a cutoff line is that we cannot think that we would have been better off not being born *unless* our life is really terrible, not worth living. The implications of this widely held view is that Parfit's Z-world is indeed *repugnant,* or that only severely handicapped children can sue for damages for having been born by a negligent wrongful act.

Now, if value is person-affecting, then the value of life is obviously also person-affecting. And naturally the chief candidate (although never the sole one) for the object of these "effects" is the subject of this particular life. That is to say, life is of value only if it is good *for* its subject. What makes a life good for its subjects is a question into which I cannot and need not enter here. My own view is that it cannot be grounded in any universal conditions and factors. In other words, the standards of life's value are *constituted* by the subject of that life. The reflexive nature of value is more particularly manifest in the case of the value of life than in that of other values, because it hardly allows for a paternalistic attribution. We may say (within a person-affecting approach) that stopping the destruction of the rain forest is good for Brazilians, even if they do not admit this; but we can hardly say that a life in a concentration camp is worth living even though those living in it believe that they would be better off dead than alive. Yet, even if it could be a matter of paternalistic judgment, the value of life would still remain "person-affecting."

Accordingly, suicide in the person-affecting view is a matter that can be morally judged only in its effect on the subjects themselves (do they *really* want it? is it really in their interests?), or on other actual people. It cannot be said to be bad because a life is lost "to the world," that is as an impersonal reduction of overall goodness. And it would be even more absurd to condemn an act of suicide in the name of those potential offspring of the suicide who are deprived of existence because of the premature death of their potential progenitor. If that view is correct, then there is no obstacle to extending it to the collective sphere: a decision of humanity to commit suicide, either by active self-killing or by universal abstention from procreation cannot be treated as morally wrong, either if based on an allegedly incorrect judgment of what makes human life on the planet worth living, or on the interest of future generations to be born. The contention quite popular in certain historical periods that we should not bring children into such a bad and corrupt world may sound ridiculous or unappealing to most people, but there is to my mind no rational argument against it. The choice of life is no more *rational* than the choice of suicide, either on the personal or on the collective level.[28]

If that is the case, then it seems that all the attempts to apply a cutoff line in the discussion of the ethics of procreation are misguided, as no *prior* judgments of the value of a potential person's life can be adequately predicted or paternalistically imposed. Furthermore, the whole notion of a minimum quality of life seems to be borrowed from social theories of distributive justice, that is, it is typically comparative in nature. But my life is not valuable to me only if it has a certain average or universally shared amount of certain properties and goods. It is a noncomparative, absolute, idiosyncratic, subjective character or quality that makes my life either worth or not worth living ("in my eyes"). Believers in the idea of a minimum line as a basis for population policies and family planning might be challenged by the thought-experiment that *we*, the actual people, leading what we consider worthwhile lives, are seen by other happier agents, from a different planet, as living well below their notion of subsistence level. Actually, we may think of such comparisons in our own world, which is characterized by such varied objective conditions of human life and by no less varied personal attitudes toward the value of life even when the objective conditions are the same. How can we know that we have not already reached Z-world? Or, alternatively, why should the Z-world people not be able to be relatively happy with their lot and shudder at the prospect of there being a ZZ-world so much below *their* Z-standard of living?

The prior philosophical question that must be asked is to what extent is the whole issue of the worthwhile life relevant to genethical decisions. On the one hand it appears that the value we attach to the fact that we are alive has to do with a certain quality of our living and that below a certain minimum we would not consider our lives as worth living (and might deliberate suicide). This seems to entail that at least for those who from a subjective point of view regard their lives as not worth living, it makes sense to regret having been born at all. This is the Job-like situation, in which a person curses the fact of his or her birth, or sues those who negligently brought it about. But further consideration makes such regret problematical. For if regret means in this case "being better off not born," who is the subject of this better state? The answer is that there is no such subject, and hence—at least within a person-affecting view (which is the only relevant one in Job-like contexts)—such a judgment cannot make sense. A strict interpretation of the person-affecting principle makes the question of the minimum quality of life irrelevant to genethical duties and rights, as even the most misera-ble people who wish not to live cannot say that they would have been better off not conceived. Regretting one's very existence is therefore logically incoherent although psychologically understandable (being an extrapolation of other kinds of regret at having such a life rather than another). Job should be understood as rhetorically expressing the ex-treme pain of a life that has become not worth living, and perhaps a wish not to exist. To make this point in another way: where in literature or in everyday life do we find the opposite expression, namely of being happy to have been born? It would sound strange, even from people leading a happy life. Celebrating one's birthday is not an expression of gratitude towards one's beneficent parents.[29]

A softer version of person-affectingness claims that the fact that suicide might be painful or contrary to a person's religious belief, would make the preference of nonexistence to existence difficult to realize and hence justify the complaint at having been born at all. This is a serious qualification of permissive person-affecting neutrality regarding the pro-creation of miserable people. It calls our attention to a possible situation in which a person is forced into the game of life with no power or option to quit! Indeed, life is always forced upon its subject, but if it is forced in such a manner that its subject cannot even *post factum* resist it (by quitting), then it might be considered a wrong. The reflexivity of the value of life implies that although becoming alive is itself of no value, once alive, you may value the fact that you are alive only if your life is above a certain minimum level. If you cannot even cut short your life when it is considered not worth living, then not only your coming into being is forced upon you (which is inevitable), but also your remaining alive (which should not be so). For the purposes of our discussion it might be wiser to assume the second, qualifying, interpretation, and as is common in recent genethical literature limit the discussion to the creation of persons having a life that is worth living, slightly restricting the permissiveness of genethical policies.

Parfit is quick to notice the important distinction between the issue of the incommensurability of the values of life and death (which makes the issue of suicide so difficult) and the issue whether the act of giving life can be a benefit (or a harm) (Parfit 1976a, 110). The former is an ethical problem of how to make comparisons between life and nonexistence (both death and nonconception); the latter is a logical problem of the assignability of a subject to the states compared. But in dealing with the second question Parfit assumes that prenatal nonexistence (not being conceived) and postmortem nonexistence (being dead) are of the same logical status, and hence that either both can be handled by a person-affecting conception (i.e., it is equally coherent to wish not to have been born at all as it is coherent to wish to die), or that neither can be handled by such a conception (implying that there is no evil in death, as there is no subject to suffer it, in the same manner as there is no subject to suffer nonconception).[30] This is a mistaken symmetry. As Nagel has argued in his classical discussion of the Epicurean and Lucretian attempts to alleviate our fear of death, death has a subject, and an identifiable individual whose life is cut short contrary to his or her interests. Life is an ongoing project that consists of goals that need time. It is a unidirectional phenomenon, which cannot be viewed nontemporally.[31]

Indeed there are what Williams has called "categorical desires," which make life worth living. But these desires give positive or negative meaning and value to life only "projectively," not retroactively. These desires not only make us wish to go on living (not to commit suicide), but also to be happy that we did not die two years ago. But they cannot make us happy to have been born at all, since had we not been born there would not have been any such categorical desires. The fact that the pursuit of certain ideals makes my life worth living presupposes the fact of my existence and hence does not mean that it would have been bad for me not to be given the opportunity of pursuing those ideals by not being born. We owe gratitude to one who saves our life; we do not owe our parents such gratitude (for having been saved from the limbo of nonexistence). Life itself, irrespective of any desire or satisfaction is often considered as a good for its subject. Only a simplistic view that conflates interests and conscious mental states can brush aside the evil of death by arguing that the dead cannot suffer from being dead. However, nonconception has no such subject. When Job curses the day of his birth he can visualize a world with no Job, but not himself better off not conceived, and hence only an impersonal view can handle the preference for not being born.

So I agree with Parfit that there is "no failure of reference" in Job's musing, as long as it occurs in the value-neutral case of imagining a world "without me having been born into it." This is a meaningful thought because it can be given an impersonal interpretation. However, in *evaluative* contexts, saying "I could have been better off not born" does not make sense, as it typically involves a person-affecting concept. The logical conditions of assessing the value of one's birth are different from those obtaining in making other (e.g., ontological) counterfactual statements.

The fact that birth cannot be regarded either as a benefit or as a harm is further supported by the hopeless attempt to articulate *any* kind of means for measuring the benefit or the harm. This problem goes far beyond the usual difficulties of measuring benefits and harms done to persons in the course of their lives. For if one is on the whole very happy with one's life, how much of this happiness should one ascribe to the bare fact of being created? True, it is a necessary condition for all the good in that life. Does that mean that it should be regarded as the greatest (only?) benefit or fortune? Or is it just a small "trigger" that was necessary, but hardly of any meaning and value beyond the very moment in which it took place? These are absurd questions, which do not call for serious answers but rather an admission of the special problem involved in treating life as a gift. The same, of course, applies, *mutatis mutandis,* to harm; especially as we cannot rely on any argument for an asymmetry of benefiting and harming in that logical issue. This explains the hopelessness of formulating any criteria for the compensation of the alleged victim in wrongful life cases, as we have noted in chapter 1. And again death is different. Being saved from it creates an attitude of gratitude as it can be seen as a beneficent act. The damage of premature death can be even roughly (alas, only very roughly) assessed (e.g., by calculating the overall net balance of happiness or income the identifiable individual could have enjoyed had he or she not suffered premature death). There is no conceptual barrier to extending tort law to negligent acts leading to death.

The conclusion of this chapter is generocentric: existence is not a moral predicate; to be cannot in itself be either good or bad, a subject of duty or prohibition, a right or a wrong. This applies to being as such, which according to a volitional concept of value cannot have any value, and specifically to *human* being, which due to its reflexive nature can have value only from the point of view of an existent human being—that is, *post factum*. Thus, in family planning, it is basically the interests of the parents which are determining factors in the decision whether or not to have children (parentocentrism).[32] It is their attempt to extend themselves beyond the bounds of their mortality. In population policies it is ideally the interests of the present generation that guide the decision whether or not to continue the human race (generocentrism). It is the attempt on the part of humanity as a collective to give meaning to its life in terms of an ongoing enterprise or project. In the theological case of creating humanity as such, it is some sort of divine interest or will that makes God create Man (theocentrism). It is the expression of a transcendent wish to infuse value into the valueless nature through the existence of valuers.

The problem of theodicy is meaningful only within an impersonal framework of axiological discourse or from God's (theocentric) standpoint. From our point of view as human beings, there is no sense in putting God's creation of humanity to a moral test, for the same reasons that wrongful life cases have been shown to be philosophically groundless. Of course, from God's point of view justifying the creation of Man is a meaningful issue, and God's regret in Noah's time for having created Man makes perfect sense. The person-affecting interpretation of theodicy does nothing to undermine its importance as a theological issue, for the believer cannot remain indifferent to a situation in which God is responsible for the creation of a world that is in some sense bad "for God." It is the same critical judgment that we pass on parents who decide to create a defective child: it reflects badly on them. The problem with this analysis is that such "bad reflection" itself assumes some value standard: which again must be either theocentric, or anthropocentric. In what sense can we say that creating a defective child is wrong because it reflects badly on the creator? If it is sadism, what is wrong with sadism? If it is the harm and pain done to the "victim," then person-affectingness says there is no victim; if it is the interests of the creators, the way these are harmed is explainable in the human sphere (sadistic parents damage themselves and potentially other existing actual human beings), but hard to explain in the case of God. However, a person-affecting view casts doubts on the abstract, impersonal Leibnizian notion of "the best possible world." There is no way to compare "worlds" evaluatively, since being person-affecting, the value of each world is only "for" its inhabitants, whose identity is world-dependent, and hence the value of the worlds is incommensurable.[33]

In nonintentional descriptions of the evolution of humanity, no agency is involved and thus no value can be ascribed to the process of the coming into being of people (of volitions, and therefore of values!). It is here that we reach the limits of explanation and justification: value itself becomes a given *fact* that cannot be evaluated. But once there *are* human beings, the question of their continued existence, the question of their own wish to have descendants, the type of people who are going to be created, their number and identity—all become relevant and pressing. The handling of genethical issues in such *im*pure contexts is surrounded by further difficulties, which are the subject of the next two chapters. The purely generocentric solution to genethical problems of existence will have to be qualified and subordinated to ethical considerations in deciding the number and identity of future people.[34] But the uniqueness of pure genesis problems lies in the fact that if moral issues arise only when there are subjects who are affected by actions, then the very existence of subjects cannot be considered a moral issue.

CHAPTER 5

Numbers

THE POLITICIZATION OF GENESIS PROBLEMS

Genesis problems of existence and genesis problems of numbers are doubly interrelated: on the one hand, any decision to produce new people involves a decision as to their number (even if this is only one, as is standardly the case in any particular choice at a particular time in the context of family planning); on the other hand, any decision regarding the number of desired people (as in the context of demographic planning) implies a preference for the existence of human beings over their nonexistence. Usually the choice of existence takes priority over the decision regarding numbers, as the latter arises only after a positive choice is taken regarding the former. Yet, such a two-phase decision procedure does not characterize all genesis choices. Sometimes the question whether or not it is desirable to have (more) people in the world is dependent on their number, thus undermining the attempt to attach a clear priority to existence over number. For instance, parents or societies may rank the existence of x children as better than the existence of 0 children, but that of 0 children as better than $x + n$ (or $x - n$) children, believing that beyond a certain degree of population density (or sparseness) human life becomes undesirable.

Nevertheless the conceptual distinction between the issues of existence and of numbers is firmly grounded in the significant difference in the type of reasoning which bears on each of these issues. Existence is a pure genesis problem, which characteristically appeals to metaphysical rea-

sons, to personal ideals, to beliefs in the value of the human enterprise, or
to the deeply rooted human attempt to escape mortality. The question of
the number of people to be created is, however, usually dealt with in
terms of the welfare of future people, the carrying capacity of the planet,
the ratio between the will of present people to save for posterity and what
they think is the minimum standard of living owed to their descendants.
Distinguishing between the two types of issues becomes theoretically
imperative in generocentric genethics, which grants moral status only to
actual people. For, as we have already seen, only when genesis choices
refer uniquely to potential people can they be treated as *pure* genesis
problems and be decided on fully generocentric grounds. When the people whose existence is deliberated are partly potential and partly actual,
the problem becomes typically *impure,* namely, combining genethical
(generocentric) reasons with ethical (other-regarding) obligations.

Deciding the number of future people is a typically impure genesis
problem in more than one way. First, population policies always involve
actual people other than the procreator(s), that is, actual third parties.
For as we shall see, our choice of how many people will make up the
next generation affects the amount of savings and conservation imposed
on members of the *present* generation. Secondly, population policies
cannot take all *future* people as potential, since some of them are absolutely actual (i.e., their existence is independent of any voluntary choice)
or at least relatively actual (i.e., their existence must be taken as given
for some of the people in the present generation even if not for their
immediate progenitors, for whom they are potential). Thus, since I do
not live on a desert island, my child is going to be born into a world
populated with other children, some of whom will be "inevitably" born,
and others born to parents who have chosen to beget them. Thirdly, if
children (or a certain number of them) are considered a public or social
good, decisions regarding their procreation cannot be made on the sole
basis of the interests and desires of their parents. As a public good,
future children must be treated as actual.

The impurity of the genesis problem of numbers introduces, therefore, conceptual as well as practical complications to the idealized portrayal of the subject in chapter 4. The generocentric solution to the
problem of existence, which was suggested in that chapter, is applicable
to the divine creation of human beings *ex nihilo*—and maybe to family
planning in ordinary circumstances. But it must be supplemented by
ethical principles and constraints before being applied to population
policies and demographic planning. The shift from the abstract and

totally idealized context of the question "is it good to have human beings at all?" to the muddier context of the question "how many human beings should there be?" transforms the genesis problem into a markedly *political* problem. The choice of the number of future people in a society (or in the world) is political in the sense that it relates to choices that cannot be made independently by individuals. The politicization of genesis decision making is called for by the features cited in the previous paragraph as responsible for the impurity of the problem of numbers. Basically, the genesis problem of numbers involves problems of *coordination* and *distribution,* as well as the protection of the rights of future (actual) people and the promotion of a collective (public) good. All these goals can be secured only through the political process for the following reasons.[1]

As long as we live in a world in which some of the children are born "inevitably," that is, to parents who have no control over reproduction, the state will have a duty to protect the rights of these future actual people. One effective, even necessary, means for doing so is the control of the rate of population growth in the group of those who have control over their reproductive behavior. Such a political intervention in matters of procreation raises difficult ethical issues, because it limits the reproductive liberty of some people in order to safeguard the rights of the offspring of other people. These difficulties are of a distributive nature. They belong to the principle by which the right to procreate is distributed in a society in which some members are required to restrict the exercise of this right in order to guarantee the welfare of the children of those members who have no control over the exercise of this right. We will see in the following sections the difficulties in formulating a fair scheme of distribution in such real-life situations.

But once everybody in society achieves the level of full control over reproduction, all future people become potential. What procedures for solving genesis problems can be devised in such a case? One possibility is to shift the role of the state from the regulation of procreation on the basis of fair distribution of the right to parenthood (combined with the protection of the rights of future actual people) to the coordination of the exercise of the right to parenthood among equal and symmetrically situated presently actual people. In such a situation the political problem becomes that of coordinating the behavior of equal players in a game in which certain goals can be maximized only through enforced cooperation. As we have already shown, the actual-potential distinction is often relativized: your future children are potential for you, but actual for me (once you decide to beget them). But the same applies symmetrically to my future children. In such an idealized game, there is no way to work out principles for the determination of the number of future people. This might lead to the procreation of a quantity that everyone would find undesirable. The role of the political process in such a case would be to enforce a procreative policy of some sort, which would maximize the utilities of the actual procreators (rather than protect the rights and interests of future actual children, as in the previous case). In technical terms, this is essentially a collectivization of reproductive choices, making *all* future people potential *for everybody,* that is, overcoming the self-defeating effect of the relativized actual-potential distinction in a noncooperative context. In such an idealized situation of bargaining over the number of offspring each couple should be allowed to have, all future people become *absolutely* (viz., nonrelatively) potential.

The political process is also an effective (though morally controversial) way to rationally fix the ratio between the number of future people we wish to have and the amount of savings and other burdens that we are willing to impose on ourselves. As we shall shortly see, there is no *a priori* or absolute "optimum" population size, because from the point of view of the future people, who are all potential, such an optimum makes no logical sense; and from the point of view of the actual people of the present generation there are endless alternatives of various ratios between population size and standard of living, depending on the value attached to number of people and that attached to the sacrifices involved in creating them and the quality of life wanted for them. A strategy of separate attempts by individuals to maximize their own idiosyncratic preferences regarding that "optimal" ratio would surely prove counterproductive. Hence the need to "politicize" the genesis decision in the demographic intergenerational sphere.

And of course, if the existence of future people in a certain number is considered a "public good" (good for us, the present people), then it is only through cooperation and coordination (either voluntary or political) that these values can be assured. Letting individuals realize their personal preference for the continuation of themselves, their families, or humanity at large would not guarantee the public good of the existence of future generations. For with no communal regulation, the number of people brought to life might be either too large or too small to enable them to survive, let alone to lead that kind of life which we all want them to have.

Real-life procreation contexts never provide us with examples of absolutely pure genesis problems. Family planning is a relatively pure case, especially in comparison with population policies. But even there, issues of coordination, distribution, bargaining, and collective choice may arise. This is not only because family planning typically involves at least *two* individuals (the prospective parents), but also because the interests of already existing siblings must be taken into account, as well as the conception of the "ideal" number of children in the long run (beyond the decision about one particular child), and because of the economic ramifications of any reproductive choice for the life of the family as a whole. Demographic planning is an extrapolation of family planning, which is structurally analogical to it. Nevertheless, family planning is not usually considered a political problem, because it takes the form of a joint decision based on love, altruism, sympathy, shared values and ideals, rather than on bargaining between competing anonymous individuals motivated by partly exclusive self-interested life plans. Consequently, family planning is to a large extent protected from political interference through the right to (and the value of) privacy.

To conclude our comments about the shift from genesis problems of existence to those of numbers: potential people have no moral status. Pure genesis problems involve only potential people. Hence the only moral reasons guiding the creation of new people are generocentric or parento-centric. However, real-life genesis problems, especially those concerning numbers, involve in addition to potential people either future actual people (who are going to live anyway) or people who in relation to certain actual people are actual (i.e., who must be considered by some present people as inevitable). Although the generocentric principle applies to these impure contexts no less than to the pure ones, the only way to protect the interests of the yet-to-be-born (actual) children and to decide who is potential and who is actual, and who is potential or actual for whom, is through a mechanism of coordinated choice. This naturally calls for "a political ascent." The nature of the political mechanism is, of course, highly controversial, and the particular reasons in favor of various procedures of political choice cannot be elaborated in much detail here. They belong to the difficult balancing of parental rights, the value of privacy, the extent to which a society has obligations to the consequences of procreative choices made by individuals who are protected in their choices from social interference, and so forth. Should political bargaining take the form of a majority vote, allow more free play for individual preference, appeal to paternalistic modes of enforcement? We will see later how the unique status of genesis decisions makes these questions particularly hard to solve.

We should mention, however, the nonpolitical alternatives to the political forms of coordination of genesis behavior, the free market being the most obvious candidate. Parents in that case choose the number of their children according to their preferences and the costs of rearing them. This nonpolitical mechanism of regulating the population size is expected to internalize some of the externalities involved in demographic expansion. The distribution of the family size in society would be similar to that of any other commodity in a free market. The problem with such a mechanism is that it must deny children of any rights against *society,* such as schooling and health care, since these inevitably lead to a parallel right of society to intervene in the "market of procreation." To many people this sounds morally wrong, because the children involved (e.g., those born to parents who prefer large families even at the price of a low standard of living) are innocent parties who should not pay for their parents' follies. Although children do not have a right against their parents not to be born, once they exist, they have rights against them; and if the parents cannot respect these rights, it is widely believed that society ought to respond to these rights. Thus society may have a say regarding the procreative behavior of its members.[2]

The three following sections of this chapter have the following structure. First, the abstract theoretical question of the very relevance of numbers to genethics is discussed within a generocentric framework. It is suggested that even if the existence of future people is considered good, this does not necessarily entail a principle of "the more, the better" or any other "quantitative" rule. Subsequently, in the next section, it is argued that even if the number of created people does make an ethical difference, the issue of fixing the optimal number in genesis choices evades both theoretical and practical solutions. Finally, in the last section, it is argued that even if the notion of optimum population size were theoretically coherent, extremely difficult ethical and political problems of distribution and coordination, paternalism, and social intervention would remain, which could make the implementation of any allegedly "right" population policy too costly or immoral.

DO NUMBERS COUNT?

Ethical theory has always been an arena for the struggle between maximizing principles and deontological or distributive constraints on such principles. On the one hand, holding that a certain value is desirable calls for its maximization (the more of it, the better); on the other hand, the business of ethics has also been conceived as the articulation of constraints on the enterprise of promoting value—be it in the form of distributive or retributive justice, virtuous character, political rights, or moral duty. Medical ethics has more recently raised the issue of the constraints on maximization of the unique value of human *life* in various forms. One of them has to do with the question whether or not saving the lives of more people is always better than saving fewer lives. The context of human life makes the problem of the competition between maximization and rights more acute, since on the one hand the value of life is universally held very high, whereas on the other the individual's right to life is also universally recognized as basic, natural, or inalienable. Thus, there has been much debate over the "trolley examples," in which the life of five persons can be saved by diverting a trolley to another track and thereby killing only one person, or over the more active deed of handing over the innocent person to a ruthless enemy who would consequently spare the lives of a whole community under siege.[3] The very realistic medical analogues are tragically too obvious to require illustration.

Basically, the question whether or not numbers count in these contexts involves the tension between maximization of value, which is achieved by *aggregation,* and individual rights, which by their very nature resist cumulative operations. If I have a little boat that I can use to save the life of one person on an island threatened by floods, or the lives of five people on an equally threatened and equidistant island, where should I go (assuming that I have time or fuel to go to only one of them)? From an impersonal point of view, I should opt for the island of the five. But from the point of view of the solitary person, the fact that she *happens* not to be on an island with other people does not reduce the weight of her right to life relatively to that of any of the five; that is to say the *right* to life (unlike the value of life itself) is not something that can be *aggregated.* From that point of view, the only moral way for the boat owner is to act with equal respect for each individual, for instance to cast a die, giving an equal chance to each in an equal claim for help.[4] This might appear to many an irrational or even immoral strategy, yet medical cases from the emergency room support our nonaggregative intuitions. Only in rare contexts of "triage" do maximizing principles override the principle of "first come, first served," or that of assigning priority to the patient in greatest medical need of help, or the special responsibility owed to a doctor's "personal" patient. In medical ethics numbers usually do not count.[5]

This whole issue of the relevance of numbers in decisions regarding the saving of lives is raised here because it is used as an argument supporting an impersonal view of ethics. Thus there is an argument that if we take the person-affecting view too seriously, we reach the conclusion that there is no reason to give priority to the saving of a group of one hundred people over the saving of a nonoverlapping group of fifty people, because no one of the first group can be thought of as worse off than any of the second group. Since such an unqualified conclusion is patently irrational, it seems that we must adopt an impersonal view of the value of life, which would allow for aggregative considerations.[6] I believe this argument is wrongly applied to genethics. Without taking sides in the debate over the question of the relevance of numbers in the context of saving lives, I wish to argue again that there is no logical symmetry between saving lives and creating lives. Thus, the person-affecting view does not preclude the aggregation of utilities of different individuals, as long as these individuals are *actual*. The question whether numbers should count in saving lives has to do with the conflict between the "utility" of being saved from death (which can be aggregated) and the right to be saved (which presumably cannot be so aggregated), but it has nothing to do with the issue of impersonalism as it is understood here. The person-affecting view can logically allow for trade-offs between the aggregate welfare of groups of individuals, even though there might be ethical grounds for not letting such comparisons decide questions of rights. As we have already noted, actual subjects of moral consideration can also be collective entities, such as groups of people—whether collectives that are irreducible to individual subjects or aggregates of individual persons.

In other words, from the point of view of person-regarding theory of value there is no logical barrier to the extension of *intra*personal aggregation of, for example, the experiences of an individual in his or her prudential calculus to the *inter*personal aggregation of utilities or preferences in welfare economics or in the political principle of majority rule.[7] What is ruled out is such an extension into the "*trans*personal" sphere, that is, to *im*personal aggregates of value of whatever kind. Choosing to save the lives of five people rather than one does not commit us to a principle of impersonal overall promotion of the value of life "in the world." It just means that we choose to affect the interests of actual people in a more effective way. Deciding to create five new lives rather than one, however, would mean a commitment to an impersonal principle of making the world a better place. The fact that numbers count in certain (most?) areas of ethical reasoning does not mean that they count in genethical choices.

Not counting numbers in judging the morality of population policies may raise serious ethical objections in the same way as disregarding a potential person's handicap in the genesis problem of existence. As we have seen in chapter 4, a consistent person-affecting view has to confront the difficult challenge of the asymmetry argument and the slave-child example and deal with the underlying impersonal intuitions involved in these cases. Similarly, we will presently see, the question of numbers poses equally difficult problems for genethics. The various modes of aggregation of the value of individual human lives lead to intriguing or even paradoxical results.

Let us start with the conceptually neat and idealized case in which all reference to actual people is for the sake of the argument ignored. For example, the genesis problem disregards the generation overlap and its implications for population policies. (For an ultimate form of such an idealization think of human reproduction as involving the birth of a new generation at the exact moment of the disappearance of the previous one, rather like male bees who die immediately after completing the sexual act.) A generally utilitarian framework will serve us in tracing the logic of genesis decisions regarding numbers.

Total utility is an easy impersonal guideline. We should beget that number of children which would increase to the maximum the overall utility or happiness in the world (we may add, "across generations"). That is to say, the ratio of the two variables over which we have control, numbers and utility, should be decided by the maximal product of their multiplication. The trouble with this suggestion is that it leads to the possibility at least of a world populated with a huge number of people enjoying a very low quality of life (if indeed, empirically, the great numbers would be able to compensate for the individual low standard of living). This is Parfit's Repugnant Conclusion. Average utility avoids that danger. Procreation is guided by the injunction to promote average utility, that is, the "use" of future people as a means in the promotion of overall utility is proscribed. But whereas total utilitarianism appeared to be too "liberal" in guiding reproduction, the average version seems to be too restrictive, for it would forbid happy people to procreate if their offspring would be even slightly less happy than they themselves are. In some stages of human history, and in innumerable cases of family planning, such a restriction would certainly lead to the end of procreation (and of the human race).[8] In other words, the two competing versions of utilitarianism undermine each other: the total version is willing to sacrifice average utility; the average version is willing to sacrifice total utility.[9]

The conflict between the two versions of utilitarianism is manifest in Parfit's Mere Addition Paradox (Parfit 1984, chap. 19). Should we add to the present population more people, whose life would still be worth living, but of a lesser quality than ours? The overall utility in the world would be increased, but the average utility reduced. In order to rule out any complicating factors of distributive justice (involved in the gap between our standard of living and that of our descendants), Parfit assumes that the life of the future additional people would be fully independent of ours, like that of Native Americans and Europeans before 1492 (Parfit 1984, 420). Of course, as long as we stick to our original idealization of the absence of generational overlap, distributive problems of justice, fairness, and envy should not raise any concern, since only on an impersonal view, applying the principles of justice intergenerationally, can any comparisons create claims.

Nevertheless, the question remains of the comparative degree of justice between two alternative future generations that consist of different people. Here too, the strict person-affecting view suggested in this book does not allow a preference of one over the other, because justice is itself a value only *for* (actual) people. In other words, genesis problems in the pure and abstract context of such idealized conditions must treat both the notion of total utility and that of average utility, as well as that of degrees of social justice and equality, in impersonal, non-person-affecting terms. This runs counter to our program for genethics. It leads directly to absurd conclusions such as the requirement to take into account the standard of living of ancient Egyptians as well as that of people in the distant future in deciding whether to have a child now (Parfit 1984, 420–421), or to extreme restriction over procreation in order to achieve a more equal society. It is, I believe, Parfit's insistence on impersonalism which gives rise to the Mere Addition Paradox. In a person-affecting framework there is no place for the comparison of the value of *possible* worlds defined by different ratios of average and total utility.

Yet, demographic planning must deal with the fact of generational overlap and with the fact that at least some of the future population is going to exist anyway (i.e., its number is beyond our control). In other words, the groups being compared in the effort to increase total or average utility are not actual people on the one hand and potential people on the other, or two alternative groups of potential people, but rather actual people versus a group of partly actual, partly potential people. Yet we are immediately confronted with the problem of identity: who are the potential and who are the actual people. This is a particularly puzzling problem because the population policy that we select is going to affect the identity of those future people, and hence the way the line distinguishing between actual and potential people is drawn.

Peter Singer tries to avoid this problem by abstracting the issue of number from that of identity. He argues that if we know that at a certain point in the future there will be 1 million people over whose existence we do not have control (i.e., future actual people in our terminology), then it seems that we are not allowed to add another million people by our choice if they would lower the standard of living of the original million. But then, he continues, once we realize that by adding the extra million we change the identity (though not the number) of the "original" group of people who are going to exist anyway, we cannot—in a person-affecting approach—say that the addition would be worse off for anyone. As this sounds counterintuitive, we must refer only to the number of that group and disregard the identity of the individuals constituting it. Accordingly, it is wrong to add N people to the original group P, who enjoy an average standard of living A, if *no* subgroup of P + N containing P people (not necessarily the original individuals of the P-group), would have A or more (Singer 1976, 88–89 and passim). This is a softer version of the person-affecting view, which claims that we can speak of happiness only *of* people, though these are not necessarily "identifiable."

Singer's suggestion definitely agrees better with common intuitions regarding population policies than do strictly impersonal versions of utilitarianism. The addition of potential happy people (N-people) can compensate for the decrease in the average standard of living of the future actual people (P-people). But how? If the P-people are going to be the same people after the N-people are added (Same-Number, Same-Identity), then we violate Singer's own thesis that future actual people should not be "sacrificed" for the promotion of impersonal average utility. However, if the P-people are going to be different due to the implementation of the population policy of adding the extra N-people (Same-Number, Different-People), then *any* subgroup of P + N is going to consist of *potential* people, which would rule out the relevance of comparisons between alternative populations. Singer could argue that his whole point in the amended principle described above is that the *P*-people are *not* potential, despite their "lack of identity" (or despite the change in identity following the addition of the *N*-people). But then, if they are actual, how can the addition of happy potential *N*-people offset the loss of average happiness to actual people without contravening Singer's own commitment to prohibiting sacrifice of happiness of actual people for the sake of possible ones? The extreme case that would prove my point would occur when the subgroup of *P* + *N* is that of the *N*-people. It would mean that it is all right to bring 1 million happy people into the world even though this lowers the standard of living of the 1 million people who are going to exist anyway! But the same objection would apply to *any* subgroup of *P* + *N* combining *P*-people and *N*-people in whatever proportions.

It is, I believe, the problem of the relativization of the principle of identity of individuals (discussed in chapter 4) which makes Singer's suggestion both appealing and problematic. For it could cogently be argued that the *P*-future people are actual *for us,* qua demographic planners, with no reference to the personal identity of the individuals constituting that *P*-group. But we must assign them *some* identity, *beyond* their being of a certain number (*P*). For example, they may be those people who are going to be born to Nigerian parents over whose patterns of procreation we have no control (although the identity of their children is affected by our policies). In such a case, the *P*-people are relatively actual, in a way sufficient to prohibit any decrease in their average standard of living even if another subgroup of the same size is better off. For the people in the subgroup are not going to be of the same identity as the original *P*-people, even in the more relaxed characterization of their identity (e.g., they are going to be Canadians, or partly Nigerians—partly Canadians). Once the actuality of the *P*-people is relativized to such an extent that the only identity of the *P*-people is their very number (!) we reach the limiting case in which there is no longer any basis for the distinction between actual and potential. That is to say, we cannot speak any more of the addition of *N*-people *to the P*-people, but only of the impersonal addition of *N* number of people to a *P* number of people. And then we are back to square one: impersonal comparisons of the idealized type between the average utility of two groups, different in number and in identity, which we have shown not to make sense.[10]

This discussion again proves the intricate connection between existence and number on the one hand and identity on the other and points to the difficulties in settling the substantive issues concerning the relativization of the actual-potential distinction. In the sphere of population policies, this is exactly where politics enters the debate. The question "do numbers count?" proves abstract. Demographic planning raises the question "numbers *of whom?*" or "numbers of people under what description?" Any decision regarding the status of future people (are they actual and have present moral claims over us, or potential with no such claims) is bound to involve reference to their identity. Uniquely genetic, or "personal," identity might be too strong for the morality of population policies. But reference just to "numbers" is logically too loose; for lacking any other identity, "their" welfare cannot be compared to that of the potential persons whom we consider adding to the world. Future persons must be similar in their character, properties, personality traits, chances, health, geographic location, national or ethnic affiliation, or any other pertinent conditions, for such comparisons to be meaningful. The vital role of identity in genethics will be further elaborated in chapter 6.

This discussion also allows us a better understanding of the idea of relativization of the actual-potential distinction. Although I have no suggestion for a general rule by which such a relativization may be carried out, it would be, I hope, agreed that the relevant description under which a person is considered as either potential or actual varies. For the minister of population (or of economic planning) the person might be "an Israeli, expected to be born in 1999." For the parents of "this" child, it is "the son or daughter of middle-class Jewish parents with certain genetic makeup, having certain ideals that they plan to inculcate and identity that they wish to implement in their prospective child." Finally, for the individual, it is the unique "I," with a much richer repertoire of identity fixing properties (e.g., gender). Substitutability conditions apply accordingly: for the minister of population there are more individuals who could "stand for" or be substituted for the one denoting the respective person (hence the relative weight of number and personal identity). For the parents, it might be a boy or a girl, but the substitutability conditions are stricter (the child cannot be of a different race or religion or genetic makeup). Finally for the person concerned, it must be "him" or "her," that is to say, only *this* individual having those traits thought to determine identity. This is the most restrictive perspective. The minister of population is thus less bound to the welfare of the individuals in the society and more concerned with the general welfare of the future generation as a whole, implying a special interest in numbers. Parents are much less bothered by numbers (although they play a role in family planning) and more constrained by the kind of individual life their child is to have. The actual individuals (once born) are concerned only with the welfare of their actual selves. It is as if the constraints on the kind of persons they want to create, could they be their own creators, are absolute: it must be *they* and only they! No wonder that from this point of view numbers never count.

OPTIMUM POPULATION SIZE—A MYTH?

The conclusion of the preceding section was that in pure genesis contexts, namely when all future people are absolutely potential, all considerations regarding their desirable number can only be "generocentric." This means that we are morally permitted to beget children who will make us happier although the average utility in the world might be lowered or the total utility not increased as it might have been had we adopted another population policy. We may even create a new generation that due to its numbers is not as just and equal as ours (or as another generation that we could have created). But once we deal with demographic planning in impure contexts, generocentric considerations are constrained by the existence of future actual people (or at least relatively actual people). But how do these constraints work? There is no optimal number of people in pure genesis contexts. Person-affectingness means that the idea of an optimal number of people does not make sense in the same way as the best of all possible worlds cannot be made to make sense in a volitional theory of value. Is there an optimal population size in real-life cases of the *im*pure sort?

If the question of population size emerges *after* the question of existence has been positively decided, we can at least say that there are limiting cases of too many or too few people, namely those numbers that would make human life not possible. This can be given clear empirical meaning. Human life is hardly sustainable (in the long run) with only two people on the planet (which is unfortunately a less sheltered environment than the Garden of Eden). It is no more sustainable with a trillion people. Both the injunction "be fruitful and multiply" and the contrary one "detonate the population bomb" are partly directed at preventing the entire destruction of humanity. But there is something rhetorical or misleadingly propagandistic in many of the currently popular cries of alarm. For empirically it is hard to conceive that humanity would reach literal (total) annihilation because of overpopulation or underpopulation. Even if overpopulation brings with it mass starvation, epidemics, wars, pollution, and other catastrophes, it seems that there will always be enough people (even in "alarmingly" small numbers) who will go on with the business of life and its reproduction. So for someone strictly concerned with the sheer survival of any form of human life, even the most "irresponsible" population policy cannot be ruled out.

But in any case, the extreme upper and lower limits of population in terms of conditions for the very survival (existence) of humanity, cannot serve even as rough guidelines for the *best,* the ideal, or even the desirable number of people, which lies somewhere within the vast span of alternatives between these two poles. It is when criteria other than mere biological survival dictate our thinking about numbers that the question of optimum population size becomes interesting. Philosophers have sometimes settled for a solution of compromise between the separately untenable and conflicting criteria of the total and the average principles of utility discussed in the previous section (Narveson 1973, 86). For example, it is permitted to decrease slightly the number of people if by that we substantially increase the average quality of life. And vice versa: it is desirable to increase the population tenfold if the standard of living only decreases by 3 percent. These "mixed" solutions to population problems (attempting to avoid both the Repugnant Conclusion and the opposite case of a very small number of extremely happy people) appeal to strategies of *discounting* the value either of the number of extra people beyond a certain level or the quality of life beyond a certain standard. For example, after a certain number of people is reached (typically the current one!) there is no extra value in adding further people to the world. Or, alternatively, once the total utility in the world can be promoted only at the cost of lowering the average standard of living below a certain minimum reasonable level, procreation should stop (Attfield 1987, chap. 9).

Derek Parfit has systematically sorted out the different combinations of the value of quantity of happiness and the value of quality of life (Parfit 1984, 401 ff.), as for example the extent to which added numbers can compensate for the relative misery of existing people. But Parfit, with all his eagerness to avoid the Repugnant Conclusion, honestly admits that none of these "combinations" works. We need not go into the reasons for this failure, as all these "possible theories" of the relative weight of quality and quantity are impersonal, that is, they treat both average and total happiness as values abstracted from the subjects "bearing" them.[11]

Nevertheless I shall mention an interesting view based on a concept of discount, namely the idea that the fewer human beings remain in the world, the more weight should be given to their number in relation to the quality of their life. This, to put it bluntly, amounts to treating human beings as a scarce resource, or procreation as yielding decreasing marginal returns (up to a point of zero). Thomas Hurka, who has developed "the variable value view" (following Leibniz and Thomas Aquinas and the idea of the Great Chain of Being), argues that Noah's obligation to procreate after the deluge is infinitely stronger than our obligation, even if the addition of his children adds less total or average utility to the world. In our case, creating happy people might be good, but not obligatory (Hurka 1983, 496–497). The intuitive appeal of this view to person-regarding theorists is that in large populations, such as ours, the more efficient way to promote overall utility is by multiplying the standard of living rather than by multiplying the number of people (with the same average as we have). But this is misleading, since the same principle leads Hurka to prefer in Noah's case multiplying population rather than the welfare of existing people (p. 504)! This serves to highlight the impersonal basis of Hurka's whole argument, namely the supreme value of the continued existence of humanity. In pure genesis contexts at least, generocentrism allows us to adopt the principle of *après moi, le déluge,* whereas Hurka proposes *après le déluge, secure posterity first.*[12]

Two disciplines have struggled with the question of optimum population size long before philosophers became interested in it. Being based on the ratio between two variables—the number of people and their welfare (quality of life)—it is not surprising that the idea of optimum population size has been discussed by population theorists on the one hand and economists on the other. Each of the two disciplines has started from a different variable: the Malthusian demographer from the causes of population growth and the problems of controlling it; the economist from the problem of savings, namely how much should one generation save for the next. As we shall see, the issue of the number of people and that of the quality of life are inseparable, and the choice of an optimum cannot proceed on the assumption that one of the two variables is fixed, given, or decided on independent grounds.

But if that is the case, how can two variables yield an optimum? Most theorists dealing with population issues have not been aware of this logical difficulty and have preferred to concentrate on the substantive empirical problems of either controlling population growth or ensuring saving and conservation for future generations. The definitions of optimum population level that try to combine the two parameters do so in a typically vague manner. Take, for instance, the following definition of optimum population size as one that

> lies within limits large enough to realize the potentialities of human creativity, to achieve a life of high quality for all men indefinitely, but not so large as to threaten dilution of quality, the potential to achieve it, or the wise management of the ecosystem. (S. Fred Singer 1971, 3)

The concept of optimum in this definition is too indeterminate to have any theoretical or practical value. But beyond that, it is also insensitive to the person-affecting nature of the ideas of a "high quality of life" and the "wise management of the ecosystem." "High" is relative to the number of people in the sense that although the quality of life of a larger number of people might be lower in absolute terms, it could be seen as "high" or at least "high *enough*" in the eyes of the people of the larger number. The same relativization applies to the ideas of the realization of potential creativity and the relationship between human population and its natural environment. Furthermore, the idea of *indefinitely* guaranteeing a certain quality of life for humanity presupposes that the value of the perpetuation of the human species is an integral part of the concept of an optimum. But demanding both intergenerational equality (in the quality of life of each generation), and "high" quality, together with the indefinite continuation of the species, may be asking for too much. Our generation can fix the optimum size of the next one on the basis of some conception of a high quality of life. But the next generation will have to decide whether this optimum is viable for its descendants. Only under ideal conditions can we hope to maintain all three conditions: a high quality of life, intergenerational equality in the quality of life, and the indefinite perpetuation of new generations. Reality might require the sacrifice of at least one of these conditions in order to satisfy the other two. Our thesis suggests that not only might it be inevitable but that there is nothing morally wrong in compromising any of these three requirements, and that it is on generocentric grounds that the decision regarding which of the three should be sacrificed is made.

The above definition also assumes that the notion of optimum is intergenerationally constant, that is to say that once the optimum is achieved it can be indefinitely maintained. But this is true only if the *rate*

of population growth as well as the level of technology and the environmental circumstances that make that standard of living possible are kept
constant. This would be an implausible constraint, not only because it
involves the indefinite enforcement of a certain pattern of procreation
but because it is insensitive to the possibility of technological advances
that would promote the standard of living and changes in the environment that might reduce it. Such factors would call for a change in the
"desirable" number of people, entailing a different pattern of procreation in a particular generation. But the change in the number of offspring would also mean that the next generation (being larger, for example) would have to reduce its rate of procreation to a lower level than
the original one, in order to avoid overpopulation (lowering of the high
quality of life required by the definition of the optimum). Changes in
technology and in environmental conditions together with the "inherited" demographic effects of procreation patterns of the previous generation on any given generation make the notion of optimum typically
"fluid" and time-dependent. As in Nozick's critique of "patterned"
theories of justice, the freedom of individuals to go on making procreative and economic decisions *after* the optimum is achieved, prevents
the pattern from being frozen and enforced throughout time. Thus, a
concept of optimum might require criteria for judging *changes* in the
numbers of people, rather than for fixing the numbers in the abstract
(Adams 1989, 480).

The "person-relative" nature of the notion of optimum population
size is manifest in the difficulty of judging *our* own population size in
terms of its "distance" from the optimum. For as we have shown in the
case of the incoherence of the idea of a Parfitian Z-world, there is
something tricky about treating our own situation as one of overpopulation. Obviously we can think that the existence of a large number of
poor people in the world makes it worse for *us,* and that we would have
been better off on a less inhabited earth. However, this optimum cannot
serve as a guide for deciding optimum population size, because it works
only as a criterion for actual people. It indicates the numbers of people
desirable for actually existing individuals, but not for potential ones.
That is to say, our world cannot be considered overpopulated from the
point of view of the imaginary planner who is responsible for population size.[13] Theoretically, one could retort that the optimum population
size is that which consists of people, none of whom—once actualized—
can say that they would have been better off with a different number of
surrounding fellow-beings. But this number is also indeterminate; for

first, there might be many such "optima," and secondly, the number of fellow-beings is itself a constitutive factor in the judgment of what the good life is (and hence of the judgment whether a different number of people in the world would have made my life better or worse).[14]

Concern about overpopulation is, historically speaking, relatively new. This, however, cannot serve as an indication for a notion of an optimum population size (as if the pre-Malthusian world was closer to the "right" size, and that only in the last two hundred years has "an excess" in people been created, raising the alarm of overpopulation). For the reason for the alarm might be different, namely the *rate* of population *growth* leading to unpredictable and uncontrollable consequences for future people, rather than the current *large number* of people. As with the Z-world, we—the present generation—tend to project our values and expectations onto future people, thinking that a world with more people than there are today would be intolerable. This mode of "projective" reasoning is not only legitimate, it is the only one available to us according to the generocentric view adopted in this book. But it cannot claim to draw its validity from any impersonally objective or *a priori* criterion—let alone from a reference to potential people's interests.[15] The strict person-affecting view does not allow us to say that we are worse off than previous generations because of our larger numbers, since many of us would not have been here at all had the world not been "overpopulated."

The abstract idea of an optimum population size cannot therefore make sense any more than the analogous concept of the ideal size of *a* family or *a* society. For unlike the idea of an optimal daily calorie intake, which is determinate (at least on the basis of a certain conception of healthy nutrition), the very change in the number of people in a human group often changes the criteria of optimality. So it seems that the notion of population optimum is beset both by the indeterminacy of the reference group of individuals "for whom" any particular number of fellow-beings is said to be good (or optimal) and by the indeterminacy of the criteria by which such a number is judged to be good (or optimal). Optimal calorie consumption is, in contrast, valid for an identifiable group of people, and a deviation from it does not itself create a new nutritional standard that replaces the older value.[16]

Lacking an abstract concept of an optimum, that is, a notion of the ideal number of people *tout court,* we must appeal to a relative concept, which I would refer to as *functional.* A population size can be best only *for* certain people, or in the light of a certain function, ideal, goal, or value of people. Thus, for the Chinese—both presently living as well as those planned for the future—it might be better to have a smaller population. For Australians, it might be argued that a larger population would be good. These judgments are based on highly complex generalizations concerning the relationship between the current number of people and the prospects of attaining a certain standard of living or achieving certain political and cultural goals. Our person-affecting thesis forces upon us such a shift from an absolute notion of an optimum to a functional one, since an impersonal optimum based on "all things considered" (viz., both numbers and values of potential people) would inevitably be indeterminate. The following definition captures this point:[17]

> Optimum population size = the population size and/or density at which the value of some other normatively selected variable is maximized.

This definition does not explicitly specify whether the "normative variable" is impersonal or person-regarding, but it nevertheless pays tribute to the value-relative nature of the idea of an optimum, and to the fact that it cannot be dealt with in an abstract manner.

Classical discussions of the optimum issue specifically refer to these normatively selected variables. Plato thought that the ideal state should consist of 5040 households because this is a number which can be easily divided by all numbers from 1 to 10! Although this criterion of optimality might sound as reflecting an obsession with arithmetical neatness (or alternatively as an oversimplistic pursuit of practical convenience), the deeper reason behind it is the commitment to the value of a fixed and permanent distribution of land (Plato, *Laws,* 737–740). Aristotle is naturally more emphatic and explicit in developing the functional aspects of the idea of an optimal population size. Like ships and animals, which have a particular function to which their respective "size" is subservient, so has the *polis.* Self-sufficiency, military capacity, economic welfare, governability, and law-abidingness—all point to both the upper and lower limits of population size (Aristotle, *Politics,* bk. VII, chap. 4). In our terminology, genethics is subordinated to ethics. First, the idea of the good life is articulated; only then and on that basis, the desirable number of people able to live up to that ideal is specified.

However, I have mentioned Plato and Aristotle not just by way of historical curiosity. It should be noted that they both discuss the question of optimum population size in the context of a "closed" society, an independently defined political entity (a polis or an ideal state). Their typically functionalist attitude to the issue makes their proposals a weak model for the more "global" problem of the overall population in the world, which is our modern concern. For it is obviously much harder to discover an "ergon" for human society as a whole, a goal for the collective consisting of all human beings in the world. Human society is too varied and diverse in its capacities, potentials, values, sources of identity, cognitive attitudes, and histories to be able to share specific goals as a community. It is an "open" society, in both size and values. It is not a task-oriented organization, constructed or sustained for a certain purpose or driven by a common motivation. It is self-sufficient by definition and in a morally neutral sense. I believe that much of the confusion concerning the difficulties in arriving at a cogent notion of optimum population size arises out of the rash analogy between the two levels of human collectives.

However, many attempts have been made to fix the normative variable in a way that would be relevant to the human species as a whole (present and future). Typically these attempts fall into the two categories mentioned above: those that—like Plato and Aristotle—start with a conception of the good and then work out the optimal number, and those that take a certain number as either given or desirable and then formulate a savings policy (including investment for the future, conservation of resources, and transmission of knowledge and technology). And of course there are attempts to combine the two approaches by some method of mutual balancing of value and numbers.

An absurdly extreme normative conception would take as a goal the prevention of misery. Some of today's demographic warnings regarding the dangers of the "population bomb" point to the vast human misery in the world as an indication of overpopulation. But if that is an indication, then the world has always been overpopulated, since misery has accompanied human existence from its inception (Dasgupta 1974, 109). Furthermore, such a view means that the optimum level of population should be fixed at zero! As in the case of Negative Utilitarianism, the safest way to avoid pain and suffering is not to have any subjects capable of suffering pain. A more reasonable version of this view is specifying a certain threshold of suffering, beyond which numbers should not increase (or decrease, if that is the cause of the aggravation in the human condition). Finally, the most person-affecting version would require not to add any more people if the misery of any *existing* person is increased.

A modest normative principle for population optimum is the survival of the human species. As we have already noted, as long as survival is not defined in terms of any particular quality of life, almost any population size can be treated as optimal (which virtually means that there is no optimum). For Malthus, we might say, the optimum is the population equilibrium, in which there is no natural growth. For growth inevitably leads to overpopulation, defined in terms of absence of food to sustain human life (viz., starvation). Malthus is not so much concerned with the improbable total annihilation of the species as with the moral superiority of avoiding overpopulation by abstention from procreation over achieving this end through the mass death of existing people in hunger and war. This accords perfectly with our view of the asymmetry between killing actual people (or letting them die) and abstaining from conceiving potential people.

Some demographers would say that an optimum population size is that beyond which, even if we do not suffer, we pawn the future of our descendants by forcing them to either restrict their desired procreative behavior or to lower their standard of living. This is the typical strategy of alarmist theorists, who find it difficult to convince us that we have already passed the desirable level (for that would mean that it would have been better if some of us did not exist). And again, the person-affecting view does not allow us to say that there is any wrong in the fact that our children will have a lower standard of living because there will be more of them. And in any case, they will be able to restrict their number of offspring so as to offset the trend toward "overpopulation." Of course, the problem of distributing the burden of population control between generations is complicated and cannot be coherently formulated if future people are potential. But as many of the future people are at least relatively actual, their claim to reproductive rights cannot be ignored by the present generation.

Other criteria of optimum population size consist of environmental factors, such as the carrying capacity of the earth, or the harmonious equilibrium between man and nature. But the carrying capacity of the earth is not fixed, or given, but partly dependent on human intervention (including agriculture and the building of dams—not only the use of chemicals and nuclear power!). Furthermore, the notion of carrying capacity is typically relative to human values and preferences, and these are constantly changing, sometimes due to changes in the balance between the number of people and the available resources. So although one can say that the country of Oz can have only an x number of people, because of its limited road infrastructure, $x + n$ people could be made equally happy either by the invention of a more efficient method of mobility, or by adapting to a preference for less mobility.

Both theology and evolution tend to characterize the optimum in terms of the maximum. "Be fruitful and multiply" enjoins humans to procreate as much as possible. (What is the limit of this "possible"? Maybe the carrying capacity of the earth, if we wish to reconcile the religious injunction with current recommendations of population control.) Evolution tends to favor those that have the best chances of procreating, perpetuating the gene pool, or maintaining the diversified gene pool. These concepts of optimum are hardly amenable to ethical discussion, for it is not clear why there should be more people rather than less in the religious sphere (more God worshippers? more of the image of God in the world?); and the value of the diversified gene pool might turn out to be an aesthetic ideal, which again cannot be given a person-regarding account.

The more technical definitions of optimum population sizes in the demographic and economic literature select as their normative variable some notion of welfare or standard of living. That is to say, in contrast to the strategy of adjusting the production effort and the standard of living to the independently fixed number of children (as, e.g., in a traditional Jewish family), they take as their starting point a certain level of income or welfare and work out the maximum number of people who can enjoy it. Thus Paul Ehrlich, the well-known population theorist, who has constantly been warning us of the "population bomb":[18]

> What must be done is to determine how much "good" should be available for each person. Then just how many people can enjoy that much "good" on a permanent basis can be determined, at least in theory. That number of people would then be one "optimum" population size for our finite planet.

Again, this approach understands "finite" as "closed" or rather "fixed in resources," rather than allowing for unpredictable ways of stretching the carrying capacity of the planet. But even if that assumption were plausible (and the earth could be said to have reached the ultimate limits of what it can sustain in human terms), our deeper objection would remain: no conception of "good" can be fixed for potential beings, that is to say as a guide to the decision how many new people to create. It is only in the name of our own welfare or that of the future actual people that we can use such a notion of "good" as constraining procreation. And we should not paternalistically prescribe to our children the conception of "the good" used by them in *their* procreative behavior. So although this definition of an optimum is powerful in guiding our real-life population policies (taking into account generation overlap and the inevitable existence of many of the members of the next generations), it is useless in purer genesis contexts.

Economists naturally tend to define that "good" in economic terms:

> The optimum population is that population which, with given natural resources, state of arts, and standard of working time, would secure the largest *per capita* output. (Dasgupta 1969, 295)

But the quality of life, and hence the desirable number of people, is not only a function of average output (income or utility). Instead of the highest *average* of whatever value, people might strive for more *justice,* or equality. And instead of judging the quality of life in terms of output or income, they might seek intimacy, unhampered wilderness, personal and social security, and so on. The proponents of the ideal of "Small is Beautiful" are willing to forgo some degree of economic welfare (output, income) in order to secure other values.

In any case, Dasgupta himself objects to the definition quoted above, because it might lead to the unacceptable consequence of a drastic reduction in population. He accordingly adopts a "total" criterion of optimality, namely "the maximization of the total discounted welfare of all generations from now to infinity" (p. 295), and fixes the right rate of savings as that which would secure that overall maximization. Thus, production and reproduction, we might say, are combined in the common enterprise of achieving an impersonal (and "eternal") goal.[19] But looking at both savings and procreation as subservient to an abstract transgenerational goal implies using people and whole generations as tools for the promotion of an impersonal good, including the willingness to bring in new people "so as to accumulate capital in the interest of posterity."

Realizing the ethical and conceptual implausibility of the impersonal approach to demographic planning, Dasgupta himself, in his later work, converts to a person-affecting view. This inevitably leads him to more skeptical conclusions concerning the concept of an optimum population size. In a masterful article (to which out of the literature on the ethics of population my own views come closest), Dasgupta denies the validity of Sikora's "extra-person-obligation," or what he calls the principle of "Pareto-plus."[20] There is no moral obligation in the addition of an extra person even if existing people are not affected by this addition and the life of the new person is worth living (thus adding to the total welfare). For person-affectingness does not allow either the application of contractarian principles to potential beings, nor the impersonal evaluation of agreeable states of consciousness as such (and the implied assignment of the same value—zero—to both the miserable standard of living and to total nonexistence). Thus, Parfit's Repugnant Conclusion is avoided.[21]

But Dasgupta is not satisfied with the skeptical conclusion that there is no "definite rule for optimum population" (Dasgupta 1974, 118). In his view what gives rise to this skepticism is the pure genesis context (Dasgupta 1988, 117). In real-life demographic policy making there is an existing generation of actual people of a certain number and preferences. In my terminology, this fact provides an ethical basis for genethical decisions, that is, it specifies the reference group of actual persons as required by the person-affecting conception. Yet, although it seems that only a purely generocentric principle of population policy can arise out of such a shift from "Genesis Problems" to "Actual Problems," Dasgupta stops short of such fully fledged generocentrism. This is reflected in his willingness to give some weight (although to a lesser extent) to potential people.

Dasgupta's reason for assigning comparative weight to potential people is that actual people have *both* categorical goods (which make their lives worth living) and conditional goods (which are good only on the condition of their being alive), whereas potential people have *only* the latter (p. 119). But I believe this reasoning is based on a serious fallacy: like categorical goods, conditional goods are goods only *for* actual people; they are not good as such, in the sense that the more of them "in the world," the better. It is true that unlike categorical goods, they do not justify going on living, but that does not make them ascribable to potential beings. Enjoying my morning cappuccino is indeed "only" a conditional good, which is good only if and as long as I live. Still, it is only good *for me*. The pleasure of a morning coffee cannot be a reason for creating a coffee-loving person. Dasgupta, who denies the intrinsic value of agreeable states of consciousness (abstracted from their subjects), cannot hold that potential pleasures can serve as a reason for creating a subject to enjoy those pleasures.

This hardly perceptible move of assigning *some* weight to the living standard of potential beings leads Dasgupta to "compromise" his initial person-affecting commitment and to go on to an unacceptable analysis of the population dilemma in the non-genesis context. By counting the welfare of the actual parents as twice the weight of the welfare of their potential child, Dasgupta argues that if by remaining childless each parent will have a welfare of 40, whereas by having a child (with a prospective welfare of 15) one parent will have 30 and the other 45, the rational choice is procreation. For the sum total of childlessness is $(2 \times 40) + (2 \times 40) = 160$, whereas that of procreation $(2 \times 30) + (2 \times 45) + 15 = 165$. The rest of Dasgupta's argument, which leads to an ingenious solution to the problem of rational choice in contexts of incoherence in the moral ordering of possible worlds, need not concern us here. For the solution is based on an implicit surrender to the impersonal comparability of states of affairs involving potential people. Generocentrism, as we understand it here, holds that childlessness in the above choice is absolutely superior to procreation (assuming of course that the benefits and pains of both childlessness and of raising a child are properly included in the welfare of the parents as expressed by the specific numeric values). We can put our alternative view in Dasgupta's own terminology (p. 121): the fact that "there *is* no overall moral ordering" does not deny the possibility of *rational choice,* but it is so only on purely generocentric grounds.

The conclusion of the present section is that from a philosophical point of view, that is, as a pure genesis problem, the notion of optimum population size is incoherent. There is no abstract way to determine the ideal number of people—either in any single generation or in a set of consecutive generations. A person-regarding conception cannot allow abstract comparisons between demographically different worlds any more than a comparison between the existence and nonexistence of human beings. In that respect there is no logical distinction between the genethical issue of existence and that of number. Accordingly, *sub specie aeternitatis* there is no meaning to the world being "overpopulated." Overpopulation is also a person-affecting concept, and as such can apply only to actual beings. Similarly, from a generocentric point of view there is no duty to potential future generations to secure any particular standard of living, such as a certain minimum, as much as possible, maximin, a standard equal to what we have, or a slight amelioration of our standard. A savings principle cannot be formulated independently of genesis choices, that is, as long as the number of future people remains undecided.[22] By analogy to a rich family of industrialists: it sounds fair to demand that each generation not touch the capital, or even to demand that each generation transfer to the next generation at least what was inherited from the previous one. But does this mean that the number of children be decided so that these principles of savings can be followed?

When population policies are designed, however, in impure, real-life contexts (involving both generational overlap and the existence of future actual people), a normative generocentric principle must be selected. This can relate to the way children affect our lives or the way we want their lives to be. It can be based on a particular balance between the quality and quantity of happiness, the love of children, the need for an extra work force in the economy, national aspirations, religious beliefs, availability of resources, and so forth. Even more importantly, the generocentric determination of the optimal population policy usually takes into serious account the welfare of the future people, at least as we want them to see it (and as we strive to inculcate in them). When we choose to restrict population growth "for the sake of our children," we are actually paternalistically deciding for them the standard beyond which life on earth becomes bad or undesirable. Thus, the idea of a "population bomb" is not meaningless. It derives its meaning either from the threat posed by overpopulation to future actual people, or from the fundamental values that we hold and wish to pass on to our descendants.

But once we concede that there is no one, absolute, and impersonal, optimal population size, we also realize that different people have different views about the desirable number of people (an indefinite number of incommensurable optima). This fact calls for the contemplation of interpersonal strategies of efficient coordination and fair distribution in the collective enterprise of deciding the number of future people, either by means of market mechanisms or through the political process.

COORDINATION AND DISTRIBUTION

Deciding the number of future people in impure genesis contexts is a typically coordinative and distributive issue: it involves either the choice of strategies directed at achieving an agreed optimum (if there is one), or the principles for compromise in (the more widespread) cases of conflicting conceptions of desirable population size. The purpose of coordination is to guarantee that the goals of each party in the procreative enterprise will be hampered as little as possible by the procreative behavior of other parties. The purpose of distribution is the fair allocation of the benefits and the just imposition of the burdens involved in the process and outcome of begetting children. I have little to say here about these substantive issues, and in this section I shall try only to outline schematically the particular conceptual and ethical difficulties that make these issues even more controversial and theory-resistant than other problems of distributive justice. In chapter 7 I shall address in more detail some of the concrete principles and social and political conflicts involved in the implementation of population policies in our real-life conditions.

The greatest problem lies in drawing the line between merely potential people and future actual ones. The problem is logical, as we have already noted, and is characterized by the following circularity: the ethical distributive issue can only be dealt with after the relevant reference group of people is fixed (viz., of actual people); but determining the reference group is itself partly a matter of ethical values (e.g., the ethical constraints determining the degree to which I have "control," or "say," over your reproductive choices). Defining who is "actual" is *the* problem in the coordination of procreative behavior in the *inter*generational sphere. Even if we, members of the present generation, agree on an optimum population size, can we impose it on our descendants? Can we be sure that they will also agree that this is indeed the optimum? Are we allowed to paternalistically condition them to adopt our notion of the optimum? Should we ignore the quite realistic possibility that their technology together with unpredictable changes in environmental conditions would make our definition of optimum outdated? And even if the next generation can be treated as more or less "given" to us (in its number and values, which are both to a great extent decided by us), this surely does not apply to more distant future generations. Still, they too might be affected by our present population and savings policies. In chapter 2 we saw the limitations of contract theories of distributive justice in solving genethical problems involving potential people. No imaginary congress of representatives of all generations can be devised so as to yield distributive principles. Coordination is also a problem in respect to actual people, for if they are not around yet, there is no one with whom we can coordinate our policies.

Assume that we have reached the conclusion that the optimum population is x and that this would be an acceptable standard also for all future generations. Currently we are $2x$ people. Over how many generations should the effort to curb population growth be spread so as to attain x? Our generation (implying having roughly only one child per couple)? Over that number of generations which would adopt a policy of slightly less than zero growth (just two children per couple)? Some other standard? And why should the more distant generations (after x is achieved) be exempt from sharing the burden of balancing the population? But, not all generations can be assigned their share, because they are indefinite in number. Furthermore, some future generations might *prefer* having even fewer children than required by the principle of the distribution of the depopulation burden. Should the distribution of the burden of depopulation be sensitive to subjective preference—for example, by demanding more restraint on the part of those who are less eager or less interested in having (many) children?

One meta-principle in the effort to formulate intergenerational guidelines for population is the often-entertained idea of *discount*. The further a certain generation is located in the future, the less we should (and indeed can) take its interests into account in our population policies. This idea is based on our ignorance of their numbers, their preferences, their technology, and their environmental circumstances (e.g., natural resources). In our terms: once we have decided the number of *our* descendants, they become actual for us. But we might also know quite a lot about their prospective preferences regarding the number of *their* children. In that respect we have to take the interests of our grandchildren into account no less than those of our children. But beyond this two-stage accounting, it seems difficult to iterate transitively this reasoning, implying that beyond the second or third generation people become (for us) more and more potential. Psychologically this may also have to do with the fact that we can personally know or "relate" only to people of the next two or three generations.[23] We feel that on the one hand, demographic choices are of crucial importance to future people, yet on the other hand cannot be shared with them. But from a person-affecting point of view this feeling is of course groundless. Take as an illustration the fact that none of us feels resentment toward past generations (e.g., from the Industrial Revolution onward) whose reproductive behavior is responsible for the presently (or at least potentially) overpopulated world.

The *intra*generational problem of distribution and coordination is conceptually easier but proportionately more difficult in the moral and political sense. Even if there is an objectively justified notion of an optimum population size, how do we distribute the responsibility of achieving it within our generation? First there is the international dimension. Should people in overcrowded parts of the planet take extra responsibility for reducing the overpopulation to which their contribution is larger? Or rather should the economically better off countries take their share in reducing numbers by helping to raise the standard of living of poorer countries, a most effective and proven means for reducing population growth? There are even extreme voices calling for a denial of help to third-world countries because such help would lower the infant death rate and lead to a larger future population, ultimately resulting in even more deaths from starvation. Even if the argument is arithmetically correct it is morally unacceptable precisely because of generocentrism (i.e., the morally "privileged" status of actual babies, born now, in comparison with *their*, relatively potential, offspring).

Although in the international domain the size of population is usually discussed as a public *hazard*, within particular societies or nations populations (even larger than existing ones) are often seen as a public *good*. This is due to the fact we have already noted that societies and nations (unlike humanity as such) have more definite "functions," goals, ideals, to which certain population sizes might be more or less conducive. But again, the distributive problems look insurmountable. Should the childless pay for bringing up children (education, health, incentives for larger families)? As old age pensioners they would benefit from the existence of future people who would produce the income necessary for pensions (see especially George 1987). Should those classes that have more children pay or rather be paid by the public fund for their reproductive preferences? How should the burden of numbers be distributed among the rich and the poor, the young and the elderly, women and men? To what extent should the satisfaction of raising children be taken into account?[24]

The general distributive problem in the attempt to achieve a certain population size in the light of certain social or collective ideals (even when there is a consensus regarding these ideals) is related to the basic tension between public goods and individual autonomy. Population size is typically a public good; procreation is typically a matter of the private choice and personal expression of individual couples. It is therefore widely acknowledged that public demographic policies, even those most enlightened and directed at the "public good," must be strictly constrained by personal rights. This is reflected by the unacceptability of various political means that could efficiently affect demographic trends, means that would be fully acceptable in other domains of social policy. Thus, centrally planned Platonic matching, forced sterilization, the criminal punishment of parents for deviating from a certain number of children, the genetic (or social) screening of potential parents—are all considered morally repugnant. However, direct and indirect incentives for either increasing the number of children in a family (positive incentives) or reducing the number (negative incentives), mainly through taxation regulations, are not only considered legitimate (as a matter of principle), but are inevitable, in the sense that whatever a government does in its taxation, welfare, and education policies directly or indirectly affects the reproductive behavior of its citizens. Other legislative means, such as a minimum age of marriage or the status of abortion and contraception, are more controversial and sometimes considered as an invasion of privacy not justified even by urgent demographic needs. So it seems that the distinction between compulsory and voluntary means is not sufficient to separate legitimate and illegitimate means of controlling population trends.[25]

The issue of "licensing parents" is a focus of the tension between the deep personal interest in having children and the public good. For although parenthood is usually held to be a natural or universal (and unconditional) right, society is often held responsible for the welfare of its minor members who are born handicapped or to parents who are incapable of taking care of them. Does society in these cases have the right to restrict the right of parenthood? As we have seen, even if it has, it is not "in the name of" the future child. It is only because of the special burden incurred on *society* by the irresponsible reproductive behavior of the parents. One may understandably argue that political interference with procreation is so dangerous in the sense of a slippery slope that we are better off avoiding it completely (even at the price of further burdens on society). But this cannot apply to every kind of public effort to influence the reproductive trends. Education, propaganda, creating and encouraging access to certain institutions, are all legitimate means for attaining what is considered a demographic public interest. It is an illusion to think that "letting nature take its course" is a solution to the tension between public good and private rights in the case of procreation (as if by the help of an invisible hand, the "right" population size would be reached). If there are considerations making a certain number of people in a given society good *for* its current actual members, then the invisible hand will not lead to this optimum—neither conceptually nor empirically.[26]

If licensing is considered repugnant in the case of natural parenthood, why is it usually considered acceptable in artificial parenthood (government control over artificial insemination, *in vitro* fertilization, and surrogate motherhood)? And if, as those granting a moral status to potential persons believe, there is a right to be born healthy, why should not the state *force* parents to refrain from conceiving children when early screening discovers a serious genetic disease in the family? Generocentrism seems to dissolve these widespread inconsistencies by relegating the discussion of these matters to the distributive level of actual people involved in a standard conflict between public good and private interests and rights. Since the child's welfare is not a reason to interfere in procreation, but *only* society's good, we can explain why we tend to severely limit the right of governments to invade the privacy of procreative decisions.[27] (Note that the state is believed to have not only a right but also a duty to interfere in the way parents treat their children after they are born, i.e., in cases of maltreatment. This again proves the relevance of the actual-potential distinction.) In other words, the reasons justifying social intervention in parenthood are not related to the welfare of potential children but rather to the interests of other actual individuals (present or future) and to the balancing of the deeply respected intimacy of reproductive choices by individual couples and the burden to society involved in the outcome of such choices.[28]

Another way of justifying government intervention in procreation is to argue that curbing population growth cannot usually be expected to strike the individual as a self-interested or as a benevolent act (Miller and Sartorius 1979). In terms of the view developed here, the state paternalistically intervenes to defend the interests of the group of future actual people consisting, for instance, of all the firstborn children of our generation, that is to say their right not to live in an overcrowded world. This is a paternalistic intervention that achieves a coordinative goal. If I know that you are going to refrain from begetting more than one child, I am willing to do the same so as to secure a better world for both our children. The state acts as a Hobbesian guarantor of game-theoretic solutions (threatened by "defections").

We may conclude that the determination of the number of children is a matter that can be guided only by generocentric principles. Yet, these belong to two partly incompatible kinds: public interest and private rights. The coordinative and distributive problems of procreation are particularly difficult; the stakes are very high, both for the public good and for the life of the individual. Overpopulation can be disastrous (for actual people); restriction of family size can involve the curtailment of the deepest preferences of the individual, the undermining of his categorical desires (which make his life worth living and meaningful). There is no clear-cut solution to this tension, but a general criterion can be formed on the basis of *partitioning* reproductive decisions into the private and the public, leaving the individual with as much liberty as possible to decide the size of his or her family, and society with the responsibility to influence the macro-trends in population growth. This implies that the state may work through the *social* medium of taxation, incentives, and education, rather than the more "personal" means of legislating for the individual (forced sterilization, legal prohibition). This would leave the individual with enough space to exercise the liberty to procreate, even if that would involve certain monetary costs for the state.

Although this chapter has dwelt on the complex relationship between genethical issues and ethical (distributive) principles of population policies, it is our argument that in the end the issue of the number of future people in the abstract is no more amenable to ethical theorizing than is their very existence. Although it might seem at first that existence is an impersonal issue, whereas number is a person-regarding matter, our discussion has shown that they belong to the same level of (gen)ethical discourse. It is not the case that we first decide the issue of existence and then proceed to fix the number of future people. The latter is no less a genuine genesis dilemma than the former.

CHAPTER 6

Identity

"Pinocchio, you wicked boy!" he cried out. "You are not yet finished, and you start out by being impudent to your poor old Father . . ."

"I deserve it," Geppetto said to himself. "I should have thought of it before I made him. Now it's too late!"
C. Collodi, *The Adventures of Pinocchio,* chap. 3

SHAPING PERSONS' IDENTITY AS A GENESIS PROBLEM

Much philosophical attention has been paid to genesis problems in the context both of the existence and of the numbers of future people. Equally ample discussion has been devoted to the ethical questions involved in the formation of people's identity by biological or educational means. Surprisingly, however, there is almost no philosophical study of the issue of *identity as a genesis problem*. The aim of the present chapter is to examine the formation of human identity or nature as one of the most interesting aspects of genethics, with the double aim of achieving systematic completeness of genethical theory and of illuminating through the principles of genethics the particular limits on the morality of education and genetic engineering. However, by first trying to explain the relative neglect of the genesis aspect of identity formation (or, alternatively, of the identity dimension of genesis problems) we may gain a preliminary insight into the issue at hand.

Empirically, we might surmise, the identity of human beings has usually been considered as lying beyond the moral sphere because of the slight control we have over its formation. It is as if once we decide to beget a child (or once we decide the number of children we want to have), the irreversible and uncontrollable process of the creation of *a* (particular) child is initiated. This, of course, is doubly wrong. On the one hand, we are gradually mastering the very biological process through which the nature and identity of a child is determined. On the other, we can safely claim that human beings have always had an extensive command over the identity of their descendants, although less in the biological sense than in the social and psychological dimensions. In other words, the traditional neglect of identity formation as a genethical issue can be ascribed to the fact that in the past we either had absolutely no *biological* control over the determination of new persons' identity, so that it never occurred to us to have any moral dimension, or we had such an extensive *social* control over it that we almost took it for granted, thus ignoring the ethical dilemmas involved in education as part of the creation (genesis) of people.

Philosophically, the question of personal identity is multifaceted. Amelie Rorty has usefully listed the different issues discussed by philosophers under the title of personal identity: the unique nature of human beings (as against other living creatures), the criteria of individuation (i.e., the numerical distinction between individuals having "the same" properties), the conditions of reidentification of individuals through changes in time (that is to say problems of "survival"), or the cluster of characteristics which constitutes the essential core of the self (Rorty 1976, 1–2). We might add that the first three kinds of interest in personal identity relate to it from a third-person ("external") angle and are accordingly metaphysical in nature; the fourth tackles the problem of personal identity from a first-person ("internal") perspective and is accordingly of a subjective nature. Aristotelian attempts to define the uniqueness of the human species, Leibnizian criteria for numerical distinction, or Parfitian exercises in determining personal survival (to illustrate the first three kinds of identity issues) are all matters of objective, metaphysical criteria; the question "what makes me what I am?" is, however, answered by the subjects themselves, who thus choose, project, or create their identity, that is to say it constitutes the very criteria of their identity.[1]

In genethics we are naturally more interested in the last (fourth) issue of identity. For even if the objective conditions of human identity can be tampered with, the moral significance of such manipulations is mediated by the subjective attitude of the person whose identity is manipulated. In an impersonalist conception of ethics one might argue that it is morally wrong or bad genetically to change the essential traits of the human species, or to split one person "amoebically" into two identical ones, or to subject an individual to Parfitian teletransportation (the first three identity issues listed above, respectively). But for a person-affecting conception, such as the one endorsed here, what really makes

an ethical difference is—as we shall see in the following sections—the
changing of a person from his or her point of view. For it is typical in
this case that *someone* is affected for better or for worse, that is, from
the point of view of his or her volitions.[2]

It is, therefore, the *creation* of identity, rather than the conditions of
change in it, which is our subject matter. It is identity in the sense of a
gradual process, rather than of a yes-or-no state, which concerns us. For
it is a biological and psychological fact that human personal identity, in
the sense of "who I am," is formed in a long process, over which there is
much human control. Unlike genesis problems of existence and number,
which are typically "one time," and usually irreversible, the shaping of
people's identity (in the sense of individual character) extends over time,
is subject to revisions based on feedback, and refers to a constantly
changing object. The crucial importance (both theoretical and practical)
of the identity dimension of the genesis problem is due to the logical
impossibility of separating identity from existence. One cannot decide
to beget a child without at least implicitly deciding some aspects of its
identity. A human being is not created as an empty slot or as a *tabula
rasa,* namely, with no biological and psychological traits. Furthermore,
the decision to create it never terminates the process of its genesis, as so
many aspects of its identity remain to be decided in later stages of its
development.

The ethics of identity formation presupposes that there is a process
that can be controlled, thus calling for genesis choices. But the control
over the gradually evolving identity of individuals can be exercised
either by the subject or by another party. The subject can exercise such a
control only in later stages of this evolution and usually only to a limited
degree (e.g., by deciding to undergo a sex change by surgery or hor-
monal treatment, by radical conversion, by emigrating to a completely
new society and culture). Other parties, typically the parents, exert a
deeper control over the identity of a newly created being, because they
have the power to forge it at earlier stages, when the individual's character is much more malleable. And as we shall presently see, the earlier
the interference, the deeper are its effects. The difference between self-
formation of identity and the formation of another's identity is that only
the latter calls for moral constraints and involves rights and corresponding duties. But the former can and will serve us as an illuminating
analogy through which the very problem of identity may be analyzed in
genethics.

Deciding the identity of another person, unlike the choice of one's own identity, raises the question of *paternalism*. In the strict sense, paternalistic interventions are justified in terms of the good of other people, who—for some reason—do not realize what is good for them. This, in turn, presupposes the actual existence not only of a person, but of a set of "real" interests that constitute that person's existence. Being good *for him* or *for her,* the paternalistic act must appeal to an actual subject under a certain character-description, or volitional identity. Consequently, a genesis choice of bringing a new person into existence can never be justified in paternalistic terms (e.g., of this person's good), for as we have shown (in chapter 4), coming to exist cannot be viewed as a good for the subject. But if persons already exist in some way, can choices regarding their identity be considered paternalistically justified? If the decision makers are the subjects themselves, the answer is of course negative, as the decision is made on the ground of what the people concerned conceive as their true interests.

But if the decision is made by another person, the question of paternalism is more difficult to settle. Sometimes parents decide to instill in their children certain identity-fixing characteristics in the name of the children's interests; sometimes they cannot appeal to such interests, because these themselves are the object of the parents' intervention. Only in the first case can the parents' action be called paternalistic. The second, which is the typical genesis formation of another person's identity, is not paternalistic, because it "generates" the very volitions that are the basis for further and later paternalistic actions. It creates the very criteria of "good for someone." What might be thought of as the deepest kind of paternalism is not paternalism at all. In the same way as it is misleading to treat the very creation of human beings as paternalistic (creating people without consulting them), so it is misleading to describe the decision of their identity as paternalistic.[3] Genetic engineering and education in its deeper aspects will thus be shown to be fallaciously represented as paternalistic.

The particular genethical problems of identity formation call for a new approach to personal identity in its dynamic change. I shall refer to this as the *concentric* view and describe it metaphorically as considering identity not as a cluster of identity-fixing traits but as a hierarchical, regimented conception, according to which human beings are gradually formed, layer by layer, from "core" to "surface." Identity in the genethical context is not determined by any essential nucleus providing an "all-or-nothing" condition of personal identity. Unlike the traditional search for the essential core of personal identity through a process of peeling off the nonessential traits surrounding the core, our approach seeks to trace how the very core constituting the gradually evolving identity is shaped. Rather than the retrospective isolation of what precedes the peripheral accretion to the essential primary self, genethics is concerned with the way in which the prospective process of the formation of the self is guided.

Being concerned with identity *formation,* the genethical concept of identity is incremental in nature. It views the growth of personal identity as a tree-like process, in which every node of branching is defined both in terms of the various options for new offshoots and in terms of the constraints on branching imposed by the nature of the already existing stem. Unlike essentialist views, it does not take any particular set of traits as the final ("static") criterion of identity. Unlike the cluster theory of identity, it does not define identity in terms of any modulation of a set of traits that forms a certain minimal cluster. It is dynamic in taking the surface-core distinction as stage-relative: once certain features become essentially characteristic of a person, they constrain further developments of the *same* person. In that respect they become part of the person's essential core identity. Branches become stems for further branches. But before they are so installed in the individual, that is, when they are subject to choice, they may be considered as peripheral.

We will illustrate this view in the next two sections of this chapter; however, we should note here the connection of the concept of genethical identity to the actual-potential distinction, which serves us as a basis for the analysis of all genesis problems. In the same way as the existence of a person is treated as potential as long as it is dependent on a human choice, so also is personal identity in the sense of the profile of traits characterizing the individual as a particular person. Thus, from the point of view of a decision taken at a particular node, the various possible branches that can be cultivated are potential, whereas the existing stem is actual. And, as will be illustrated below, those branches that are *bound* to grow out of the stem (whatever we do), are also actual, although not yet existing (analogously to the future-actual person in the sphere of existence). The actual-potential distinction in identity formation is dynamic and relative, that is to say it *shifts* with the formative process. An identity-fixing trait can be potential at one stage of personal development, but become actual at a later stage. More and more identity-fixing traits are joined by this process to the core of the person's identity. And thus the core is constantly enriched and expanded. The ethical implication of this enrichment is the increase in the number of constraints on the further development of personal identity. The number of possible options (possibility defined in terms of existing, actual traits) is continuously narrowed down throughout the evolution of identity. The individual's character is forged, its profile crystallized.

Ideally, there is an end to this process of identity formation, a certain stage at which the tree of identity-fixing traits of character is fully grown and in which all further changes in one's life and circumstances do not entail an identity change. This is the end of both biological and social intervention in the genesis of identity. Yet, it applies only to external intervention (of genetic manipulators, parents, or state educators). It does not apply to the subject! Unlike existence, in which the only practical expression of the subject's dissatisfaction is suicide, personal identity is to a large extent controllable by the subject, who can change it. From this subjective point of view, the constraints on "branching" are different. Thus, an individual might *go back* and cut existing branches in his own identity tree and grow others in their place. This partial change of identity, in which it is morally wrong for others to engage (being "manipulative," "brainwashing," violating autonomy), is permitted to the individual (although it is sometimes considered as "lack of integrity," lack of character, reflecting on the superficiality of the traits that had seemed to belong to the core of the personality). But it may equally be considered a change toward a better, more coherent organization of the subject's life, character, and identity. The genesis power of human beings can be self-directed—either negatively (as in the case of suicide), or by making oneself different to what one actually is (as in radical conversion). But this genesis power cannot ethically be applied by external agents to an actual individual—either in the form of killing (total annihilation) or in the form of forced identity change (the annihilation of part of the individual, or of the individual under a certain identity-description).

The present discussion consciously bypasses the substantive philosophical issue of the list of identity-fixing traits and the individuation criteria of these traits. We leave this question open not because it is unimportant, but because it is too large for the more modest purpose of this study. I may even add that in contrast to Parfit, who explicitly diminishes the moral importance of personal identity, the view presented here is wholly dependent on the reality and importance of identity in the sense of what makes people essentially what they are, that is, what from their point of view would be considered a change so radical in their life or character that *they* would not consider the result to be themselves any more. Parfit, upholding an impersonal approach to ethics, can play down the issue of personal identity, because value is ultimately a quality of the world. Consequently, moral duties are not necessarily defined through an identifiable individual, but rather through states of affairs.[4]

A person-affecting view, however, must take seriously the issue of the identity conditions of the persons affected. The morality of genesis choices in the case of existence cannot ignore the question when does human life begin (conception, viability, birth). Similarly, the morality of genetic engineering or education cannot ignore the substantive issues of what makes us what we are, and at what stage does a further enforced change count as an attack on our very identity. However, the general (formal) argument applies to any possible theory of both the beginning of human existence and the formation of personal identity, and hence the substantive issue can be left open.[5]

Approaching personal identity from the first-person perspective is natural for a volitional theory of value, such as the one adopted in this essay. For if value (either life itself, or a certain kind of life) is viewed as related to the subject *for whom* it is valuable, the very identity of this life and its subject is a volitional concept, that is, a function of what the subject of the life in question wants or would want from his or her point of view. But this particular point of view is also partly "generated" by the process of child rearing and education and in that respect cannot be constrained by any person-affecting considerations. Unlike genesis choices of existence and number, which concern purely potential people, the genesis of identity is concerned with beings whose identity is partly actual, partly potential. And the dynamic nature of the evolution of identity means that the ratio between the actual and the potential itself constantly shifts toward the actual. But in any case, a person-affecting view must take personal identity into account in treating the difference between the self and others as more significant than that between the present and the future selves. For only in the latter case is there a common "core" of identity-fixing traits, from the point of view of which the changes of the self are judged and evaluated. The common stem of the various possible branches of a person's biography gives it a moral standing, a basis for comparison of alternative branchings, a necessary condition for the ascription of "good (or better) *for*." These conditions do not exist for the comparisons of different biographies, which consequently can be compared only on an impersonal basis.

The concentric conception of identity may be seen as a weakened form of the Kripkean conception. Both are "genetic" in claiming that personal identity relates to a certain origin that through a historical chain determines who a person is; yet the concentric view regards the genesis of identity as a process, a gradual evolution, and is interested not only in the metaphysical question of who a person is but also in the practical and ethical question of what counts as a change in the identity of an individual and what can be done to a person without bringing about such a change. The concentric conception is "gradual" in the sense that it introduces the idea that there are various dimensions of identity which are formed one after (and on the basis of) the other.

The two remaining sections of this chapter will illustrate in some detail the applications and implications of the concentric approach in the analysis of genesis problems of identity. The first section discusses the formation of identity through *biological* means, that sort of identity over which we have gained some control only lately. The other raises the problem of the psychological and social shaping of the individual personality through *education,* a universally exercised power that humans have always had. The distinction between the two types of identity formation is justified not only as being based on different means but also as relating to different stages in the evolution of personal identity. The first is earlier, and hence—according to the tree metaphor—deeper. It is also, for empirical reasons, "irreversible" in a relatively stronger sense than the second.[6] It is closer to the decision to bring about the very existence of a human being, and hence is usually seen as a more typical genesis issue. It is also much more often suspected as reflecting a human *hubris,* an attempt to "play God." Nevertheless, our point is that these are mostly differences in degree, and that the analogy between genetic engineering and education as two parallel means of creating people is stronger than is usually conceded.[7]

Identity formation is a continuous process, but its crucial stages, at least from the practical point of view (i.e., those over which we have control), belong to childhood. It is thus child rearing in the primary form of the way a child is brought up by its parents which raises the most widespread issues of identity formation. Yet, other stages are of no less theoretical interest, as well as of a growing moral concern. Human existence in earlier biological stages (fetal and even preconceptive) has become partly malleable. Furthermore, intervention in the "natural" biological process of the identity formation of human individuals may often have long-term effects on the evolution of the *species,* that is, it transcends the enterprise of forging *personal* identity. It is in that respect too that genetic engineering goes deeper than education. Yet, in genethical theory we should not disregard nonbiological forms of control over the identity of collectives, societies, and communities. These political and social means of shaping human identity on a transpersonal level may be no less effective than the shaping of the identity of an individual. On this level, identity is no longer a first-person problem, but rather pertains to the Aristotelian question of what kind of beings we are, or rather what kind of beings we want ourselves to become and our descendants to be.

THE RADICAL MOLDING OF PEOPLE: GENETIC ENGINEERING

Genetics is naturally the most conspicuous subject for genethics, at least in the latter's identity aspect. Yet it is often considered the most controversial kind of genethical choice. "Engineering" and "manipulation," which are the common substantives of the adjective "genetic," allude to artificial interference in a natural process on the one hand and to paternalistic exploitation of human beings on the other. Many factors of genetic intervention in identity formation make it morally suspected. First of all, it is *new*, that is to say we have no firmly entrenched intuitive responses to some of the emerging technical and medical possibilities offered by science; nor is there a tradition of ethical discussion of the matter. Being new, it is also risky, as much of the technology is experimental and its effects unknown. This includes the unpredictable effects on the system of values of future people which we usually take for granted as a basis in planning for *their* future (Golding 1972, 98). Secondly, in some of its uses, genetic engineering offers the option of a *deep* change in the identity of the evolving human being, that is to say a radical deviation from the "natural" course of events. It involves a "softening" of the traditionally regarded hard core of human identity, both on the individual level and that of the species. Thirdly, genetic interference has a potential long-term effect on the nature of the *species* at large, that is, further generations and the gene pool. Fourthly, and connected to the previous factors, genetic engineering is *irreversible*, that is, not subject to reconsideration either by the engineer or by the subject undergoing the change. Fifthly, and again derived from the previous factors, tampering with the natural biological process of the evolution of both the individual and the species is considered as a form of metaphysical *trespass,* an abuse of human power and knowledge, a self-destructive plan to change the course of natural selection, an arrogant attempt to transcend the religious role of humankind in the universe, the illegitimate desire to assume the function of a creator.[8] Finally, much of the repulsion regarding genetic engineering arises out of concern about the abuse of power by a particular group of people in society, who might come to hold the key to the creation of the future generation, thus monopolizing all genethical *power* in the present generation. This concern is more of a distributive nature. In the formation of future people's identity we should not only be humble in relation to natural (or supernatural) forces but also in relation to other actual individuals interested in forging the identity of their offspring.

But we have gradually become reconciled to the idea that some forms of genetic interference might be not only legitimate but positively beneficial and even morally commendable. It is, however, particularly illuminating to analyze the cases in which common resistance to biological intervention is lessened or is even replaced by active support. Genetic *counseling* is almost universally advocated as a method of preventing the birth of a defective child. Although parents are given the freedom to choose whether to conceive a child, counseling makes their choice more informed and responsible. No particular opposition applies to this mode of preconceptive "gentle" genetic control over natural processes, mainly because it does not involve any identifiable human subject, that is, it is concerned with a purely potential being and in that respect does not differ from choices regarding the existence and number of children. Genetic *screening* is a slightly more active intervention in natural processes. It can take the form of the laboratory examination of separate gametes or a zygote, fetal tissues, and so forth. The result of such examination can serve as the basis either for active genetic intervention or for the discontinuation of the developmental process. This method is more controversial since some people regard it as a violation of the sanctity of human life, assuming that there is already such life in an identifiable and hence morally relevant form. Finally, genetic *engineering,* the most active and hence the most dubious method, consists of the manipulation of the genetic makeup of an evolving (human) being. It is specifically an identity issue, because the existence of a particular, identifiable, individuated creature is given; it is actual. But here too, there is a difference in attitude toward negative and positive forms of engineering. The former and less dubious procedure is sometimes referred to as somatic cell gene therapy, in which a deleterious gene is removed, thus preventing defects and suffering; the latter involves the attempt to shape a creature having a set of "desirable" properties, a "better" being than normal human beings.[9]

A critical examination of this variety of attitudes to different forms of biological control over the identity of future people must take as its theoretical basis the distinction between actual and potential. But in the case of the genesis of identity (in contradistinction to that of existence) particular care should be taken not to confuse "potential" in our genethical sense (viz., being dependent on a human choice) with "potential" in the biological or metaphysical sense (viz., "in the process of becoming a certain entity if certain background conditions obtain, or are not interfered with"). Those traits that are inevitably going to evolve in individuals because of their genetic makeup are (at the early stage, before their manifestation) potential in the biological sense, yet—in our genethical terms—they are actual. They become potential only once we gain the knowledge and power to prevent their occurrence, to change the predetermined genetic course of events.[10]

On this basis we can now directly confront the problem of genetic intervention from a generocentric point of view. Genetic intervention is morally constrained only by actual people. Actual, in this context, means both existing people ("us") *and* the people whose identity is being shaped, the people under the description of all their *actual* attributes and traits (i.e., those over which we have no control). More specifically, we have to consider any genetic "manipulation" against the background of the set of traits which the "person" already possesses or that he or she will inevitably turn out to possess. This is the person-affecting principle in the context of identity formation. In the case of genetic counseling, such as that sought by the prospective mother in the wrongful life case of chapter 1, the person affected is only the mother, because there is no child yet, under *any* description. However, in cases in which a harmful gene is removed from a zygote, there is already a core of identity-fixing traits *in relation to which* this gene can be said to be harmful. In other words, although a zygote is only a potential human being in the metaphysical sense, *part* of its identity is in genethical terms actual. This incomplete but actual identity justifies the ascription *to* this person of the value or disvalue of certain genetic interventions.[11]

This generocentric approach to genetic intervention provides us with only structural guidelines. It makes sense only in highly idealized imaginary cases or in relatively simple ones (such as the removal of specific disease-causing genes). What we so far do not have is a theory of personal identity in which the various genetic components are assigned a defined role. This is due both to the philosophical debate regarding the general nature of personal identity, as well as to the lack of scientific knowledge regarding the genetic basis of those attributes that constitute identity. In other words, we so far know very little about the actual way the "tree of human identity" evolves. However, genethical theory suggests the kinds of *tests* by which substantive moral issues of genetic engineering *would* be decided.

I believe that with the future development of techniques of gene replacement, "negative" genetic control will become not only morally acceptable but even imperative. In the same way that the removal of a particular gene causing a disease is thought of as morally justified, so would the removal of a gene that makes people aggressive. In both cases we appeal to the first-person identity of future individuals: on *its* basis we may say (or rather *they* may say) that they would be better off without the disease or the tendency to aggression. The person who is said to be thus better off is the person constituted by all the other (prior) identity-fixing characteristics. Such gene removals can even be considered as the person's right, and refraining from the appropriate genetic treatment could in principle be the subject of a wrongful life suit (or rather a "wrongful identity" suit!). A child would justifiably claim that *it* could have had a better genetic makeup. Of course, the same argument can be extended to the more positive forms of genetic intervention. Take Nozick's imaginary supermarket, in which we may select whatever genes (and character traits) we wish our child to have. If there is already an identifiable being, parts of whose identity are already formed, then it would seem that, other things being equal (e.g., the costs of various options), we have a duty to buy our offspring those supplementary elements of genetic equipment which would be best from the point of view of the already existing traits.

On the other hand, if either the negative or the positive form of genetic interference is directed at genetic material that is itself constitutive of the person's (future) identity, then the person-affecting view must insist that it cannot be morally constrained by any reference to the subject (though of course the interests of the parents or of society might be involved).[12] If the shopping spree in Nozick's genetic supermarket is aimed at building a genetic makeup *from scratch,* then the only limits on the shopping parent (or engineer) are those of personal taste, price, effect on others, and so forth. The potential person can have no more interest in having a certain identity than in being born. Within a person-affecting view it is only the interests of actual people which can dictate the choice of identity of new people. Beyond the general debate on the legitimacy of applying principles of distributive justice to genetic endowment (should I be compensated for my low I.Q. or for my ugliness?), we can affirm that people cannot logically have a right to any genetic endowment, if that constitutes their identity. So even if I might deserve some redistributive share for my genetically transmitted disease, I cannot claim anything for not being a Mozart.[13]

But we should note that part of our identity is determined by the environment into which we are born. This, no less than their genetic makeup, is an identity-fixing feature of human lives. And if we, parents or engineers, have no control over the natural and social environment in which the future individual is going to live, then it must be treated as belonging to the "core" identity and must consequently serve as a constraint on our hypothetical choice of a genetic makeup. Thus, we would have to select in the genetic supermarket only those traits that are compatible, adaptable, and efficient in such *given* environmental conditions. An aggressive character is harmful both to the future social partners of the individual and to the individual herself, only if it is predicted that the future society in which she is going to live will indeed treat aggression negatively. The same applies to positive attributes like a high I.Q., ambition, beauty, and so forth, which are all good *for* their subjects only within certain social conditions and conventions.[14] But even the judgment that a disease-causing gene is "harmful" is dependent on the assumption that the individual in question is going to be aversive to pain and handicap, an abbreviated life, and limited freedom (that is to say that all these features belong to the "identity core"). From what we know about the in-built features of human beings (independently of social conditions) this is a pretty safe assumption; but it is nevertheless conceptually true to say that *if* human beings can be created so as not to care about longevity and pain, then what we now call "disease" would not be considered a harm, and no person-affecting reason for genetically preventing it would be morally required.

With such wild thought-experiments we reach the logical limits of genethical theory. Choices of identities for future people that are absolutely free from any prior constraint, due either to the individuals' future makeup or their environment, make us really Godlike. The completely free creation of human identity presupposes full control over *all* identity-fixing traits and conditions (that are compatible with the result still being called "human"). Yet, this would always be empirically impossible, since even the most controlled form of creation is constrained by both the "raw material" in which it is mediated and by the surrounding circumstances and conditions of the created object. Future people cannot ever be treated as literally *empty* slots. The idea of creating people with no prior constraints makes no more sense than building with Lego pieces that have no size, no color, no shape, no consistency— all these being subject to the creative process itself. This is especially true in the most extreme case in which the creator is not even bound by the constraints of creating a *human* being, that is, by human-specific properties.[15]

Note that genuinely total control also entails the absence of other equally powerful engineers of identity. Once we introduce other genetic planners into this sci-fi picture, we are faced with coordination problems of the same type as those mentioned in chapter 5 in the context of population policies. The analogy of genetic engineering and population planning as two genesis problems can be illustrated by the idea of "a perfect baby," which is as incoherent from a person-affecting point of view as the notion of "optimum population size."[16] If a particular genetic makeup can be good only for its subject, and if this very makeup constitutes the subject's identity, then the idea of an optimal combination of genetic attributes cannot make sense. There is no best of all possible human beings in the impersonal sense (as there is no best possible world). We mention these purely fictitious cases both because they are theoretically significant and because they have the same structure as the much more common practical problems of standard identity formation through education, as will be suggested in the next section.

The strong tendency we all have toward an impersonal approach to genetic engineering cannot be ignored. Much of the opposition to unrestrained genetic interference is based on a genuine concern for what seems a typically impersonal value—the quality of the gene pool, or the smooth working of natural selection. The possibility that much of the variety of the human gene pool might be lost in an overly regulated process of genetic transmission is often considered as catastrophic, since variety is the grist for the evolutionary mill. But some of these concerns can definitely be translated into a person-affecting language. We might be justified in believing that even for our eugenically programmed offspring, the existence of a minimal variety of human character would be thought of as desirable. In other words, genetic variety is good for future actual people. Only if we instill in all our descendants a character that would prefer homogeneity would the price of genetic uniformity be considered worthwhile. In that highly remote contingency, there would indeed be no argument against the loss of genetic variety, as there is no argument against the voluntary discontinuation of the human race. Similarly, from a person-affecting view there is no value in eugenics, that is, in the impersonal betterment of the gene pool. Human beings have an interest in *their having* better genetic traits—not in *there being* a better reservoir of traits for potential beings.[17]

We may say that the deeper one goes in the concentric layers of human identity, the more potential are the identity-fixing attributes. This implies that there is less of a *prior* core in terms of which the manipulation of attributes can be restricted. This is also the sense in which long-term genetic interference with the gene pool is in Elster's terms "global," namely the total opening of the process of the creation of human nature to radically novel possibilities and configurations of traits. It is understandable why precisely in those circumstances of unconstrained creative liberty we tend to withdraw to the more restrictive and the less threatening conservatism afforded by *im*personalism, such as the alleged value of "natural" processes, the appeal to a metaphysical concept of essential human nature, the wrongness of interfering with chance, or of preempting the future exercise of free choice, and so forth. A person-affecting view has to account for our aversion to such radical changes in human nature. As will be suggested in chapter 8 below, the basic motivation for having children and for the continuation of the human race is associated with the continuation of ourselves, our survival. But for that goal to be realized, we must (pro)create beings in our own image and likeness, that is to say creatures who are going to be human in that they are somehow similar to us, especially in the basic traits that we consider "essential" (not in the traditional metaphysical and impersonal sense but in the sense of the type of persons we *want* to be).

The limits on genetic engineering do not therefore lie in any scientifically or metaphysically defined core of essential human nature, but rather at the point where we would stop treating an offspring as *ours* (see Chadwick 1987, 125–127). Since this is a volitional criterion, there is no universal way to fix this point in advance. But it is an interesting thought-experiment to take genetic inheritance (which so far has been a strong criterion of parenthood) and gradually to weaken it by imaginary genetic changes. At what stage would we, the parents, stop seeing the ensuing child as *our* child? At what stage would we consider the radical artificial leap in the evolution of humankind as tantamount to the creation of a new species, that is, to the end of the human race? These questions are analogous to those of the personal identity and survival of an individual, widely discussed in the philosophical literature. Although the answers to these questions are highly subjective and varied, they point to the person-affecting criterion, which is the only alternative to impersonal attempts to explain the limits of genetic interference in human nature.

Genetic engineering is a context in which our common intuitions are rather violently challenged by wild thought-experiments and menacing science fiction. But we can turn to less dramatic areas where the genesis of genetic identity is decided, in order to test our general generocentric thesis. Matchmaking is, of course, the most "natural" way to create children with a specific identity, and it has often been suggested as a eugenic means (typically in utopias, but also in a recent experiment in Singapore). But modern medicine has lately supplied us with a wide range of options of artificial methods of reproduction, which although originally meant to enable the very creation (existence) of human beings, also compel us to choose their identity. In artificial insemination from donor (AID) or *in vitro* fertilization (IVF), matchmaking becomes much more controlled and sophisticated. Surrogate motherhood and techniques of long-term freezing of eggs or sperm open up possibilities and call for moral choices and legal arrangements that have become all too real. For example, the ability to draw from a bank a frozen egg and frozen sperm, both anonymously donated many years earlier, and match them because of a promising potential makeup, is a form of genetic control over identity with no genetic engineering required.[18]

The extensive literature in medical ethics usually discusses the questions of parental rights, the status of the donor, the role of the state, and the obligations of the doctors involved; but we are interested here in the status of the (potential) child. From the point of view of a woman trying to conceive through AID, it is psychologically natural to think of the identity of her future child as already somehow fixed and to look for the "best" father. But, of course, we know that the genetic role of the father is no less crucial in the identity formation of the child than the mother's and hence that there is no sense in the attempt to secure *for* the child the best paternal genetic inheritance. State regulation of sperm banks cannot be justified in the name of "the best interests of the child," but only as a protection of the woman using the bank's services and *her* interests.[19]

Still, the exact combination of genetic qualities that fix identity cannot be abstractly formulated. I would have still been *I*, had my parents genetically caused a change in the color of my eyes. It would *not* have been I, had they—immediately after "my" conception—brought about a change in the sex of the embryo. But in between these two extreme poles there is an indefinite number of possible configurations of traits that separately and in combination contribute to the way I see myself as a unique individual. Knowing so little about the connection between genes and first-person identity, we feel confused when confronted with remote fantasies of genetic supermarkets. What I am suggesting here is only the structure of correct reasoning about the subject. It will always be necessary to build a "tree" of the evolving identity and then to isolate in that tree the traits that belong to the stem (viz., those already fixed and actual); on that basis, choices of further traits (branches) would be made—on the one hand constrained by the stem, on the other hand free inasmuch as they do not run counter to the interests of the individual under the identity of the stem. The problem is that the botanical metaphor does not do full justice to the complexity of the evolution of human identity. For in human beings identity is partly malleable *retroactively,* that is later branches can change the nature of earlier stems! This is due not only to greater reversibility in the process of human identity formation than in that of a tree, but also to the fact that we are concerned here with first-person identity, in which the subject partly decides his or her identity, a decision that may be applied also "backwards." This flexibility is less apparent in the genetic element of identity formation and more in the social and cultural conditioning taking place after birth. But it has repercussions for genetic engineering as well. For instance we are allowed to change the sex of a human organism at an early stage despite this being a property definitely belonging to the core identity. For the adult person with the "new" sex would not regret our decision, being—from a first-person perspective—identified with this sex rather than with the "original" one. This serves to show how human identity formation is more complex than the simple linear or hierarchical picture suggested by the tree image.

If we are correct in the person-affecting approach to the creation of people, then the idea of "licensing children" is unacceptable, that is, the determination of a certain genetic standard below which children should not be produced. Licensing parents on the other hand has the limited sense of allowing people to rear children (which with genetic engineering might start long before birth) only if they can prove that they can minimally provide for the interests of their offspring, but only the *actual* interests (namely those that form the core of the person's evolving identity). Good (or morally acceptable) parents are not those who can raise a child to have any particular ideal character as an end-result, but rather those who respect the already actual "core" identity of the child in the process of further developing it into a fully grown human personality. This view tallies with the basically parentocentric thesis that has been offered here as the framework for deciding the existence and number of future people.

THE SUBTLE FORMATION OF IDENTITY: EDUCATION

Discussions of genesis problems have tended in general to concentrate mainly on the dimension of existence. Genesis as a problem of numbers has been only marginally addressed by population theory. Least of all has the genesis of identity attracted theoretical interest, and this has usually focused on the ethics of genetic engineering. But the most universal form of creating new people, at least in the sense of making them what they are, is education. The reasons why the genesis aspects of education have been overlooked have to do with the fact that unlike genetic engineering, education works on the relatively peripheral areas of the concentric structure of human identity; it is more reversible, it does not directly affect the fate of future generations, it is less risky (although not necessarily less dangerous), and above all it is more "natural," even inescapable. Thus, philosophers of education have discussed in great detail the problem of paternalism, the nature of the child's autonomy, the relation between state and parents in the education of children, the goals of education, the very justification of education, and its content. In our terminology, education has been conceived as a practice involving *actual* people: parents (with certain rights and duties), society (with certain interests and ideals), and children (with needs and rights of their own). However, the aim of this section is to explore the subject of education as a practice involving *partly potential* persons, that is, as a process of identity formation.

It is therefore education in the sense of the way in which identity-fixing traits are implanted in the child that exclusively interests us here (rather than teaching and learning, training and the acquisition of skills). Education in the genethically relevant sense concerns the upbringing of a child in the literally *formative* years of its biography. The concept of *Bildung* is one example of this sense; Aristotle's idea of moral education and the creation of a well-rounded "virtuous" personality is another. Casting the national or religious identity of young people is yet another typical case of education in the genethical sense. In this deep sense, education is usually practiced by parents, though society, through its powerful institutions (schools, churches, laws), also plays a role in the identity formation of its younger members (most dramatically exemplified by totalitarian regimes using methods of mass brainwashing). And unlike the genetic stages of identity formation, which proceed on a natural, spontaneous course, unless actively interfered with by human engineering, the social, cultural, and moral molding of human identity never "happens" by itself. It is always the product of human conditioning. Rearing children, as a partly intentional and contrived process, for which adults are forced to assume responsibility, can never be completely left to nature. The extent of control over the way children acquire their basic character is still very much greater than control over their genetic makeup. In that respect, despite similarities between the biological and the social genesis of human identity, there is still, for the time being, a difference in responsibility between nature and nurture.

But there is a more crucial difference between the genetic and the educational modes of identity formation. Education is directed at a human being at a stage in which the identity is beginning to be crystallized also *by that person*. Genetic engineering is constrained by genetically actual traits, which determine the subject's third-person (objective) identity. Education must take into account also actual volitions (attitudes, preferences, interests) which constitute the gradually evolving first-person (subjective) identity. It is as if genetic identity is forced on the child from the outside, whereas education works mostly from the inside, through the identity consciousness of the subject. The upbringing of a young baby rather resembles "external" genetic manipulation in a fetus. But the older a child grows, the more "internal" its education becomes, that is to say the more mediated by its conception of itself as an individual.[20]

This internal nature makes education a unique case among all other genesis issues. It is the only genesis process that is confronted by the principle of *autonomy*. We have seen in chapter 2 that respect for a person's autonomy in the Kantian sense cannot serve as a principle for creating (the existence of) people. The same applies to deciding their numbers as well as their genetic makeup. We are here concerned with autonomy only in the very limited sense of the individual's power, right, and value of deciding the type of person, character, or identity he wants to have for himself (rather than the freedom of choice within the biography of an individual with a "given" identity). In an adult, autonomy is most typically expressed by the power of the subject to reassess the nature of his "identity-tree," that is, to redraw from a first-person perspective the borderlines between character traits that are identity-fixing ("essential") and those that are not. In a younger person (e.g., an adolescent) autonomy is exercised by a kind of partnership relation between the subject and other parties having the power (and the right) to instill in him or her identity-fixing qualities. The ethics of education is concerned with the child's participation in the choice of new identity branches rather than in the retroactive restructuring of the whole existing identity tree by the fully autonomous adult.

Liberal thought in general and liberal theory of education in particular hail autonomy as the highest value and goal. From the specifically genethical standpoint autonomy is of unique importance, as it is the capacity of the individual to take part in the creation of what he or she is. So when parents bring up their children and shape their identity, they usually want them to have not only a particular set of traits but also the second-order trait of being able to choose their own identity. Parents wish their children to eventually become independent self-determinators, partly because they expect to die before their children. But the deeper motive for the cultivation of genethical autonomy in children is that it is the basis for the same genesis power that is exercised by the parents in both begetting and rearing children. And if *we,* as autonomous beings, want to have children so as to somehow extend ourselves, then we naturally want our children to have the capacity enabling *them* to do the same—first, regarding their own life; then, regarding procreation of further descendants. To put it succinctly, the wish that our children become autonomous is of the same structure and arises out of the same motive as wanting them to have the biological power to reproduce. These are two parallel expressions of the motive behind the creation of new people: the one on the level of existence; the other—on the level of identity. Unlike the creation of an artifact, procreation and education have as their goal a "product" that will be able to continue the creative process on its own. Raising a being without the capacity for self-formation is like genetically programming an offspring who has no reproductive capacity: both are logically coherent options, but highly implausible from the point of view of the parents' motivation for having children.

Note that we have so far referred only to the generocentric (parentocentric) justification of the value of autonomy in child rearing. Since the view of this book is that no impersonal value can be attached to the fact that autonomous beings exist in the world, autonomy must be a good either for the procreators or for the subjects themselves. If, for some strange reason, the autonomy of the developing child is not considered a value by the parents, then we must turn to examining its value for the child. But the person-affecting value of autonomy is particularly hard to decide. For on the one hand, autonomy is surely highly regarded by autonomous people (both for themselves and for their children); on the other hand we strongly believe that it is the interest of the yet-non-autonomous child to become autonomous, that is to say that there are certain in-built human properties that can flourish only under the conditions of autonomy. But what are these properties? Is it our biological nature that predetermines the value of autonomy, regardless of psychological profile or religious and moral upbringing? This is partly an empirical question relating to the biological or psychological basis of the "need" or interest in being autonomous, and partly a conceptual question concerning the nature of autonomy.

These are difficult questions, which cannot be decided here. All that can be said in this context is that a certain capacity to make rational choices, to exercise freedom of choice, to be able to reconsider the value even of the deeper ("identity-fixing") commitments and life plans is of value (for all we know) *for* any being with the biological and psychological makeup of humans. This core, which we cannot change (or do not want to change), imposes on us, as educators, a duty to cultivate autonomy. Obviously, this duty cannot be based on the idea of respect for autonomy, but only on the grounds of respecting *other* actual personal traits that "call" for autonomy. These might have to do with the as yet unknown structure of the brain, with the cognitive faculty of critical thinking, with the moral capacity to distinguish between right and wrong, with curiosity or with creativity. These imply that human beings have a genetically inherited tendency to autonomy, a natural need for it, or an in-built potential that must not be blocked. Another kind of actual property is the social and political circumstances in which children are going to find themselves in the future, and which might make autonomy a valuable equipment for them as adults, in their relations with other people. The ability to deal effectively with the natural and social environment is a value for any individual regardless of most other identity-fixing properties that the individual might have, and it creates the person-affecting parental duty of developing autonomy.

But of course we can think of a "creature" (we might not want to call it "human") who would not have that kind of core identity calling for the cultivation of autonomy: an efficient pleasure machine, a happy slave, a blind follower of a fanatic religious sect. And despite the claim of many philosophers for the universality of the value of autonomy, we must admit that it is in a way a culture-dependent value, and that in many cultures throughout human history autonomy has not been held in high esteem.[21] This means that the decision to create an autonomous being cannot always be justified in terms of the interests of the person created. But the question still remains open whether the "interest" in autonomy belongs to nature or nurture. The formation of a nonautonomous identity is permitted as long as this does not violate any other actual property of the developing being. At the stage of genetic engineering it is doubtful whether such actual properties limiting our right to create such a person already exist. By the time human beings reach the age of being educated, it is quite certain that they have acquired those actual properties that require autonomy or have even developed some form of actual autonomy.

It is today widely agreed, both by philosophers and education theorists, that autonomy is meaningful only against the background of a certain range of options. From a genethical point of view we can say that the absolute freedom of choice with no constraints of any kind makes no sense, because there is no one to make the choice! A chooser must have an individual identity, and the features constituting this identity drastically limit the range of options. So inculcating autonomy in a child must be accompanied by the gradual creation of a set of character traits, interests, tastes, beliefs, and values which would serve as a basis for the exercise of autonomous choice and self-determination. But there is no optimal set of traits and interests which best serves the development of the autonomous individual. People holding different conceptions of themselves and of the world can have an equal power of autonomy.[22]

Thus autonomy cannot be the criterion according to which values and beliefs should be cultivated in the child. These are decided either by *prior* features of identity, or—as is often the case—by the parents' system of values or by what society holds as worthwhile. In any case, leaving the formation of identity to take its "natural" course evades genethical responsibility without securing autonomy. A consistent educational strategy of noninterference, of cultivating "negative" freedom, of letting "the child" decide for itself, is morally wrong since it makes the process of identity formation completely random and uncontrolled. Molding the deep features of the child's personality and individuality is not only permitted, it is inescapable and necessary for the evolution of a genuine autonomous agent.

Education is, therefore, neither paternalistic in the negative sense of the word, that is, forcing upon someone an idea or a value that is contrary to his or her real volitions; nor is it paternalistic in the positive sense of forcing a people to do something that is really good *for them* (though for some reason they do not see it). Education, as the creation of identity, is not paternalistic at all, because by definition it is concerned with the shaping of those very interests and volitions that will later serve as the basis for claiming that a certain act was paternalistic in either the negative or the positive sense. If we look at the development of a human individual we can say that paternalism cannot be exercised in the very first stages of the process. In other words, the genesis of identity from scratch, or the molding of a *tabula rasa*, cannot be considered paternalistic; nor can it be exercised on a fully developed personality, because then it becomes plain compulsion. This implies that parents-educators combine the power of free creation of a character and the duty to respect and help realize the already given ("actual") aspects of the child's personality.[23] Paternalistic behavior in education can only refer to the interests of the child—either present or future (including those that we plan to instill in the child!), rather than to our generocentric projections in creating those interests, or to the interests of society in having citizens of a certain type.[24]

Approaching education as a genesis problem casts new light on the issue of justifying education. First we may state that education is not just a right and a duty, but also a *necessity*. And it is probably inevitable that we shape the particular character of our children to a more far-going extent than that recommended by a Rousseauesque theory (which regards the core identity of human beings as mostly "natural" and "inborn"). Being exposed to human environment and parental model is in itself a formative condition for the child, and in that respect a form of education. Secondly, the *duty* to educate is genethically justified in terms of the superiority of controlled identity formation over the unregulated process of random exposure to the environment. The duty to educate is also derived from the actual interests of the child, which require adult support for their satisfaction, as well as from society's demands that individuals be prepared for life in a particular social setting. Thus, parental duties refer either to the demands of other actual human beings or to the already actual character traits of the child. Finally the *right* to educate is genethically derived primarily from genesis freedom that cannot be constrained by potential persons or potential identity-fixing traits. Insofar as we have no duty toward the child to raise him or her as a particular kind of person, our genethical right is absolute. The only controversial problem involved in the right to educate is distributive: *who* should have the power to form the identity of young people? In other words, how should genesis power be distributed between parents and the various organs of society?

The problem here is that more than with the biological creation of human beings, which is motivated by personal forces, the determination of the identity of children is a matter in which it is difficult to separate individual (parental) and social stakes. Education is both a process of individual parental creation and a collective enterprise of creating a social world, social ways of life, the realization of communal ideals. And education is not just a combination of two separate motives— parental and social, because the parents' educational goals are themselves mediated and conditioned by social norms and values. In any event, the social nature of human life requires a coordination of the genesis process of identity formation, a guarantee of a minimal homogeneity in the nature of society. The genethical approach to education may help in drawing the line between the right of individual parents and that of society in child rearing. Parents may be said to have *genethical* rights to bring up children according to their liking, since they are their biological origin. That is to say, the right to procreate (genesis of existence) is complemented by the general right to educate (genesis of identity). Were there an impersonal ideal of a human personality (or identity), or a duty toward potential children, a much more central role could be assigned to society (or to professional experts) as the promoter of that ideal or the protector of the rights of potential children. But we have rejected those suggestions. And therefore the genesis power and interests of the parents should be respected, that is to say not subjected to state (paternalistic) control.[25] Yet there is also the *political* right to educate, which arises out of collective ideals and the coordinative function of social institutions. These justify the social control and regulation of some aspects of identity formation in children. Particularly it applies to basic moral traits and the preparation of individuals for life in a certain kind of society. The difference is that genethical rights of education concern behavior toward potential (evolving) people whereas the corresponding political rights concern behavior toward actual people (present or future, the educated subject or his fellow citizens).[26]

In an excellent discussion of the central role of education in democracy Amy Gutmann outlines the political constraints on how children are brought up in a democratic society and offers an illuminating taxon-

omy of the theories dealing with the distribution of the right to educate
between parents and the state (Gutmann 1987, chap. 1). She presents a
view that is close to our genethical approach: "If education is what gives
us our distinctive character, then we cannot determine the purposes of
education by invoking an *a priori* theory of human nature" (p. 22).
Gutmann is particularly concerned in this context with "the politically
significant features of human character," that is, the principles of education derived from the interests of *actual* society and its values. That is to
say, she focuses on the division of educational authority between parents and state rather than on the standing of the child. However
Gutmann's sensitivity to the genethical paradoxes of paternalistic enforcement of state values on citizens is manifest in her doubts regarding
the preservation of personal identity when allegedly objective values are
imposed by the state (p. 26). But Gutmann seems to base her opposition
to state control of education on a form of moral relativism ("our good is
relative to our education") rather than on the denial of impersonalism.
"Realizing *the* good life" cannot be the state's justification for paternalistic education, not because, as Gutmann says, we differ in our moral
convictions regarding the good life (p. 28), but because the good life is a
person-affecting notion.[27]

The liberal theory of education has traditionally claimed that education should be limited to the cultivation of the natural right and capacity
of the child to freedom. The basic notion underlying this conception has
been value-neutrality, namely the avoidance of any inculcation of parental "prejudices" in the child. Gutmann, like many other contemporary
critics of liberalism, both in political philosophy and the philosophy of
education, is suspicious of the viability of the ideal of neutrality (pp.
36–38). However, her critique is of a normative nature, grounded in her
denial of the singularity of freedom among the repertory of social
goods, whereas our opposition to the idea of neutrality is logical, that is,
grounded in the incoherence of the exercise of freedom with no prior
determination. This difference may be due to the fact that Gutmann is
more interested in the exercise of freedom of choice by an individual
already possessing personal identity in a social setting, whereas our
genethical concern is education as the formation of that very identity.
These are two different meanings (or rather stages) of education: the
creation of a subject capable of *any* kind of choice, and the cultivation
of the power in that subject to make meaningful and socially desirable
choices. It is only when she discusses the right of *society* to interfere in a
non-neutral manner in education that Gutmann explicitly adopts a gene-

sis perspective, claiming that this right is based on the commitment to "conscious social reproduction" (p. 39). This, at least implicitly, is a generocentric theory of education, although not expressly committed to a person-affecting axiology.

Education as a genesis process of identity formation can be illustrated through the simile of painting (playing on the ambiguity of "painting" both as the process or activity and as the product). When the painter approaches the empty canvas he is almost fully free in choosing between styles, themes, colors, and proportions. Still, he is constrained by the size of the canvas, the materials with which he is working, and also by certain norms and expectations of the prospective viewers of his art. Now, in the process of painting more and more choices are made and the painting becomes increasingly crystallized. Correspondingly, there are more and more constraints on the painter in the way he adds lines and colors to the painting. Stylistic and iconographic demands for consistency narrow the "potentiality" of the picture. In later stages of the creative process, only a radical retroactive reassessment of what the painting is all about can justify a sharp deviation from the original plan. Artistic creation is a self-binding process in which the creator gradually loses the original freedom of choice between purely potential alternatives. Every choice creates a layer of actual aesthetic reality that must be "respected."

Thus, when a child is born, it has only the biological and genetic qualities that are the raw material for the educational process. It also "has" prospects of living in a certain kind of society. This is its core identity, imposing on the parents the duties of feeding and providing shelter, as well as satisfying the child's other inborn psychological and physiological needs. But at this primary stage, the parents do not have an obligation to give the child any particular national identity, religious belief, native tongue, or aesthetic tastes and moral views. These are all part of the child's potential identity, and the parents are fully free to choose them *for* the child. However, once a certain national or religious identity has been implanted, the parents incur a duty to respect it (their own creation) and to satisfy the desires and interests of the newly created identity-fixing dimensions of the child's personality. Thus, for instance, having given a child a Christian identity, parents have to provide it with suitable Christian education; or having raised it as an Italian, they have to take its interests into account before deciding on immigration to a foreign country. From a generocentric and person-affecting view it is meaningless to say that a newly born child has a right to be brought up as a Jew or as a Christian. But converting ten-year-old children is rightly considered a violation of their autonomy.[28]

The fundamental problem in this account of education as a genesis process is that we have no theory of what belongs to the core identity. In other words we do not know how to draw the line between nature and nurture in identity-fixing properties. Biological needs are easy to locate on one side of that divide and religion or national identity on the other; but autonomy, curiosity, *arété*, or ambition are much more controversial. The doctrine of natural rights, for example, views freedom and possessiveness as belonging to the core. Others would say that they belong to social conditioning, that is, to education, and hence can be either inculcated or not, according to parentocentric motives and interests. The richer our concept of what "humans as humans" are, the less genethically free are we as educators. The more we believe in the biological determination of character traits, the more we have to treat educators as guardians rather than gardeners. The more we believe that the individual can revolt against and change the social structure, the less we are bound as educators by the predicted nature of the society in which our child is going to live in the future. But in any case, educators are not just custodians of a natural process of personality *growth*. Unlike plants (and animals) which are fully fixed in their identity by their natural-biological traits, which gradually become manifest and actualized, human beings also "grow" through nurture and self-determination.

The key to the problematic nature of drawing the concentric circles or layers of identity lies in that aspect that is *not* conveyed by the painting simile. A painting never gains life in the literal sense of the word. Themes, colors, shapes, and compositions never become independent determinators of aesthetic identity; they always remain vehicles in a creative process whose end-result is externally conceived by the artist. Education, as the formation of individual identity, is not merely a process that is guided by a conception of a certain desired *product*, but is also a form of interpersonal relationship, in which the originally "inert" and passive party gradually acquires a set of *internally* determined volitions and interests, or a self-determined conception of identity. This first-person concept of identity is naturally associated with a person-affecting view of value; for if the good we do by our educational effort is nonimpersonally ascribed to actual people (primarily those whom we educate), then the way they define themselves is obviously relevant to the way we judge the success of this effort. We are therefore concerned with a volitional concept of identity, that is, the way individuals regard the boundaries of their own identity, rather than with the metaphysical or legal concepts, which are decided independently of what persons conceive in themselves as essential to what they are.

Although there are no universal criteria for first-person identity, there are certain indications or tests for the application of this concept. Take first *envy*. We might distinguish between two kinds of envy: person-envy and property-envy. In the former, we envy someone else in the sense that we want to *be that person*. In the latter, we envy a property of his or her personality, a quality of his or her life, a circumstance of his or her biography; we want to *have it*. The first is an irrational attitude, since being somebody else cannot be good for us. The pathology of this destructive form of envy consists in the wish to be someone else while miraculously maintaining at the same time some form of the original identity of the self. Drawing the person-affecting analogy between existence and identity we may say that such envy is suicidal! The second form of envy is more natural and psychologically less destructive. It consists of a coherent fantasy of being myself with some better properties and conditions of life. Thus, I can envy Einstein for his intelligence, reputation, success, moral integrity; but I cannot want to be Einstein. The concentric view of identity also accounts for the gradational aspect of envy: the closer a property is to the core the less can it be an object of envy. This may explain why we usually envy people who are close to us in some important way: we can more easily imagine ourselves in their place. We rarely envy Napoleon or Socrates; we often envy a relative or a colleague, a friend or a neighbor. We do not envy a dead person, nor an unborn one. Our fantasies of being another, of escaping our disliked selves, must always have at least a narrow basis of continuity of identity.

Or take *regret*. We can look back at our past choices and regret having taken one course rather than another. But we cannot look back at the history of our identity formation and regret its course. It is conceptually misleading to talk of different potential identities as a smorgasbord out of which an optimal selection could be made. For identities can be good only for actual people, namely people with a particular identity. We therefore cannot regret having been born in the twentieth century, because that is one of our identity-fixing properties. Nor can we regret having been born either male or female, or in general with the overall combination of traits that constitute our unique character, what we conceive as essentially *us*. But again, these attitudes have a gradational aspect: relatively to a hard core of identity-fixing properties, we might regret not having been born in the other sex, or in another culture. We can regroup the identity-fixing properties in various ways so as to form new "cores" on the basis of which a wish to have a particular identity-fixing trait changed can be imagined.[29]

Another indicator for first-person identity is our attitude toward our parents for what they did to us, namely *complaint* or *gratitude* (or both). We have already mentioned the incoherence of "wrongful identity" claims. But as identity is a gradational concept, the lack of ground for such claims is not as clear as in the parallel wrongful life cases. There is a sense in which a complaint for having been born Ethiopian has no meaning, since this is an identity-fixing property. However, being more peripheral in the concentric hierarchy of identity-fixing properties, being Ethiopian can be evaluated on the basis of properties of the even more inward core, for instance, the interest in having basic nutritional needs satisfied. This makes a possible complaint coherent, as long as the more peripheral property is not necessarily linked to the inner one (e.g., the parents could have immigrated, thus giving an alternative national identity to the child which would have been better in terms of its inner core identity). In more general terms, we can never be appreciative or resentful toward our parents for the kind of identity tree they constructed, but only for the consistency or inconsistency of the hierarchical relations between the core and the concentric periphery of our identity. Identity trees are not developed *for us;* we are rather created *as* identity trees.

Finally, there is the desire to *go on living,* to survive. There is little solace in being told that after our death our intelligence will survive as part of God's Intelligence, since even if we view our rationality as an important element in our identity, our individuality is lost in such a metaphysical prospect. When considering the universal will to survive, we should therefore note that people desire to go on living only under a certain description, under minimal identity conditions. Our categorical desires accordingly play a major role in the first-person conceptions of our identities, and their continuity and satisfaction are conditions for our desire to go on living.[30]

The individual's power to take part in the genesis of his or her own identity lends first-person decisions regarding one's life a genethical dimension similar to that of genetic engineering and education. Indeed, by the time humans acquire the power of self-determination most identity-fixing properties are already deeply entrenched in their personality. Still, human beings have the power to tamper even with these traits, and they sometimes exercise this power. An adult's decision to undergo sex-change by surgery is a dramatic and rare example. Religious conversion is a less dramatic change in identity, but also much more common. Immigration, especially a move that involves a complete change in values and lifestyle, is also a pertinent case. The intriguing effect of freely chosen "leaps" in identity arises out of the unexplained motive for such changes. For being a total conversion, there might be too little in the "old" identity to explain the wish to adopt the "new" one. Conversions break the layer-by-layer rationality of identity formation. Unlike the hierarchical, Neurath-ship-like logic of both education and self-determination, *en bloc* identity changes and abrupt conversions appear to be inexplicable. It is only natural that both subjects and spectators of such changes may try hard to account for them in terms of a hidden trait in the former identity, an invisible true self that is discovered and given its dues by the act of conversion.

The process of both education and self-determination combines manipulation of the environment together with formation of the set of preferences. In that respect there is an *adaptive* aspect to any kind of character formation. When objective environmental circumstances cannot be changed so as to better the life of human beings, there is always the option of changing subjective wants and desires so as to secure a better degree of satisfaction. But as Jon Elster has noted in his pioneering work on adaptive preferences, there is no *a priori* way to fix the proportion between the two strategies of satisfaction promotion.[31] Impersonalists can fix that proportion in terms of overall satisfaction, but for a person-affecting view this strategy is blocked by the identity changes involved in radical and constant adaptations. Impersonalism leads to the paradoxical goal of bringing up a chameleon-person who would be so adaptable in adjusting the values and preferences to reality that adaptability would become his only identity-fixing feature! However, we resist certain adaptations (in our preferences or those of our children) on the basis of their being either negatively identity-fixing or undesirable in the light of *other* identity-fixing features. Although the bounds of first-person identity cannot be clearly defined, the idea and value of *integrity* consists exactly in the existence of certain limits to adaptive changes.[32]

The genethical problems of identity apply not only to individuals but also to collectives. Society, unlike individuals, cannot be educated by other parties (colonial paternalistic rule is an interesting exception), but it can shape its own identity. Societies, and indeed the human race as a whole, can change identity or nature—either by genetic means or by social engineering. Social progress is analogous to the perfection of character; revolutions to conversions. But like the identity formation of individuals, social evolution (or even revolution) is constrained by criteria of minimal continuity of identity. First-person identity of social groups explains the scant interest we have in creating a "higher race" of *super*-human beings. We want our descendants to be eugenically, morally, and intellectually better than ourselves; but this interest is subordinated to the deeper interest we have in their being sufficiently like us. Otherwise what motive can we have for wishing them good?

PART THREE

Genethics and
the Limits of Ethics

CHAPTER 7

Empirical Constraints

The population problem has no technical solution.
> Garrett Hardin, "The Tragedy of the Commons"

MITIGATING THE COUNTERINTUITIVE
NATURE OF GENETHICS

The general underlying argument of this book has been that "genesis problems" cannot be dealt with on the same principles as other moral issues. In part 1 we tried to support this argument by exposing the paradoxes involved in the application of traditional moral principles to these problems. Granting a child legal standing in "wrongful life" cases, or laying down a duty to procreate in order to enhance overall happiness in the world are only two examples of the pitfalls awaiting those who ignore the distinction between ethics and genethics. In part 2 we undertook the more positive task of supporting the argument by suggesting the generocentric framework for the solution of genesis questions. This framework, even if proven theoretically cogent, was however shown to run the risk of yielding some puzzling, even embarrassing, results. For example, it cannot in principle rule out the willful conception of a defective child, or an irresponsibly expanding population policy leading to an "overcrowded," Z-like world; nor can it prohibit the engineering of "happy pigs" as substitutes for human beings, or indeed the total extinction of the human race by a voluntary act of collective suicide.

In the first section of chapter 3 we suggested that a possible resolution of these conflicts of intuitions regarding "futurity problems" could be found either in a revision of ethical theory which would make it applicable to these problems, or in the redefinition of the borderlines of

193

ethics in a way that would leave these problems outside the moral sphere altogether. In slightly different terms, the issue was, in what way is genethics part of ethics and in what way does it lie beyond it. The generocentric approach outlined in part 2 showed precisely how decisions regarding the existence, number, and identity of future people should either be accounted for in moral terms (the interests, welfare, and rights of actual people) or be considered as having no moral dimension (potential people as well as "impersonal values" having no moral status). In other words, to the extent that genesis choices affect actual beings, they should be judged by conventional moral principles; but inasmuch as they have no such effect, they should be recognized as lying beyond the grip of moral judgment. Thus the meaningfulness and coherence of the morality of procreation is saved by limiting the scope of ethical theory.

In this final part of the book we are concerned with two senses in which genethics points at the limits of ethics. On the one hand there are deep *empirical* conditions that serve as a natural constraining background for any ethical theory. They are "deep" in the sense that we can hardly conceive of a world in which they do not obtain, and trying to apply moral concepts in such a world would amount to a deviation from the common sense of these concepts in a way no less radical than ascribing rights to rivers or duties to animals. On the other hand, genethics is a unique domain through which the limits of ethics can be examined from a *metaphysical* perspective; for genethics deals with the very creation of the conditions of ethics, namely human beings. The motives for such a creation are, in this metaphysical sense, not merely empirical (biological or psychological), but also "projective" in nature, expressing the uniquely human attempt at self-transcendence, at establishing the meaning of life in terms of the creation of further life. The present chapter discusses the empirical considerations that make generocentrism look less threatening. The next chapter undertakes the metaphysical investigation into the ultimate nature of genethics and the methodological implications regarding the limits of ethics. The spirit of the discussion of genesis issues in part 2 was that of ethical skepticism. However, this skepticism will be shown in part 3 to be only of partial force: first because empirical considerations will show that most of our cherished intuitions can be "saved," and secondly because this skepticism is well contained by being relegated exclusively to the genethical realm (with no implications for other "standard" ethical issues relating to actual human beings).

As we have noted in chapter 3, the principled discussion of genethical issues cannot be dismissed as being "remote from reality" or overly abstract, since in its very nature it consists of choices regarding the possible molding of radically novel states of affairs. In that respect, intuitions are less of a help in genesis problems than in standard ethical issues. However, the ultimate choice between a person-affecting view (implying generocentrism) and impersonalism (granting moral standing also to potential beings) depends partly on the overall intuitive appeal of the respective views in their accounting for hard cases. In that sense Parfit is justified in confronting the two competing views with their respective repugnant conclusions (such as the Z-world for the impersonalist and the deliberate conception of a defective child for the person-affecting view). Nevertheless, although we insist on the generocentric theory as the only consistent solution to the wide variety of genesis problems, even if at times it conflicts with our immediate moral responses, it is important to note that deep empirical facts can remove the sting of repugnance from many of the hypothetical counterintuitive conclusions of generocentrism. These facts cannot indeed serve as an independent philosophical corroboration of generocentrism, but they may help in defusing the force of some of its unwelcome implications.

Recall that the most direct insight into the unique nature of genesis problems was gained through the idealization of genesis choices in *pure* contexts, that is, where the decision regarding the creation of human beings, their number, and identity is taken in a world in which there are no actual beings. But the purity of the context of choice should not be taken as implying its arbitrariness. When God creates Man, he is acting on reasons. These have to do with his own "volitions" (such as expanding his image in the world). In pure contexts these volitions, being "person-affecting," must be exclusively self-regarding. In part, they may be "empirical" in the sense of relating to the creator's nature and given motives. But being also free to choose one's own nature and values, the creator is not fully bound by his empirical nature. This is particularly true of God, who is traditionally viewed as free from any empirical constraints in his deeds. But it is also partly true of human beings, who can transcend aspects of their own empirical character and even deliberately choose parts of it. This is the metaphysical dimension of human action which is typically manifest in genesis choices, as will be shown in the next chapter.

In *impure* contexts, however, there are many more constraints on genesis choices. The very existence of actual people other than the chooser introduces two kinds of constraints: moral and empirical. In the last section of chapter 5 we examined the ethical complexity of distributive and coordinative considerations in population policies. Here we are concerned with the empirical way in which the fact that other people exist (or will exist) affects the formation of our genethical preferences. Ethical considerations make it unjust to existing people to add a new person to an overcrowded community. Empirical considerations make it less desirable for the prospective parent to bring a child into such a populous environment.

Empirical constraints in impure genesis contexts may be either *human* or *environmental*. The human conditions in which reproductive choices are made are either biological or psychological (see next section). The environmental conditions relate to the way in which the existence and welfare of human beings is dependent on environmental factors over which we do not have control (see last section of this chapter). This distinction is significant in a person-affecting theory, for it will be argued that the manipulation of those very empirical conditions is morally constrained only in the case of the human conditions. That is to say, we are morally restrained in manipulating the biological and psychological desires of actual adults in having children so as to achieve a certain genethical outcome; but we are morally free to change the natural environmental conditions so as to free genesis choices from their restriction.

Empirical conditions can limit procreative choices either by affecting our *power* to achieve desired genesis goals or by influencing the *will* to achieve those goals. More important for our purposes, their influence can apply either "horizontally," on the *intra*generational axis, or "vertically," on the *inter*generational axis. The best way to characterize the empirical constraints on these two levels is by contrasting choices made under these constraints to *ideal* choices, which are empirically unconstrained in the relevant manner. Thus, on the horizontal level, a completely solitary creator (God, a demiurgus, a Robinson Crusoe having the tools for producing a clone of himself) is exempt from having to take into account the rights and interests of his contemporaries; this does not necessarily mean that he can ignore the rights and interests of future generations (since they might be "actual"). On the vertical axis, however, imagine again human beings with all their present traits, with just one difference: immediately after procreating they die. Generations succeed each other with no overlap—both in the individual and the collective spheres. In these circumstances it seems that the life of future people would count less; this again does not mean that the interests and rights of the chooser's contemporaries do not make a moral difference (e.g., if such beelike procreation has a social cost). We may say that the Godlike and the beelike abstractions serve to purify the genesis situation from those empirical facts that obfuscate analytical argument. But as we shall see in the following sections, they can also be used as reference points in relation to which the deviation of real-life genesis circumstances accounts for many of our deeply held intuitive beliefs regarding procreation, demographic policies, and the identity formation of human beings.

GENERATIONAL OVERLAP AND THE DESIRE TO HAVE CHILDREN

The most general empirical constraint on genethical choices in impure contexts is the existence of other *actual* beings. The obvious and trivial nature of this statement attests to the universality of the impact this fact has on the way we deal with genesis issues. If we stick to the person-affecting view of value, the coming to life of humans can have value only if there is an actual being (creator) behind it for whom it is of value. Thus, the creation of humanity could be given axiological meaning if God saw it as "very good," but it is value-neutral if human beings were as a matter of fact created by a nonvolitional process like evolution, or if they just popped out into the world somehow. But, of course, the less controversial fact is that in impure contexts of human procreation there are actual beings (other than an alleged creator) whose interests and rights must be taken into account.

First, on the intragenerational level, it is a biological fact that human procreation takes two individuals. Consequently, procreative and educational decisions usually involve more than one parent. Secondly, it is a social fact of human existence that people live in societies or communities and that their very capacity to beget and raise children requires the support of a social (and economic) system. Even if the motive to have children is basically biological in nature, their number and more so their identity are decided in the light of social conditions and values. Other actual people not only play a role in our reproductive behavior but have a moral claim on us. If the society is too small to be self-sufficient in the long run, there is a *prima facie* obligation to procreate; if it is too large to survive with a certain agreed upon lifestyle, restricting the size of the family may become a moral duty. Procreation and identity formation are at least partly a social enterprise: we beget and rear children primarily in families, but also in communities. These collective frameworks both give meaning to the reproduction of human life and impose certain moral duties on individuals. And it is a psychological fact that we do not *want* to avoid the coordinative and distributive problems involved in procreation, because our motivation to have children and to raise them in a certain manner is so intimately connected to our life with other (actual) people—spouses, existing siblings, the members of our social, religious, or national community.

Secondly, and even more important, the existence of other actual people on the intergenerational axis is also a deep empirical fact, playing a major role in reproductive decisions. Despite the revolution in methods of birth control, we may safely assume that most people who will live in the next generation or two are *actual,* that is to say the product of natural processes not subjected to human control. The numbers of people predicted by demographers to live in some populous third-world countries impose a most serious moral and political constraint on any rational and responsible economic and demographic policies in richer societies that have more control over reproductive trends. But beyond this fact of the uncontrolled or unplanned birth of people, most future people are actual *for us* in the sense that we believe in the privacy of reproductive decision making, that is, in the far-reaching (though not absolute) freedom of individuals to reproduce with no state interference. Ethical values make the existence of most future people a fact lying beyond the reach of political bargaining of a coordinative or distributive kind.

This "vertical" constraint applies also to decisions regarding identity, although in a slightly less obvious way. The fact that there will be people in the future and that we have only marginal control over their lifestyle and values implies that certain of our own children's fundamental interests must be taken by us as actual. We are not free to mold the basic character and value-system of our children independently of the character of other future people and the future society in which they will have to live. Every parent is aware of this constraint, which at times might be painful because of conflict with the parent's own educational wishes. For example, rearing a completely nonambitious child in a society known to be highly competitive might be bad *for* the child. This does not mean that parents do not use education as one form of their own struggle for long-term social change: it only makes the "cost" to the child a relevant moral consideration. In terms of the concentric theory of identity formation outlined in chapter 6, the predicted or probable nature of the society in which people are going to live constitutes an aspect of their *core* identity, like certain congenital biological traits; that is to say, having no control over the social setting in which our children are going to live, we must subordinate our educational efforts in the formation of the more peripheral circles of their identity to these hard-core social facts.

But the most significant empirical fact on the intergenerational level is the biological *overlap* of generations. This means that future people are not only mostly actual, but that some of them are our contemporaries. The simple fact that we live together with our creation is perhaps the most formative factor both in our decision to have children and in the way we choose to rear them. This fact is not really a constraint in the sense of a limitation of our genethical freedom, since it serves as the positive motive and rationale for having children. Generational overlap is probably the main underlying fact of generocentrism or parentocentrism. It highlights the dominance of the self-regarding motives behind most genesis choices. Similarly, the failure of impersonalist intuitions can best be captured by testing them in the imaginary case of *non*-overlap. Could the impersonal reasons for preserving the human species, for promoting a particular ideal, for completing an unfinished project be strong enough to move us to beget children if we had not the opportunity of living *with* them? (Assume also that beelike "parenting" involves some cost—in money, career, or health. Would anyone want to pay it in order to have such "postmortem descendants"?)

Again, this point applies to both the existence, the number, and the identity of our children. It is a universal cultural fact that human beings desire to have children and that they raise them more or less "in their own image." Empirical research enumerates a wide variety of motives for having children: economic need (children as work force), security (for old age), status, power, psychological stimulation, expression of primary group ties (love), companionship, self-realization, the preservation of lineage, the continuation, multiplication, or expansion of the self, a religious or moral duty (to God or society), even simple fun (see Hoffman and Hoffman 1973). This long list indirectly supports a generocentric view of procreation, as the list conspicuously does not consist of "altruistic" motives that is, those concerned with the good of the future child. The decision to have children is one of the most selfish of human choices, and parentocentric motives guide not only the positive choices (to create another happy child), but also the negative (refraining from begetting a handicapped child). For as a matter of psychological fact, we rarely face a case in which the parents wish to have a (handicapped) child but decide to assign an overriding weight to the "interests of the child" not to be born. It is the parents who do not want a suffering child. Generally, most of the motives reported by the subjects of such research implicitly assume generational overlap. We want to have children for our own satisfaction; we want them, therefore, to be of a particular nature (identity), that is, sufficiently similar to us; and we want them to be of a certain number, such that we can maintain that kind of quality of life (for us and for them) which would secure that satisfaction.[1]

Our attitudes to genesis choices are formed in the light of what *we* stand to gain or to lose. We take pains to conserve for the next generation mainly because we want to converse with it.[2] We want not only to multiply but also to see ourselves multiplied. We want to help form the identity of new beings, but only through a process in which these beings become a kind of partner. We derive satisfaction from the rearing process no less than from the end-result. In a deep sense, the welfare of our children serves as a major factor in the assessment of our own welfare. This applies also to the collective level of genethical choices. Societies thrive only if they are proportionately stratified as regards age. A "generation" is not a group of procreators of the same age, but rather a community of people of various ages sharing together a historical period, a life. As a matter of empirical fact, it is also economically true that because of generational overlap our children can save for us no less than we for them.

These considerations belabor the obvious and are worth mentioning only as a reminder that Parfit-like examples of the intentional conception of defective children, despite their theoretical interest, are of limited force. The biological and psychological conditions in which human procreation takes place cannot indeed decide the philosophical problems of the status of potential people, but they can at least defuse the relevance of some imaginary implications of theoretical principles. Generational overlap makes many of these hypothetical acts of "harming" future people *irrational* and counterproductive. We are going to be worse off having to raise a handicapped child, or living in an overpopulated world, or aging in a society in which the younger generation is not well equipped for taking over economic and political responsibility. For people in a third-world society, the fact that the population of their country is going to double in just twenty-one years is of major concern, not because of abstract impersonal reasons but because they themselves will suffer from the outcome of such a trend.

The possibility of the complete extinction of the human race is therefore horrifying not so much because of metaphysical (impersonal) reasons, but rather because of the extreme pain and suffering it involves for the last generation. The universal desire to procreate and the fear of being left to die in an empty world make it unimaginable that human beings, as we know them, would ever agree on collective suicide or on total abstinence.

The general philosophical point of generational overlap may be conveyed in the metaphor of a relay race, in which runners partly overlap on the course in order to hand on a torch. Unlike the race, in which the goal is to pass the torch, and the "overlap" just a means of doing so effectively, human procreation is primarily motivated by the satisfaction to be obtained from the interaction taking place in that overlapping segment. Furthermore, as an "inversion" of the means–end relation in the athletic case, one may sometimes suspect that the very idea of a torch to be handed on by procreation is one of the ways of making the overlapping segment meaningful. One might even think that the duty to serve a transgenerational ideal or value is itself an "impersonal" *illusion,* which happens to be very effective on the generocentric level. The alleged moral wrongness of bringing a defective child into the world or of overpopulating it or of leaving it completely empty of humans plays an important social and political role in preserving the individual and collective interests of actual people—both present and future. Impersonalism, in this view, turns out to be a practically constructive fallacy.

The succession of generational partial overlaps introduces a relation of *transitivity* into the attitude of presently existing beings to their future descendants. For as we know that our children will be biologically and psychologically quite similar to ourselves, we must assume that they will have (and indeed we want to instill in them) a desire to beget children. In simple terms, one of the chief satisfactions of parents is to see their own children beget children. This empirical fact entails the extension of the notion of *intra*generational considerations to three (maybe four) biological generations (which roughly cover the average lifespan of human beings). If our welfare includes the prosperity of our offspring, and if their welfare also is partly constituted by the prosperity of their descendants, then generocentric considerations extend beyond our immediate successors. However, this transitivity argument has limited psychological force. Few people can claim that they are personally interested in the lot of the children of their great-grandchildren. The force of parental sympathy gradually fades out with time. One may claim that this makes no difference, since the successful relay of the torch requires only the succession of particular overlaps (rather than *one*, the first, runner maintaining the overlap relation with *all* the following runners). But that will not always do. For example it would not be sufficient to preclude a policy that would benefit the next two generations but perhaps endanger the more distant ones (Barry 1977, 279; Routley and Routley 1978, 145).

This is only one reason why the empirical fact of sympathy with the next two or three generations cannot serve as a *philosophical* basis for the ethics of procreation and population policy, even within a Humean theory. The Rawlsian form of deriving genethical principles from such a "motivational assumption" has also often been criticized (see chapter 2). But having said all that, the deep interest in our descendants' welfare that derives from the fact of generational overlap and with the partial extension through transitivity should be seen as a powerful *empirical* constraint on genethical principles, at least in certain cases. Take, for example, saving. Neither on the individual nor on the collective level are we really concerned with the lot of distant future descendants. We save for our children and grandchildren. In this case transitivity guarantees that even in the long run the natural parental wish to see one's children at least as well off as oneself could support a principle of just savings. These considerations serve to mitigate the repugnant implications of abstract generocentrism and the egoistic moral permissiveness derived from philosophical skepticism regarding a unified theory of savings and procreation (as argued for in chapter 5). Indeed, one might view limited sympathy (to the next two or three generations) as exhausting the issue, that is to say, there is no "problem" of justice or intergenerational savings rate beyond what people are actually motivated (by sentiment) to save. According to this view, the psychology of parental concern for their descendants *is* the philosophical basis for the ethics of procreation.

We may say in general terms that the constraints of deep psychological motives, the lack of crucial knowledge regarding the nature of people in the future, and the limited capability to change the course of genesis processes even when motivations change and epistemological barriers are broken—all put the potential "horrors" of generocentrism in a less dramatic perspective. This is a methodologically significant advantage of generocentrism, since the alternative impersonalist approach leads to many consequences that cannot be similarly mitigated (such as the duty to procreate happy children or the prohibition of the conception of a child slightly worse off than the average existing person). Ignoring those deep empirical truths leaves us with no intuitive basis to assess genethical issues. Just imagine parents having full knowledge of the nature and needs and values of all their distant descendants. Such a state of affairs would change the whole psychology of procreation in ways that we cannot predict.[3]

ENVIRONMENTAL CONDITIONS: DEEP AND SHALLOW ECOLOGY

The previous section dealt with empirical *human* constraints on genethical freedom. These constraints were derived from deep-lying facts about the biological and psychological makeup of human beings which lie beyond our control. But no less restrictive of our genethical freedom are the *natural* contingencies of our nonhuman environment, over which we also have only limited control and power. The limit of our genesis powers arises in both cases from the dependence of our existence and prosperity on external factors with which we interact. Thus, as we are dependent on other actual people in pursuing our lives as procreators, so are we dependent on natural resources for the success of our genesis goals. We might say that a certain equilibrium between human beings and their natural environment is empirically necessary no less than social cooperation with other individuals.

Again, if we want to gain an insight into the force of environmental constraints on genethical behavior we may contrast the human situation with that of an omnipotent creator operating in a complete void, that is, with the control and liberty to create both human beings *and* their natural environment. Since there are two variables in such a pure genesis context, there is no one (optimal) solution to this creation dilemma. For example, God could have created us with no need for oxygen, freeing us from the health hazards of a polluted atmosphere; alternatively he could have created the world with a virtually infinite amount of oxygen (like sun rays) which would have made carbon dioxide harmless. But human procreators are much more constrained in their reproduction, as they have no such powerful control over nature. The range of possible equilibria between human beings and the natural environment is very narrow, even for modern humanity in its modern technological phase.

Nevertheless, scientific and technological progress, especially associated with industrialization and intensive agriculture, have given us more elbow room in the way we manage the equilibrium between humans and nature (demography and ecology) than at any earlier period. In other words, some aspects of the formula for fixing the ratio between quantity of life (the number of future people) and quality of life (available natural resources, ecological conditions) stand to be chosen by us. We may take a certain level of environmental quality as fixed, or as a minimal limit (floor), and decide the number of future people according to the carrying capacity of the environment at this standard. Or, alternatively, we may take a certain number of people as fixed (or as a maximum), and use nature so as to sustain that number of human lives. The philosophical issue is what type of constraints apply to this manipulation of the two variables: are they *a priori* or "just" empirical?

This very issue has divided environmental philosophy on the theoretical level and has concrete practical repercussions for the environmental movement in its political struggle. The two opposite approaches to the issue have been described by Arne Naess as "deep ecology" and "shallow ecology" (Naess 1973, 95–100). The deep approach offers a total model, in which man and nature are related in a way that would make man lose his identity outside that relationship. It is based on respect and veneration for nonhuman forms of life and treats the richness and variety of biological species as intrinsic values. Humanity is considered to be part of nature rather than its ruler, and much of its prosperity and satisfaction is derived from the partnership with and dependence on natural forces. Shallow ecology, on the other hand, fights pollution and resource depletion for the sake of the health and affluence of people in the developed countries. It is more geared to the efficient use of the environment than to working for the environment. Naess does not conceal his hostility to the "shallow" approach, referring to it as management ethics rather than environmental ethics, and thus highlighting its selfish, socially unjust, and exploitative nature. Shallow ecological policies are unjust both because they ignore the plight of underdeveloped countries and because they are short-term (i.e., disregard the rights and interests of future people).

Naess's distinction has been very influential among the more radical environmentalists. But it can also serve as a starting point for our discussion of the constraints on genethical choices (with which Naess is not specifically concerned) because it lies at the heart of the debate between impersonalism and person-affecting views. Unlike the logically tricky question of whether the very existence of human beings is good within a person-affecting axiology, which was the subject of chapter 4, the question of the value of nature is clear: does it derive its value from the way in which volitional beings are affected by it, or does it have value independent of the existence of the effect on such beings? Deep ecology seems to treat nature as we argued genethics must treat future actual people, that is, as claimants for full moral consideration. In that respect, the relationship between human beings and their natural environment and other species should be governed by principles analogous to the principles of distributive justice for all (actual) human beings. Shallow ecology, on the other hand, treats environmental constraints on demographic policies as empirical, that is, like the constraints imposed on our reproductive behavior by the predicted desires and interests of our actual descendants.

A more sophisticated mapping, following Naess's distinction, is offered by Routley. Shallower views, which anthropocentrically take humans as the sole subjects of value, are divided into the unrestrained and the shallow. The former holds that humans may do whatever they like to the planet, permitting the brutal exploitation of nature. The latter is sensitive to the potential damage of such unrestrained exploits to future people, using the theory of externalities of modern economics. Deeper views, which assign intrinsic value also to nonhuman beings, are divided in their turn into the intermediate and the deep. The former gives priority to human interests over those of nonhumans such as animals, although it grants them some moral standing (e.g., Peter Singer's views). The latter holds that nonhumans should have equal moral standing with humans, and hence that there are cases in which environmental considerations reign supreme. This is Routley's own view of biospecies impartiality (Routley 1984, 326–327).[4]

My view lies somewhere between the "shallow" and the "intermediate" views on this map. It is shallow in the sense that the natural environment does not count as a moral partner, imposing ethical constraints on our behavior. But it is not shallow in the unrestrained or the selfish version of Naess's portrayal, for it takes very seriously the rights of future actual people (even those in the distant future) let alone the rights of contemporaries living in the geographically distant underdeveloped world. It is person-affecting in the enlightened sense of counting the long-term as well as the indirect effects of certain uses and abuses of natural resources. For such an "enlightened shallow" approach it is not only the economic or practical effects that count, but also the aesthetic or scientific, that is, any effect that would be of relevance to the wide interest of human beings in the environment. Beauty of landscape and variety of species are of equal concern to person-affecting approaches to ecological issues as the maintenance of energy sources for future generations or securing the conditions for their healthy survival. This is a wide conception of "externalities" in the ecological calculus, which regards nature as valuable in the same way as works of arts or scientific truth are valuable—intrinsically good, but always person-affecting, for example, as ideals for human beings. "Shallow" in this sense does not mean instrumental, let alone exploitative. However, the view proposed in this book is not committed to pure anthropocentrism and hence is willing in principle to allow the rights of animals to play a secondary role in that calculus. To the extent that the suffering of animals creates a moral constraint on our behavior, this suffering can be held as bad *for* the animals, that is, bad in the "person-affecting" sense. In that respect my view goes beyond the "shallow" according to both Naess and Routley.

The gap between the deep and the shallow is wide, and I can think of no direct arguments that could decide the issue in a way convincing to the opposite party. Proponents of the deep approach, since the "Land Ethics" of Aldo Leopold, have sincerely believed that nonhumans have a moral standing and an impersonal value. Thus, views have been suggested that animals have rights, that every kind of life is sacred, that trees have moral standing, that it is morally forbidden to obstruct the natural course of rivers, even that the whole planet should be viewed as an organism having a life of its own, and hence an ultimate value.[5] Most environmentalists believe that the fact that nature is now believed to have a moral status, and that man must be seen as just a part of the biocommunity or biosphere, calls for the establishment of a new ethics, transcending the traditional, anthropocentric one.[6] But it has not yet been shown what the principles of this new ethics would look like, especially in genethical matters, where there is a conflict between the good of human beings and the "interests" of the ecosystem.

One way of course is to say that human interests cannot be fully separated from ecological conditions (the "interests" of the ecosystem). But that is perfectly compatible with the shallow conception, indeed the very point of its enlightened, long-range version. As human beings (the moral subjects) are part of the biological and physical world, their welfare is "mediated" by environmental conditions and ecological balance. Contrary to the deep environmentalists' standard accusation that the shallow approach is *selfish,* the enlightened version (unlike the "unrestrained" one) calls for the preservation of nature both as an obliga

tion to future (actual) generations and as an intrinsic value (being beautiful, inspiring, scientifically interesting, and so forth). The constraints on
population growth imposed by the cost to nature's integrity are deep,
but nevertheless "empirical" rather than ethical. They operate by showing us the level of pollution, depletion, hunting, deforestation at which
our use of nature for our person-affecting purposes becomes counterproductive, self-defeating, or irrational.[7]

The reasoning behind the plea for saving the environment is of course
radically different in the shallow and the deep views.[8] But the practical
consequences of the two are much less divergent. The depth of our
dependence on and interest in nature's purity, richness, variety, and
resources makes it in many cases irrational to ignore it in our genesis
(population) policies. In that respect, the empirical facts of ecological
wisdom dictate many of the deep ecologists' recommendations. And in
those cases where the views diverge also on the practical level, I believe
that the generocentric view presented here does not sound too counterintuitive. When empirical conditions become controllable by science
and technology, most of us are less horrified at the prospect of environmental changes. Notice too that human values and preferences gradually change with regard to the desirable conditions of the environment.
We are willing today to accept many of the environmental changes
brought about by motor transportation because we have become used
to a less pristine environment.

The theoretical revolution called for by some environmental philosophers seems, therefore, to be superfluous. There is no need for a "revolutionary ethics" or a change in the whole conceptual framework. It is
true that there are special risks involved in many modern technological
interventions in the natural surroundings, especially those connected
with unpredictability and irreversibility. But these only demand extra
care—not a transformation of nature into a moral subject. Generocentrism is not necessarily committed to the idea of human *dominion* over
nature in the exploitative version often associated with the Judeo-
Christian tradition and Genesis I. It does not necessarily hold that nature was created with the sole purpose of satisfying human needs. It can
consistently declare that we are *stewards* of the natural world (in the
sense of God's commandment to Adam and Eve to keep the Garden of
Eden), but only on the assumption that more human beings in the future
will be living in this nature and relating to it.[9] Generocentrism only
means that it is man who invests nature with some sort of value, instrumental or intrinsic, and in that sense "dominates" nature. It also means

that stewardship makes sense only *for* future actual beings and that it would be absurd to create human beings *in order to* guarantee that stewardship over nature continues for its own sake.

Finally, going back to the proposition by Hardin quoted at the beginning of this chapter, we can say that indeed the population problem has no technical solution. But whereas deep ecologists derive from this fact a need for a completely new ethics, ascribing independent moral status to nature, generocentrism (shallow ecology) views the same fact as an empirical constraint on the way we treat actual people in terms of traditional ethical principles. For deep ecologists the nontechnical solution to the question of the upper limit of new people is sought in terms of the obligations we have toward the environment and its natural integrity. For generocentrism, the nontechnicality of the solution to the population problem consists of the limits of our power to manipulate the environment so as to accommodate the numbers of people we wish to have without harming the interests of existing (actual) people or undermining the prospects of the life of potential people as *we* would wish them to have it.[10] To put it crudely, empirical constraints limit our genethical freedom. The possibility that these constraints will be overcome by human technology or natural processes seems now so remote that our basic intuitions regarding genesis issues cannot but be subordinated to them. The hypothetical case of Godlike power over the empirical conditions in which our descendants will live is a serious theoretical genethical topic; but it should not be subjected to the test of intuitive response. There is a sense in which, according to generocentrism, "playing God" in genesis issues is perfectly justified, even inevitable. But we should play God in a rational manner, that is, in the light of our best interests (including the interests we want our children to have). Not to play God as an attitude of cosmic modesty toward the "natural" course of events is an irrational (as well as often immoral) approach no less than refraining from using agriculture to produce food or medicine to heal people.

Our general generocentric conclusion therefore is that the inherent problems involved in applying ethical principles to genesis issues within the framework of our empirical environmental constraints do not point to the need of a new (environmental) ethics, but rather to the limits of ethics as such. The intuitive difficulties we have with the liberation of genesis choices from ethical constraints are mainly due to the dependence of our intuitions on the general facts of biology, psychology, and ecology.[11] Yet, having conceded that empirical constraints can only play a negative role in genethics, that is, mitigating some of the possible criticism of generocentrism in terms of first-order intuitions, it remains for philosophical reasoning to deal with the positive motives for having children from a metaphysical perspective, free from empirical constraints.

CHAPTER 8

Self-Transcendence and Vicarious Immortality

Then the world in itself is neither good nor evil. For it must be all one, as far as concerns the existence of ethics, whether there is living matter in the world or not. And it is clear that a world in which there is only dead matter is in itself neither good nor evil, so even the world of living things can in itself be neither good nor evil.

Good and evil enter only through the *subject*. And the subject is not part of the world, but a boundary of the world.

Wittgenstein, Notebooks, 79e

[T]he mortal nature is seeking as far as is possible to be everlasting and immortal: and this is only to be attained by generation, because generation always leaves behind a new existence in the place of the old.

[T]hat law of succession by which all mortal things are preserved, not absolutely the same, but by substitution, the old worn-out mortality leaving another new and similar existence behind—unlike the divine, which is always the same and not another. And in this way, Socrates, the mortal body, or mortal anything, partakes of immortality; but the immortal in another way.

Plato, Symposium, St. 207–208

PRO-CREATION BY RE-PRODUCTION

Wittgenstein's ethical skepticism together with the complementary Platonic attempt to rebel against its potential nihilistic implications capture the essential vein of the underlying argument of this book. It is not only the content of the quotations which guides our discussion in this final chapter, but their juxtaposition, indeed the treatment of the second as a desperate attempt to respond to the first. Obviously, there is something artificial in such a reconstructed philosophical encounter, for Wittgenstein is not concerned with genesis problems and Plato is by no means an ethical skeptic. Yet setting the two side by side may serve us in characterizing the transition from the limits of ethics to the metaphysics of genethics.

The general problem can be put in terms of the paradoxical nature of the question: what is the value of value? If indeed all value is person-affecting, then the very existence of ("affected") persons cannot, as Wittgenstein explicitly argues, have any value. Axiology and ethics start playing a role only on the assumption that there *are* human beings. This points to the limits of ethics, that is, its inapplicability to genesis problems. However, we find it difficult to become reconciled to these limits; for we seek not only the values of things *for* us, but also the value *of* us. If our existence has no value, all other values could ultimately turn out to be empty and illusory, parochial and conditional. By taking our person-affecting values seriously we are inevitably driven to an attempt to transcend the strict limits of ethics by a metaphysical shift, namely by adopting a more comprehensive perspective of value and of our existence in the world.

Genethics is only one of the foci of such attempts to confer meaning and value to our existence through a "metaphysical ascent." People try to leave an imprint on the world so as to invest it with something that will outlast their own lifespan. They write books, engage in long-term political activites, work for the preservation of nature, build mausoleums, and in general fill their lives with creative activity that is not only life-serving but also life-justifying. This is the essence of Williams's distinction between ordinary and categorical desires. Without the latter, the satisfaction of the former would hardly give us a reason to go on living. However, even these attempts to confer meaning on our lives beyond the way these lives affect *us* are dependent either on there being an impersonal perspective from which the world as such can be evaluated, or on the given fact of the future existence of human beings. But person-affecting genethics rejects both alternative assumptions. It highlights the uniqueness of genesis choices that display an effort to transcend the closed game of person-affecting value. It does so by focusing on the creation of the *conditions* for any value rather than on the creation of value *for* people (who are the conditions for the possibility of value).

In the following three sections of this chapter we first examine the reasons people as *individuals* have to beget children. Secondly we look at the same problem from a wider, more *collective* perspective, namely the place of individuals seeking to give meaning to their lives as part both of a larger social entity and of a transtemporal succession of generations. Finally we turn our attention to the way human beings conceive themselves as part of the nonhuman world, that is, to the widest metaphysical perspective of seeing the *world* itself as part of the identity of the willing subject.

The previous chapter was concerned with the universal psychological *causes* and forces that motivate people to have children. Here we return to the philosophical (genethical) question of the *reasons* for having children (if indeed there are such reasons). Barring impersonal reasons, what are the rational considerations in begetting children, in continuing humanity, in preserving the general traits of human character as we know it, in securing the conditions of value in the valueless world? Generocentrism gives some straightforward answers in terms of the direct benefit we derive from the existence of new people, both on the family level and on the social (generational) one. But we know that some of the reasons for procreation have nothing to do with our own welfare, satisfaction, security, and pride. In other words, having children may also be a sort of ideal, believed to be of intrinsic value, lying beyond any instrumental or egoistic benefit. On the one hand, we have repeatedly argued that intrinsic values are no less person-affecting than their instrumental counterparts; on the other hand, we must analyze the nature of such noninstrumental ideals, that is, explain *how* the ideal of the continuation of myself, my society, or humanity at large affects me (us), serves my (our) volitions. Indeed, what is the rationale of these volitions themselves.

Establishing the value of the existence of humanity as an ideal is an attempt to bridge the gap between the external point of view, which—like Wittgenstein's—denies any value to human existence in the world, and the internal point of view, which seeks to ascribe meaning to the very pursuit of human value. In more metaphorical terms, if life is a game in which ethics is the set of rules for success (just, prosperous, meaningful, good, valuable), what makes the game itself worthwhile? Now if life were a game, that is, a kind of activity within the broader framework of another activity, such a question could easily have made sense. But games are games because they are "nested" in life, whereas life itself is by definition the most comprehensive framework of activity and consciousness, allowing no room for a wider framework from which it can be assessed. Once impersonalism is rejected (together with the idea of a super-game of divine creation and design), the meaning and value of life can only gain support "from within."

The typically human capacity to evaluate one's own life as a whole lies in the power of *self-transcendence*. Here we are interested not so much in the cognitive aspects of this power, namely the capacity of self-consciousness, but with the conative power of constituting value by creating and molding volitions (desires, ideals, goals). This power has more than one aspect. It is, for example, expressed in the formation of second-order desires, that is, volitions by which the existence of other volitions is evaluated, or in the articulation of ideals and goals toward which we strive and in the light of which we change our lives and character.[1] But the deepest expression of the power of self-transcendence is in genesis, that is in the creation of the very conditions of value (not just values), of the subjects of satisfaction (not just satisfactions). If indeed the person-affecting approach is true, begetting children and forming their identity creates value not in the sense of creating valuable entities, but in the sense of making the world a place in which value is at all applicable. Even though it is not a more valuable world (than a world with no human beings), it is the only world in which value plays a role.

Why should the existence of value in the world be of any concern to us? If the world itself cannot be said to be (impersonally) better with value than without it, it is again only ourselves who stand to *somehow*, "person-affectingly," gain from the continued existence of value. The clue to this mysterious benefit derived from procreation seems to lie in the idea of a wider conception of *identity*. Begetting children is a sort of self-expansion, an attempt to extend one's existence, a guarantee for a kind of continuity of the self beyond its individual-biological bounds. One way to interpret these vague goals is through an analogy with the more comprehensible desire to live, or rather to go on living. The underlying meaning of much of what we do and enjoy is related to a wider perspective of a project, a life-plan, a whole span of life. The value of at least some of our actions and satisfactions must be dependent or derived from higher-order values and satisfactions. It is in the Aristotelian hierarchy of ends or "goods" that a scheme of meaning and value is created. It is only in "a life" that human value can find its ultimate expression. The value of the momentary satisfactions of the present self is at least partly derived from their place in a larger scheme of a past and a future self. Longevity is considered a good, not just because of the larger number of aggregated "atomic" satisfactions it affords, but because of the opportunity it offers for the realization of long-term projects that bestow meaning on many of those atomic experiences.[2]

Now this "systemic" conception of value presupposes not only "a life" in the sense of a hierarchy of goals and ends, but also "a biography" in the metaphysical sense of personal identity. It is only by assuming the identity of the living subject through time that a person-affecting concept of nonatomic (system-dependent) value can make sense. But as we have already seen, the identity of persons is not merely a *given* metaphysical or biological fact, it is partly the creation of the subject. In planning our lives, we also tamper with our identity. This is the power of self-transcendence, the capacity to choose conversions or voluntarily undergo gradual changes in our personality, that is to say the power to go beyond what we are, albeit on the basis of what we actually are. But even when we do not seek to change anything in ourselves, it is from an external point of view that we look at our life as something good, wishing to have more of it. More life is considered good *for* most people, because they see their identity as potentially extending beyond the present. This explains why early death is considered a loss (the adjective "premature" in the context of death at a young age has a double sense: it refers to a life that was cut short before it had the chance to develop, i.e., change through a process of self-transcendence, and to a life which was simply short, in the sense that it did not last long enough as it was).

The desire to have children and form their identity to our liking is analogous to the attempt to extend our existence and shape our own identity. Indeed, for biological reasons it is a less effective means to preserve ourselves, since our offspring are in a deep sense different people to ourselves. Yet they are close enough to be partly an extension of ourselves, both because of their genetic similarity and because of the way we rear them and imprint in them those qualities that we deem valuable. And producing children is a typical expression of self-transcendence, as it is far-reaching in time, indefinitely extending parts of our existence and identity in future people. Our descendants can serve as such "extensions" only if they exist. But they can be *our* extensions only if they are similar enough to us: in their genetic makeup, in their general system of values, in their commitment to transgenerational projects such as the search for scientific truth or social progress (and also the very devotion to the continuation of human existence!). If family is an identity-fixing element in our self-perception, then it must also apply "diachronically," that is, in treating the *person* affected as consisting of both the ancestors and the descendants of an individual. The idea of lineage and the interest in the continuation of family lines undoubtedly plays a major role in the way we constitute our identity.

Plato articulates this point beautifully in the above-quoted passage. The pursuit of immortality is the expression of self-transcendence, namely the attempt to be more than what a person actually is. Death is the chief obstacle to such self-transcendence, although other traits (such as fixed, unchangeable properties of character) may also hamper it. Generation is the only humanly possible way to extend the individual's life and existence as such. Even if we cannot adopt Plato's general theory of "partaking," there is a sense in which we can agree that procreation is the way to partake in immortality. And as Plato argues, procreation does not make us immortal in the standard way of partaking (like being tall or just, beautiful or clever), but "in another way." I suggest calling it the "vicarious way," since immortality is achieved *through* someone else, indirectly, or by proxy. On the one hand it is the individual's life that is allegedly extended beyond its natural bounds; on the other hand it is not this individual who goes on living, but some other individual, the offspring. If divine immortality is the model or definition of that notion, then vicarious immortality is no more than an illusory, deceptive consolation for those who strive to break the limits of mortality. But divine immortality should not necessarily be taken as the metaphysically real case, and consequently vicarious immortality through human self-transcendence may be treated as the only possible form of immortality. In that case "divine immortality" becomes the illusory, idealized, merely hypothetical case, the product of philosophical abstraction.

Self-transcendence in the context of conferring meaning on our lives is characteristically a boot-strapping enterprise. It involves granting value to the existential presuppositions of value, that is, to human existence as such, to certain identity-fixing properties, even to a certain number of people. Figuratively speaking it is like pounding against the limiting walls of value-applicability, a desperate attempt to "nest" the valuing game (human existence) in a wider framework. For those, like Wittgenstein, who deny impersonalism, the valuing subject is a boundary of the world—not a part of it. The incoherence of the boot-strapping involved in the effort to evaluate our life from an external point of view is of the same type, and serves a similar function, as that of the suicide, who according to Freud imagines himself hovering over this world, viewing his older suffering self from above, and deriving consolation from the (absurd) comparison between the two forms of "existence".

If the only way to justify the value of the valuing game itself is "from within," as in the case of categorical desires that person-affectingly justify the continuation of life, then it is only the extension of the game itself which can secure its meaning. The concept of *pro-creation* illustrates the vicarious way in which human beings hope to transcend the senselessness of the valuing activity by making it last beyond their own existence. Unlike pure genesis, which creates the conditions of value (presumably) *ex nihilo*, human beings can only partake in the act of value-creation indirectly, that is, by *continuing* the existence of the preconditions of value. Procreation must be understood here in the two dictionary meanings of "pro-": it is a *positive* attitude to creation coupled with creation by *proxy*. These are also the two senses implied by the biblical text of Genesis: the blessing involved in becoming partners, or proxies, in the act of investing the world with value.

But since we "create" in the impure context of already existing human beings (mainly ourselves), that is to say we cannot create new people in an empty world, the only option left is *re*-production, namely, producing more specimens of ourselves. In other words, we can find consolation in the continuation of value only if the persons affected by it are similar enough to us, reproductions of ourselves in some deep sense of being human, having more or less the same identity-bases. The biblical text explicitly associates procreation (continuing God's act of original creation) with reproduction (filling the earth with value, spreading God's image). By being fruitful, we transcend our limited existence; but only by multiplying can we be fruitful. And in a Godless world, in which procreation cannot be considered a religious injunction to take part in a divine scheme, we ourselves are the gods, constituting value in the world by extending ourselves and our "image" through the mediation of our descendants. The logic of creation and procreation is the same; it is only on the metaphysical level, in which we reach the boundaries of value, where the distinction between the religious and the secular views becomes relevant. Religion merely pushes the issue one step further and then again faces the same logical problem of the reason for the creation of value.

However, pure reproduction in the sense of creating further exact specimens (copies) of an original cannot serve as a model for "fruitfulness" and creativity. Take again our lives as individuals, our biographies. Even those who desperately cling to life as such, who want to prolong it at all costs, are embarrassed by the prospect of the Humean thought-experiment of reliving one's life in exactly the same way over and over again.[3] That is to say, we value the continuation of our life only if it contains an element of change, progress, perfection, or self-realization. Self-transcendence involves becoming different, though within the boundaries of personal identity. So reproduction and multiplication should not be understood in the literal, mechanical sense. In both our personal lives and in our reproductive behavior we are never guided by the pure principle of "more of the same." The prospects of cloning, therefore, appear to us unsatisfactory, even horrifying. We want our offspring to be sufficiently like us so we can see them as our continuants, sufficiently similar to us so we can have a meaningful *rapport* with them. But we have no interest in exact mirror-images or in indistinguishable copies. The conception of parenthood in that respect is similar to Aristotle's idea of friendship, namely a relationship that extends our identity through an encounter with the partly different other. Self-transcendence necessarily takes some aspects of actual existence as a basis from which the desired change is judged as valuable. We want to have children not only for the sake of the preservation of pure existence, but for the sake of continued humanity (which is our "image"), namely existence under a particular description or identity.

The creation of a completely different kind of living being as our offspring, however, not only goes against the empirical conditions of human biology and psychology but also makes no metaphysical sense. Wanting to be continued in a completely different form is incoherent because it does not preserve the minimal conditions of identity which make the outcome a continuant of the origin. Thus, begetting a biologically different species, even if it were "higher," would hardly count as reproduction. A total change in identity would mean the end of humanity. There is a basic volitional structure that makes us think of ourselves as a unique species. It probably consists, among other traits, of autonomy, activity, creativity, pleasures of various sorts, rationality, fairness. We cannot imagine desiring to produce offspring who would not have these traits and capacities.

This approach to procreation also explains the sense in which we think of certain genetic or educational manipulations as *dehumanizing*. They do not degrade the subject, since it is a potential person whose identity is thus formed; but they undermine the continuity of the human species, they make *us* less human in our genesis behavior. The preservation of certain properties that we decide are essential to us as belonging to the human species is the ultimate constraint on any eugenic program; for the improvements sought for by such programs are never "impersonal" but always relate to some identifiable subject (the human race). It is therefore in the range lying between cloning (creating exact copies of ourselves) and wild genetic engineering (resulting in completely nonhuman creatures) that self-transcendence in re-production finds expression.

To conclude the argument of boot-strapping: being "thrown into the world" we can never assume the role of creators, that is, create the conditions of value in a valueless world, for we are already part of this world, with the fully developed volitional structure that is constitutive of value. The only indirect way in which we can take part in the very creation of value is by procreation, by securing the existence and fixing the identity of the subjects who are the preconditions of value. We can do so only on the basis of our own existence and identity, but we can to some extent transcend it by extending both existence (in time and number) and identity (by eugenics and education). In doing so we are playing God in the least playful way.

THE GREAT GENERATION CHAIN

The former section concentrated on *replication* as the basic means of self-transcendence. Trying to escape the threat of complete annihilation, individuals extend their very existence by reproduction, by multiplying themselves. But we have already remarked that even in the context of an individual biography human beings exercise the power of self-transcendence not merely by extending their physical lives but by engaging in self-created plans and projects. These require not only physical existence but also a notion of a *process,* a potential progress, a goal-oriented activity that justifies the endeavor to extend physical existence.[4]

When we reflect on the human interest in procreation on the collective level, we immediately see that the interest in the continuity of human existence is not so much articulated in terms of mechanical replication, but rather in dynamic terms of completion, realization, accomplishment. It is as if individuals as such are driven by strong forces of self-preservation, whereas the meaning of their lives must be understood in social terms, such as collective ideals, goals, and enterprises. As individuals, human beings are the vehicles of gene preservation; as social creatures, they are carriers of ethical values and meanings. The distinction between the individual and the social levels is however somewhat artificial, since it is always individuals (for the time being) who make reproductive choices; but it points to two different strands in the way individuals view the role of procreation in lending value to their lives.

The nonatomic nature of human values is derived from the intentional structure of human action. Much of human activity is projective, future-oriented, goal-directed. This entails both a desire to go on living and to have some sort of succession to one's life. On the horizontal axis the intentional structure of human action as we know it necessarily involves social forms, institutions, cooperation, and communal goals, for human action is essentially interactive. But more pertinent to our concern is the vertical axis, which confers meaning to human intentional action in terms of either an individual biography ("narrative") or of collective history ("tradition").[5]

Such considerations cast a slightly different light on the metaphor of the relay race discussed in the preceding chapter. Even if human beings derive most satisfaction from the overlapping segments in which the torch is passed from one generation to the other (rather than from the "impersonal" end of winning the race), it is only by treating the race and its goal as meaningful (for all the participants) that our contribution to it can be of value for us. In other words, participants in each segment of the race identify with the whole in a way that makes the ultimate accomplishment *theirs*. Replication alone, the sheer transfer of the torch, cannot suffice to make the lives of individuals meaningful.

We can easily fall here into the trap of impersonalism. For how can the value of the continuing effort to achieve certain ends be asserted if it extends beyond the lifespan of actual individuals? The general response of the person-affecting view to this challenge consists of the extension of the concept of a "person" rather than the abandonment of the condition of "affectingness." Despite the metaphysical barriers in the attempt to extend personal identity beyond the biological existence of individual human beings, our own conception of who we are is constituted by transindividual elements, as we have already seen in chapter 6. In other words, first-person identity is constructed through the mediation of collective values and goals, which involve both communal and temporal extensions. Self-transcendence implies that what happens to our descendants, projects, political aspirations, and social ideals affects *us,* even after our individual extinction, albeit in a roundabout manner.[6] This is rather like the way in which ignoring their testaments is a violation of *people's* rights and interests. In both cases there is no need to assume a mysterious form of personal existence after death. If human interests extend beyond the biological life of their subject, then in the same way as people can be "affected" after their death, so can they be affected during their life by future prospects. For instance, they can derive satisfaction from the prospect of the success of a cause to which they have been committed throughout their lives, or they can be depressed at the thought of the kind of life that awaits their grandchildren.

Edmund Burke is of course one of the most eloquent formulators of the idea that meaningful human life presupposes temporal self-transcendence, a transgenerational perspective. Much of his rhetoric is impersonal in nature:

> But one of the first and most leading principles on which the commonwealth and the laws are consecrated, is lest the temporary possessors and life-renters in it, unmindful of what they have received from their ancestors, or what is due to their posterity, should act as if they were the entire masters; that they should not think it amongst their rights to cut off the entail, or commit waste on the inheritance, by destroying at their pleasure the whole fabric of their society . . . (Burke 1968, 192)

Society is not merely a contract "for objects of mere occasional interest," serving "the gross animal existence of temporary and perishable nature" (p. 194), it is a partnership whose ends are science, art, virtue, and perfection. Since these ends are typically cumulative, they require a partnership "between those who are living, those who are dead, and those who are to be born" (pp. 194–195). Each political contract "is but a clause in the great primaeval contract of eternal society . . . connecting the visible and invisible world, according to a fixed compact sanctioned by the inviolable oath which holds all physical and all moral natures, each in their appointed place" (p. 195).

But much of the Burkean reasoning can be interpreted and justified in more person-affecting terms. A break in "the whole chain and continuity of the commonwealth" and the link between generations is a threat not only to independently existing norms and values; it is a threat to our very identity as human beings: "Men would become little better than the flies of a summer" (p. 193); their goal-directed activity would lose all ground; "nothing stable in the modes of holding property" would be possible; no sense of honor could be inculcated in a society "continually varying the standard of its coin" (p. 193). In other words, personal identity in the deep human sense is conditioned by some kind of stability, long-range commitment to standards that are not changed *ad hoc*. The evils of "inconstancy and versatility," of "the dust and powder of individuality," of the "unconnected chaos of elementary principles" (pp. 194–195) lie in the way they affect us, in their self-defeating nature, in the threat they pose to our identity as human beings resolutely trying to be more than "flies of a summer." We might say that the impersonal reading of the Burkean chain of generations starts from the content of the contract, inferring from it the scope of its membership. The person-affecting interpretation, however, starts from the analysis of what we (the contractors) are, or conceive ourselves to be, deriving the intergenerational scope of morality as well as its content from it.[7]

In that respect, revolutions and radical political changes are like conversions on the individual level. If they are too radical, they undermine the identity both of the society and of the individual in whose name the change is undertaken. If revolution creates a genuinely *new* society, who exactly benefits from it? If improvement and progress are measured not by constant standards, but by the introduction of a totally new system of standards, how can they be justified? This is the profound import of Burke's monetary metaphor of the absurdity of constantly shifting the standard of coin.

We may conclude then that the idea of pro-creation by re-production (analyzed in the previous section) is only part of the picture of the metaphysics of genethics and should be complemented by the idea of meaning through participation in a continuing project or enterprise. These are two separate modes of self-transcendence. The former consists of vicariously partaking in immortality through the continuity of the volitional conditions of value (namely securing the very existence of human beings). The latter consists of extending the notion of the affected person, by constituting essential human identity in terms of values and meanings that are in their very nature social and transgenerational. It is here that the cumulative, purposeful, and progressive dimension of what is valuable in our eyes leads the way to the Burkean concept of the chain of generations.

So even if abstractly speaking there is no wrong in the discontinuation of the human race, the very possibility of such a voluntary act of species suicide would cast a grave shadow on the ability of the last generation to invest its life with meaning. For it is hard to conceive that people would go on with scientific research, art restoration, political activity, economic investment, ideological debates, and so forth if they knew that they were the last generation on earth.[8] Although it is often said that without the knowledge that we are going to die nothing would have any meaning for us, we may also add that much of what we do in our individual lives is of value to us only on the assumption that today is not our last day on earth. The projective aspect of human behavior is vital to life's meaning both on the individual and the collective levels. With no sense of growth, hope, progress, and accomplishment, life would be senseless and the self-perception of personhood absurdly narrow and impoverished. *Après nous le déluge* is, therefore, not an immoral principle, but rather a self-defeating attitude, which leaves little point and purpose to our lives.[9]

The metaphysics of genethics lies, therefore, not merely in the great *generation chain,* namely, in the process of generating more human beings in the "replicative" sense of securing the existence of the volitional conditions of value; it also consists of the great *chain of generations,* namely, of an awareness of temporal extension (both to the past and to the future) as a precondition for the meaning of human life.[10] This is a typically person-affecting value, that is, it views the identity of actual (present) human beings as partly constituted by the heritage of past generations and by the projects that can be achieved only by future ones. Taking part in the transgenerational story is not a duty (that of keeping the story going) but an essential part of what we conceive of as *our own* story. The pertinent language for genethical choices on that level is not the language of moral duty and obligation, but that of the metaphysics of personhood and human identity.[11]

Finally, we may note the distinction between the uniquely replicative aspect of God's motive for creating man and the complementary and perfectionist motives of human procreation. The reason is fairly obvious: God is infinite and the only way of explaining his genethical choice is through the idea of spreading his image. Man is only an image of God, a paler and less perfect version of divine nature. Finite human individuals, however, can hope to transcend their limitation only through the cumulative effort of many generations. Human history is always more perfect than any individual person.

THE METAPHYSICS OF GENESIS

Securing the possibility of value by reproducing new people and establishing the meaning of human life through participation in a transgenerational enterprise are two complementary expressions of self-transcendence through other *human* beings. The value of the existence

of the preconditions of value is sought in terms of the physical continuation and the meaningful growth of human history. But the ultimate
form of self-transcendence is the attempt to view the very existence of
humanity (and hence of what we call "person-affecting value") from an
extra-human point of view. This concerns human beings' position in the
world, rather than their role in the chain of generations. From our
critical person-affecting perspective, impersonalism itself may be seen as
the ultimate feat of boot-strapping! Human beings constitute a notion
of nature in which they have a special position or, alternatively, a notion
of God in whose design they have a special status.

The most interesting example of such an attempt at self-transcendence
in the history of philosophy is Kant. As we have already noted in chapter
2, Kant's theory of value is basically person-affecting. Human reason is
the source of all (moral) value and the ultimate subject of whatever is
valuable. But then can reason itself be of value? Can the enterprise of the
moral history of humanity *as a whole* and its progress towards moral
perfection be considered a good?

Kant says that there are ample grounds for "reflective judgment" to
treat "man as not merely a physical end, such as all organized beings
[organisms] are, but as the being upon this earth who is the *ultimate end*
of nature, and the one in relation to whom all other natural things
constitute a system of ends" (Kant 1928, 92). From this proposition
Kant draws the conclusion that there is one exception to the principle
that extrinsic relations in nature (viz., of means to ends) cannot have
ulterior ends:

> This is the organization of the two sexes in their mutual relation with a view
> to the propagation of their species. For we may always ask, just as in the case
> of an individual: Why was it necessary for such a pair to exist? The answer
> is: In this pair we have what first forms an *organizing* whole, though not an
> organized whole in a single body. (Kant 1928, 87)

The fact, says Kant, that an entity (such as a human being) has an
intrinsic end (underlying its causality) leads us to the belief "that the real
existence of this product is also an end" (p. 87). But this proves misleading, because in the whole of nature we cannot find "any being capable
of laying claim to the distinction of being the final end of creation" (p.
88). We arrive here at what Kant calls "the antinomy of the principles of
the mechanical and teleological generation of organic natural beings
[including human beings]" (p. 91). And hence the question of the
"value" of the very existence of human beings escapes philosophical

solution. For it is not clear whether any *design* conferring value on the very existence of humankind can be objectively established.[12]

The difficulty encapsulated in this antinomy consists in the fact that the very idea of nature (either as a system of mechanical relations or as a teleological design) is itself a product of human reason and hence the question of the role of human existence within nature is a metaphysical issue that can never be decided. In other words, it is only by a constitutive act of reason that the role and value of reason itself can be posited. This is typically a self-transcending act of reason, through "reflective judgment," a rational function that goes beyond the "determinant judgment" used in empirical knowledge of the world. Humanity can be declared "the titular lord of nature" only through its own "intelligence and will" rather than as a matter of natural fact. The very "aptitude for setting ends" for oneself cannot therefore be evaluated independently of human reason (that is "impersonally"). The value of life to us consists in what we do "with a view to an end so independent of nature that the very existence of nature itself can only be an end subject to the condition so imposed" (p. 98, n.).

Man as a free agent, a *noumenon*, is the only being in nature that acts on ends independent of nature. But there is no sense in asking from a nonhuman point of view "for what end does he exist" (p. 99). He is the final end of nature, but only from the perspective of his own teleological, unifying, projective power of reason. On the one hand, from a theoretical point of view, there is no solution to the antinomy of nature (including the existence of humankind in it) as a system of mechanical causation and as a purposeful design. From this point of view teleology as a whole might turn out to be a delusion. On the other hand, from a *practical* point of view, humanity can be seen as investing the world with value, as striving to moral perfection, as trying to subordinate nature to its self-created ends. This is Kant's reason for replacing *physico*-theology by *ethico*-theology as a means for establishing humanity's absolute worth (pp. 108–109). The purpose and value of the existence of humanity is expressed through the existence of God, but this God is the product of human reason, of the consciousness of moral agency and freedom (p. 114). Kant's moral proof for the existence of God is a typical example of a self-transcending move, in which a transcendent nonhuman being is introduced as the ultimate ground for the meaning of human life (morality). In the nontheological terms of my argument in the previous section, it is in the purposeful (teleological) structure of human action that the foundations of genethics can be laid.

Kant may be right in claiming that if there is a final end to the world at all, it must be a human, a rational being.

> [I]f the world only consisted of lifeless beings, or even consisted partly of living, but yet irrational beings, the existence of such a world would have no worth whatever, because there would exist in it no being with the least conception of what worth is. (117)

This is a fairly direct expression of a person-affecting conception of value. But Kant warns that human beings can be the final ends of the world only if they are perceived as more than the subjects of happiness, since the existence of happiness as a natural psychological state cannot have an ulterior end. It is the existence of human beings as moral agents, that is, transcending their natural (biological and psychological) existence, that can serve as the basis for the world's worth and hence for their own worth. In other words, although there is no formal proof for the value of the very existence of humanity, it is only through treating it as the final end of the world that morality is made possible as is the nonillusory sense of the inner worth of what we are and what we do.

Kant's own critical stance leads him to awareness of the problem of giving an "impersonal" answer to the ultimate genethical question "why should there be human beings at all?" For the only possible answer to that question is in moral, that is, "person-affecting" terms. But if that is the case, then the answer can make sense only for human beings asking why they should continue the human race, and the ultimate question of the value of humanity asked in the *abstract* (is the world with humans better than that without?) remains meaningless. An attempt to ask it from a Godly point of view, that is, why *create* human beings, would only push the question one step backward, but leave the same logical problem of accounting for the value of the preconditions of value. It would require an account of God's reasons for creating humanity and indeed the world as a whole. A Leibnizian account of the creation of the world and the selection of the best possible world must necessarily be "theocentric," that is it must refer to the creator's nature and character, which already assumes the existence of value (for example, in the form of God's goodness, beneficence, and grace). As we have proposed in the introduction, creation must be in the final analysis good *for* God, or good from his point of view.

The traditional problem of theodicy may accordingly be interpreted in nonimpersonal terms: it concerns the evaluation of the genesis of the world, and of human beings in it, in the light of the nature, intentions, and aims of the creator, and not from the abstract point of view of a comparison between two states of affairs. For as we have argued throughout this book, the existence of the world and its total nonexistence are in a deep sense incommensurable, as are the existence of a world with human beings and a world without, or even a world with particular human beings and a world with *other* (nonidentical) human beings. Theodicy is a serious issue only if it regards the creator in terms analogous to those according to which human agents are ethically judged, that is, in the light of given values and norms. Even God, therefore, is bound by moral constraints (although they are, by definition, self-regarding). If God, however, is believed to have created the system of values as well as the world, then obviously there can be no evaluation of his creation. In the purest form of genesis, that is, when no agent whatsoever is involved (i.e., not even a "personal" creator), the existence or coming to being of the world or of humanity lies totally beyond the reach of any value judgment. This is the case both in an Aristotelian or Spinozistic conception of an eternally existing world as well as in a naturally evolving physical world (Big Bang) or an evolving humanity (Darwinism).[13]

On the abstract metaphysical level, pure genesis problems admit of no ethical solutions. The ultimate question why there is something rather than nothing can again be given meaning only within a theocentric framework, in which a *personal* ("volitional") God acts with certain aims and according to some existing system of values. Other attempts to treat the existence of the world as itself "ethically required" (e.g., Leslie 1983, 333–334; Jonas 1984) seem farfetched, and being examples of ethical impersonalism they serve to highlight its weakness.[14] In the same way as physics or even metaphysics cannot answer the question why there is something rather than nothing, but can only describe and explain what there is, so ethics cannot answer the question whether or not it is a good or a duty that there be human beings, but can only determine what is good and right for human beings.[15]

In the absence of convincing impersonal accounts of the genesis and the value of human existence, we are left with the man-made *ideal* of the continued existence of a humanly populated world. It is in the ultimate expansion of our identity as beings living in the natural world that a person-affecting justification of the worth of human existence can be established. The most extreme and explicit conception of human identity as mediated by the natural world (not just future generations) is the Gaia hypothesis, briefly outlined in chapter 7. This conception is not satisfied with the "totalization" of human action in communal and historical terms, but treats the relation of human beings with the natural environment as the arena in which life acquires meaning. Once the harmonious balance between human and nonhuman elements of the world becomes part of the way human beings see themselves (and the natural world), the ecological preservation of the environment becomes more than an instrumental good; it is an intrinsic value in the person-affecting sense, analogous to the value of the success of certain transgenerational projects in which we take part. Such extensions of first-person identity are, however, much more controversial than the universally shared view that the meaning of our lives is mediated by *human* history and prospects.

However, the projection of a human ideal on the world, trying to invest it with value in order to make human life meaningful, is of a limited metaphysical validity. It is true that, as Aristotle says, a supreme good, a unifying principle, must exist *if* all human action is not to be "empty and vain." But that does not establish the worth of the very existence of humans and of human action (which is the ultimate issue in genethics). It only supports the hypothetical proposition that *if* there are human beings acting in the world, then they must treat their position in it as metaphysically privileged. From a nonhuman point of view, it might very well be that there is no meaning and worth to the existence of beings who are desperately trying to give meaning to their existence. In that respect Kant's inference from the idea of humanity as "an end of nature, included in nature taken as existent" to the idea of humanity as "the end of the real existence of nature" (Kant 1928, 110) is fallacious, at least if "real" is taken in the traditional metaphysical sense.

Furthermore, unlike Aristotle and Kant, who take for granted the objective or absolute validity of reason, a more modern, post-Nietzschean view may deny this absolute and universal status of reason and together with it the implications regarding the teleological conditions of its exercise. From a skeptical, "impersonal" perspective, maybe there is no final end to our actions, no unifying principle. All our "rational" attempts to give unity and meaning to our aims might turn out to be illusory. Self-transcendence inevitably remains bound to the human (all-too-human?) point of view. To the modern mind the *fixity* of the human project and the "enlightened" assumption regarding the inevitability of human progress cannot be taken as axioms. The future of humanity is not only free from historicistic laws, but is open to unpredictable vicissitudes due to both human and nonhuman contingencies. Moreover, human history is shaped by free human agents who, among other things, exercise their freedom by their genethical choices. These choices have profound consequences regarding the existence, number, and identity of people who in their turn decide the fate of the human enterprise, leaving it deeply undetermined. Trying to extricate ourselves from the internal point of view in order to gain an impersonal insight into the status of man in the world may yield a metaphysical perspective through which man is elevated to the sublime status of the final end of creation; but it may *equally* give rise to the image of human life as no more than "a tale told by an idiot, full of sound and fury, signifying nothing."

Notes

INTRODUCTION

1. For a most comprehensive and erudite research, wholly devoted to the Judeo-Christian tradition of interpretation of Genesis I:28, see Cohen 1989. Cohen intentionally avoids the issue of image, although he admits that there is a connection between it and the issue of procreation and dominion over the earth (p. 21). He deals with the common view that sexual union is a means of *transmitting* God's image; but my own reading takes procreation as virtually *consisting of* God's image.

2. The biblical text, as well as many later interpretations, refers to the moral necessity of an ongoing human existence for avoiding "the waste" involved in a humanless world. This idea is derived from the conception of humanity as being the *telos*, the ultimate goal for all preceding creation. But this traditional idea should not be confused with our suggested interpretation of "dominion," since it presupposes an impersonally valuable metaphysical design or project that can be undermined by humans who do not assume their necessary role (of procreation). My point is that in order for any state of affairs to be described as "a waste" there must be someone *for whom* it is a waste, and it is exactly this condition that does not obtain in a natural world devoid of human beings. Again, such a world can be thought of as wasteful only in the eyes of God, for whom a certain valuable design has not been fully realized.

3. Similarly, only if creation is treated as a grand design can the world be said to "require" the existence of human beings, and their absence can make the creation of the rest of the world futile. If the world is conceived as simply a given fact, rather than an intentional creation, there seems to be no reason for treating it as less valuable if it is devoid of human existence.

4. The supreme "impersonal" value of the proliferation of God's image is often highlighted by later Jewish commentaries as the reason for treating celi-

bacy as one of the gravest sins. For our purposes here the symmetry, often appealed to, between refraining from procreation and murder(!) is of a particular interest, since it does not distinguish between killing an actual person and avoiding the creation of a potential one. For both acts are judged in impersonal terms of a transpersonal value, namely the diminution of the image of God, to which they equally lead. See particularly the discussion of the symmetry argument in chapter 4 below.

5. As Jan Narveson has suggested, the newly acquired human power of total destruction is the mirror image of God's creative power. In any case we are closer to the capability of wiping out humanity than of creating it *ex nihilo*.

6. This does not mean that theodicy—"the justification of evil"—is not a legitimate ethical subject, for it is *after* creating humanity that God is expected to make human lives as good as possible. But if the very existence of human beings involves evil, then the problem of evil becomes a typical genesis problem and would be hard to solve in moral terms.

7. As we shall see in later chapters, for the pure version we have to imagine a world in which the procreation of a new generation is simultaneous with the death of the previous generation. Such a thought-experiment might give us a fairly accurate insight into the unique status and puzzle of pure genesis choices as well as into the reasons why impure choices are often partly based on traditional ethical principles.

8. This is the theme of Nagel's book, carrying the paradoxical title *The View from Nowhere*. See Nagel 1986, especially the introduction. In chapters 8–11 Nagel deals with the issue whether there are agent-neutral, or only agent-relative values, and whether we can find the meaning of our lives in the combination of objective detachment and subjective involvement. The same issues will be discussed in chapter 8 of this book through the particular perspective of genesis contexts.

CHAPTER 1: WRONGFUL LIFE

1. When the manuscript of this book was almost completed, D. Suzuki and P. Knudtson published a book with the title *Genethics* (Cambridge: Harvard University Press, 1989) devoted to "the exploration of the clash between modern genetics and human values." The way I use the term is entirely different and refers to a much wider scope of issues (such as *gen*esis, *gen*eration, and also *gen*etics). Genethics in the aforementioned book deals with the moral guidelines for genetic research and engineering, such as the prohibition of the use of biological weapons, the duty to secure genetic variety, the warning against human hubris, and the restriction on the uses of genetic information. The present book questions the applicability of moral principles to genethical choices in the sense of deciding the existence, number, and identity of potential people.

2. *Zeitsov v. Katz* (1986) 40(ii) P.D. 85. For a detailed analysis and criticism of the two main and lengthy majority opinions in this first and so far only Israeli case of "wrongful life," see Heyd 1986.

3. Some instances of wrongful life cases in the United States, though necessarily only a sample, are: *Gleitman v. Cosgrave* (1967) 227a 2d 689; *Parker v.*

Chessin (1977) 400 N.Y.S. 2d 110; *Stills v. Gratton* 55 Cal. App. 3d 698; *Becker v. Schwartz* (1978) 413 N.Y.S. 2d 895; *Berman v. Allan* (1979) 404A 2d 8; *Curlender v. Bio-Science Laboratories* (1985) App. 165 Cal. Rptr. 477; *Turpin v. Sortini* (1981) App. 174 Cal. Rptr. 128.

4. The court in *Parker v. Chessin* recognizes this difference between the two latter categories (p. 116). So does the court in *Becker v. Schwartz,* aptly distinguishing between "wrongful birth" and "wrongful conception" (p. 898).

5. Still, it should be emphasized that abortion of defective fetuses is at most *permitted;* it is never obligatory, at least not in law. This blocks the child's claim that the doctor's duty was to abort it, a point misunderstood by Judge Ben-Porat in *Zeitsov v. Katz,* though correctly analyzed by Judge Stephenson in the Mc-Kay case quoted below.

6. *Zeitsov v. Katz* raises the intuitive doubt regarding the significance of the "slight difference" between the preconceptive case discussed by the court and a hypothetical case in which the mother is infected by a contagious disease just after conception (what we called the prenatal category). As we shall later see, this conflation of the two categories is psychologically understandable, but nevertheless theoretically untenable.

7. Feinberg distinguishes between "being harmed" and "being wronged" and argues that a child born with a serious defect (making his life not worthwhile) can be said to have been wronged although not to have been harmed and hence can sue for damages for wrongful life. However, he fails to show why unlike "being harmed," "being wronged" is exempt from the logical condition of "being worse off than one could have been," that is, the "identity condition." Feinberg's consequent conflation of a suit for being born illegitimate with the case of the production of poisonous baby food is thus conceptually problematic, as is his view that in the former sort of case adjudging damages, although "on *admittedly arbitrary* grounds," serves justice better than not allowing any compensation. Furthermore, it is not clear why Feinberg is much less inclined to recognize the legal standing of children born with "only" minor defects, as if the degree of misery makes any difference in the logic of "being wronged" (Feinberg 1984, 95–104). See also Feinberg 1980, 218, where there is a similar confusion first between actual beings with rights conditional upon their birth and potential beings, who, I shall claim, have no rights whatsoever, and second, between the moral grounds for allowing compensation and the logical problem of making any sense of such claims.

8. A funny way of putting the paradox of evaluating preconceptive nonexistence is the well-known Jewish saying that not to be born is a rare piece of luck, befalling only one out of a thousand! The comic effect of this joke is itself based on the logical incongruity of envying the unborn.

9. This argument is presented also in Chadwick 1987, 96–97, although it is logically inconsistent with the author's later statement that these cases concern a choice "between producing x with a handicap or no x at all."

10. Recall the hilarious sperm-parachutist scene in Woody Allen's *Everything You Wanted to Know About Sex,* where by fully personifying human spermata just before conception Allen toys with the idea of a preconceptive existence with all its paradoxical consequences. The logical contradiction in the

attempt of a "humanly identified" entity to determine its own identity and its very existence is the source of the comic effect. In the painful context of wrongful life cases it is the source of the sense of tragedy.

11. Tedeschi 1966, quoting the Talmud in *Sotah* 12a. Tedeschi's article on wrongful life was a pioneering work, often quoted by the courts throughout the world. My approach basically follows his thesis, which is critical of the logical coherence of wrongful life cases, yet goes beyond it as shown in Heyd 1986.

12. The amount usually accorded to the parents in such cases is much lower than that claimed by the child, especially as the parents can get money for raising the child only as long as he or she is a minor, whereas the child claims on the basis of lifelong expenses.

13. See Jecker 1987*a*, who argues that the parents violate the rights of the child in such cases (p. 232); however, at the end of her article she expresses doubts as to the existence of the relevant rights, which makes the whole argument conditional, that is, *if* the child has such rights, then they can serve as a basis for suing the parents for wrongful life. Elsewhere, Jecker argues more explicitly for the absurdity of ascribing rights to possible persons. People cannot have rights if they are not going to exist in the actual world, since their interests will never be infringed nor their freedom limited (Jecker 1987*b*, esp. 157).

14. An innovative solution to a wrongful life claim, which does not run counter either to our logical convictions or to our moral sympathy and sense of social justice, is offered by the dissenting view in *Burman v. Allan* (pp. 15ff.): the child is entitled to compensation for the losses caused by the *impaired parenthood* of his mother and father who will have to struggle with raising a mongoloid child, with all the psychological difficulties involved!

15. An uncommonly radical view, opposed to the standard way of analyzing the presuppositions of tort, can be found in the dissenting view in *Curlender v. Bio-Science Laboratories,* where the judge sweepingly states that "there should be a remedy for every wrong committed" (p. 489), irrespective of whether a worsening of the condition of the plaintiff can be established.

CHAPTER 2: THE FAILURE OF TRADITIONAL ETHICAL THEORIES

1. Note that social discount, that is, assigning less weight to the interests of future people, is also inapplicable to genesis problems, as grading the weight of the interests of persons presupposes their existence and the actuality of their interests.

2. The general distinction between distributive (saving) problems presupposing a fixed number of people across generations and population (genesis) policies that decide this number is methodologically fruitful but conceptually problematic. See Partridge 1981, 309, for a short presentation of the issue of the interdependence of the two. Partridge is more interested in the first group of issues; this book with the second. The interdependence of the two is corroborated by the fact that most of the articles in Partridge's collection refer directly to genesis problems.

3. See especially Hubin 1976/1977 for a convincing argument against the

motivational assumption and the general adequacy of Rawls's attempted "reduction" of intergenerational distributive issues to the intragenerational framework. However, Hubin is not interested in genesis problems and like Rawls ignores the conceptual dependence of the savings problem on genesis decisions (except for an unelaborated hint in a footnote on p. 82). My critique of Rawls's taking the existence and number of future people as given is analogous to Hubin's point about the fallacy of taking the circumstances of justice in the future as given (p. 74). Both are affected by the choice we are making in the present and cannot be taken as background data for these choices.

4. See also Parfit 1984, 391–393. One could argue that the duty to continue the family line, or for that matter the human race, is derived from the respect we owe to our parents who in creating us expressed, among other things, the interest in seeing the family continued into the future. But this is a duty that can hardly be derived from any contractarian principles, since we were never asked whether we wanted to be born at all, let alone whether we would be willing to pay for it (?) by begetting grandchildren to our parents . . .

5. Moreover, a conference of all *possible* people cannot reach an agreement on a principle of total utility, as Michael Bayles proposes, because—as we shall see later—it is doubtful whether or not they can wish the maximization of utility independently of their existence, which is exactly the issue that should be decided! Nor can a conference of all *actual* people reach an agreement on a principle of average utility, as Bayles suggests, since average utility often depends on the number and identity of actual people, which again calls for a decision. See Bayles 1980, app. 2.

6. Like other critics of the motivational assumption, Jane English believes that the present-time-of-entry interpretation should be abandoned and that Rawls would do better without transforming the contractors from individuals into heads of families (English 1977). But when advocating the universal representation interpretation (p. 99), English also seems to assume that the number of individuals "throughout history" is fixed and hence ignores the complexities of genesis choices.

7. See English 1977, 103, who correctly questions the status of justice as a primary good itself subject to fair (or just) distribution, although her critique is not from the point of view of genesis problems.

8. Attfield, unlike the critics of Rawls previously mentioned, is fully aware of the problems of applying the contract theory to population policies. Denying the coherence of a contract of all *possible* people, Attfield says that we are forced to transcend justice as fairness by adding maximizing (goal-type) principles of a utilitarian nature (Attfield 1983, chap. 6). But from a utilitarian point of view, he is willing to grant these possible people a moral standing (Attfield 1987, 11); this, as I will later show, is no less problematic than letting them participate in the original position. Brian Barry also rejects the adequacy of the motivational assumption and hence the present-time-of-entry interpretation, finds the conference of all actual persons a solution that prejudges the very issue, and notices the logical incoherence of a conference of all possible persons. He is thus explicitly led to a non-Rawlsian "cosmic" duty to posterity (Barry 1977, 276ff.). Typically, when getting to the stage of proposing the value of a longer

human history in noncontractarian terms, Barry's language becomes vague—
less argumentative and more emotive. But Barry is among the few critics of
Rawls who explicitly notices the dependence of the saving problem on population policies (pp. 280–281).

9. David Richards still believes that the problems of applying contract
theory to genesis issues can be overcome; he insists that all people in history
should be admitted into the original contract, both because we are allowed to
assume that humans are going to exist anyway and because potential people
also have a moral standing (Richards 1983, 140). But I find both reasons
dubious: first, the fact and especially the number of future people is exactly the
issue at point; secondly, the conference of potential people has been shown to be
an incoherent concept. Richards argues that we can consider the welfare of
future people in abstraction from their identity; that is to say their identity is
concealed from us by the veil of ignorance. But from a contractarian point of
view this is an illegitimate move, since although we might not have access in the
original position to the knowledge of future people's identity, we must take it as
fixed, as given (like all other properties of people which are not known in the
original position). Yet the identity of future people in genethical choices is not
given, but stands to be decided.

10. For a good critique of the doctrine of the circumstances of justice in the
context of intergenerational relations, see Barry 1978.

11. Diachronic theories of justice, such as Nozick's entitlement theory, do
not fare any better than their synchronic ("patterned") rivals. Although one
might be said to be "entitled" to procreate with no restriction (if by that one
does not violate the liberty and rights of others), no one can be said to be
entitled to come to life.

12. See De George 1979, 94ff. The contention there is that future people do
not have a claim on present resources and that they will have rights at all only
once they exist. But De George holds that once we decide to bring a child into
the world, we have obligations toward him.

13. This proposition runs against Kavka's version of a "modified imperative," which "would forbid the treatment of rational beings *or their creation* . . .
as a means only" (Kavka 1982, 110). My argument against Kavka's proposal
will be further developed in chapter 4, in the context of the slave-child case.

14. This idea of replication is presented in the Bible as a religious duty of
human beings, a duty *to* God. This is a possible framework for the development
of genethical principles; however being "heteronomous," it is not an option for
Kant, or indeed for other nonreligious deontological ethical systems.

15. Christine Korsgaard has called my attention to this important analogy in
Kant's philosophy and its possible implications for genethics.

16. For a very illuminating discussion of this idea, see Yovel 1980. Yovel
emphasizes the importance of history as the only sphere in which "the *totalization* of single moral works" can be achieved (p. 29). The addition of a
teleological dimension to the deontological doctrine of the categorical imperative is seen by Yovel as a logical requirement for the coherence of the moral
theory. I may add that in this Kant is following Aristotle's idea that the highest

good is the only way in which human behavior can gain structure, and hence meaning. For both philosophers, atomism, both of individual acts as well as of individual biographies, amounts to nihilism. The difference is that whereas Aristotle is content with a synchronic structure (of the virtuous life of a single agent plus a social ordering of human goals within a political community), Kant calls for a grander diachronic enterprise involving historical progress.

17. Yovel points out this injustice of history and wonders whether Kant could account for it. He correctly describes Kant as conceiving "history as if it were an organic individual, developing itself and enjoying its own product," and convincingly objects to this solution claiming that "there is no legitimate way for Kant to *personify* the historical human collectivity and assign to it a single consciousness and responsibility" (p. 145). I fully agree with Yovel's critique regarding the separation of the human individual from the alleged totality of the regulative ideal of history. But Yovel does not discuss the implications of this unsolved "puzzlement" for the ethics of procreation. He only speaks of "propagation of the moral community" in terms of education and enlightenment of given human beings, but not as a genesis problem (p. 172). In this he follows Kant himself, who in the final section of the *Lectures on Ethics* speaks of the greatest moral perfection as the "ultimate destiny of the human race," an ideal that can be attained only through proper education (Kant 1963*b*, 252–253).

18. Throughout the *Religion* Kant characterizes this goal in almost Manichean terms, namely the victory of good over evil in a conflict that is inherent in the nature of man (the fall). And again, this victory can be achieved only on the social or collective level; but that calls for "a presupposition of another idea, namely, that of a higher moral Being through whose universal dispensation the forces of separate individuals, insufficient in themselves, are united for a common good" (Kant 1934, 89).

19. Yovel explains that "the universe needs man so that he, as free and conscious creature, can *confer* its final end on the world" (Yovel 1980, 179). But it is implausible that the world needs man, as a nonhuman world cannot have any *needs*. In other words, it seems that if we take Kant's humanism seriously (as Yovel does, when he emphasizes that the moral ideal is not a Platonic idea but a projection of the human will), then moral perfectibility and the establishment of morality in the natural world can be a "historical imperative" only on the *assumption* that human beings are going to exist anyway. It cannot guide us in choosing whether to create them at all.

20. It seems that Sidgwick, who was directly aware of the competing claims of the average and the total versions of the utility principle, would agree to the "impersonal" duty of bringing a new happy child into the world as a means for the promotion of overall utility (Sidgwick 1907, 415–416). With Bentham, the question of the personal assignability of utility is harder to decide: does "the greatest number" refer to existing people or to possible people? (See Sprigge 1968, 339–340). Even if Sprigge is correct in reading the two as supporting an "impersonal" view, their theories are generally compatible with a "person-affecting" approach, which insists on assigning utility only to actual people.

For a typical impersonal view of the value of human life see also Roupas 1977/1978. Like many "impersonalists", Roupas refuses to assign rights to potential people or duties toward them (p. 163), but insists that their coming to be might have *value*.

21. See Anglin 1977, 745–754. Though claiming that the average version is no less "impersonal" than the total version of utilitarianism, Anglin—like Parfit—is willing to follow impersonalism, but unlike Parfit denies the repugnance of the Repugnant Conclusion.

22. Medical ethics grapples with the same indeterminacy in the sphere of the value of individual lives: what is the right ratio between a person's quality of life and the length of that life? Is there an optimal weighting of the two? This is a crucial but unresolved question in the euthanasia debate. For the problem of weighting quality and quantity of life in the interpersonal domain, see Parfit 1984, 403.

23. See Sprigge 1968, 338; McMahan 1981/1982, 100–102. For further discussion of the general problem of asymmetry, see chapter 4 below.

24. After the deluge, God blesses/commands Noah, using the very same wording of creation: "be fruitful and multiply and replenish the earth" (Genesis 9: 1). This may be interpreted as an evidence of God's will that the elimination of evil in the world be not achieved through the total annihilation of the "carriers" of value (human beings), that is by Negative Utilitarian means, but rather by securing (through selective measures) the victory of good over evil *within* the realm of value.

25. The general question of begetting children for the purpose of using them has drawn much attention since Gregory Kavka suggested the case of the slave child (Kavka 1982, 100ff.). We will deal with the complexities of this difficult case separately in chapter 4.

26. Parfit 1982, 114–116; Parfit 1983, 168; Parfit 1984, 358ff. And see also Kavka 1982, 97–98; and Adams 1979, 57. It is exactly this context of Different People Choice which makes the Pareto principle inapplicable in standard problems of intergenerational justice (Galston 1980, 251–260).

27. Parfit 1982, 171–172. For similar attempts see Stearns 1972, 625; as well as others, like Kavka (1982, 98–100, 106), who seek a solution to the similarly defined tension.

28. This is a fictitious example, extrapolating Elster's more realistic case of the decision to migrate from village to city, thus radically changing one's lifestyle and eventually preferences and standards of evaluation (including the evaluation of the very decision to migrate!). The theoretical difficulty lies in that the path from the rural to the industrial social form of living may be judged as negative from the point of view of the farmer, though positive from the point of view of the factory manager, even if this happens to be the "same" person at different points in time. If it suffices that people be grateful in retrospect for what was done to them, one may imagine a very wide playroom for genetic and other manipulation of the identity of future people. See Elster 1982, 231ff., for a discussion of the question whether the Industrial Revolution was a good or a bad thing, and a perceptive discussion by Glover 1979, 84 and passim.

CHAPTER 3: THE META-ETHICAL DEADLOCK

1. Dworkin convincingly argues that the method of reflective equilibrium is fruitful only under a "constructive" (rather than "naturalistic") interpretation of moral theory (Dworkin 1973, 505ff.). This highlights the differences between methods of acceptance in ehtics and in science and accords with Rawls's own constructivist account of his own theory. However, it hardly seems of much help in making reflective equilibrium a method in genethics. Put another way, beyond the question of the validity of deriving moral *norms* from natural *facts* about human beings, genethics raises an even deeper issue: that of the norms for the determination *of* those facts. In that respect, Nielsen's forceful critique of the effectiveness of reflective equilibrium to decide between a Rawlsian theory of right and Nietzschean perfectionism can be extended to apply even more convincingly to competing moralities of procreation. (See Nielsen 1982, 293ff.).

2. Raz has noted that the method of reflective equilibrium cannot assist in deciding whether to undergo a certain process of conversion, such as, from being a utilitarian to being a puritan fundamentalist, because the reflective equilibria of the two would be radically different. Raz adds that there is no reason to rely on the *present* as a better guide than the *previous* equilibrium (or for that matter a predicted future one), which makes the method logically inapplicable to decisions about conversions of that sort (Raz 1982, 322, 324). Daniels (1979*a*, 281) mentions the issue of the convergence of equilibria of different persons at different times, but does not refer to the deeper problems of identity involved in making such equilibria converge. My argument is both an intergenerational and an interpersonal extension of Raz's convincing critique.

3. Daniels discusses the "evidential" relationship between convergence and objectivity and defends the idea of wide equilibrium in terms of this relationship (Daniels 1979*a*, 273ff.). But again, convergence might be an indication of "truth" only within a group of people sharing certain epistemic and normative conditions; and these do not occur in the transtemporal, genethical sphere. And there is no escape from the "provinciality" of human psychology or biology through a constructed idealized agreement, as suggested by Daniels (p. 276), because although there is a limit to idealization, there is no conceivable limit to possible future changes in the nature of man and society.

4. A relativist objection of Kantian epistemology consists of an attempt to explain the allegedly *a priori* conditions of human perception and understanding in evolutionary terms. Once human beings are sufficiently changed (either by slow evolutionary process or by *our* swift genetic manipulation, the very notion of *a priori* is put in perspective. Archimedean points become relative to changeable epistemic or normative systems.

5. The question whether theory acceptance in science is similar to that in ethics or whether it can rely on more solid grounds of a separately based methodology cannot be pursued here. The possible difference between science and ethics in their methods of theory acceptance may hinge on the difference between the status of "truth" and "goodness" (which will be addressed below). It is thus difficult to say whether the value of achieving a *coherent system* of

beliefs and principles in ethics is a normative requirement dictated by an ideal of the sort of life which can be said to have value and "meaning," or whether it is a meta-ethical, methodological rule for theory acceptance. Aristotle's insistence on finding a supreme good that would support the system of all other goods can be interpreted in either way. Although mentioning holism at the beginning of his article, Raz does not discuss the option of taking it as the basis for a concept of truth in ethics and says little about the way the *un*connected beliefs we have can be grounded in reasons (Raz 1982, 323). Is there a nonfoundationalist alternative to justification as "a matter of the mutual support of many considerations of everything fitting together into one coherent view" (Rawls 1971, 21)?

6. Daniels suggests that the philosophy of mind is often *ideological* and that the "deep" theoretical assumptions about personal identity, for instance, which are said to be exposed by "puzzle cases," are of little help in solving moral dilemmas. He therefore suspects that puzzle cases, abstracted from the social setting, may hide the implicit ideological feature of our approach to the case at hand under the guise of revealing the metaphysically basic "facts" that supposedly solve it (Daniels 1979*b*, 276–278). I certainly agree with Daniels's point about the value-laden nature of our metaphysics of personal identity, and I believe that it is particularly pertinent to genesis issues. What is required is a wide equilibrium, in which metaphysical and ethical choices are made *en bloc.* Nevertheless, only "puzzle cases" can test the limits of idealization, that is, the point at which an imagined case becomes so farfetched that it does not satisfy those "ideological" preconditions on which we insist in the definition of the subject matter (e.g., rights of *persons,* or *human* value). In that sense, wide reflective equilibrium, through imaginary, partly contrived cases, is irreplaceable in genethics.

7. Some philosophers wish to support their meta-ethical preference for the person-affecting view by directing our attention to the repugnance of impersonal moral principles, which dictate working for the *general* happiness, even at the expense of the welfare of individuals (see, for example, MacLean 1983, 186). However, these philosophers should realize the two-pronged nature of the normative case for person-affecting views: sometimes these views turn out to have unpalatable implications, such as indifference to the possibility of reducing the general amount of suffering in the world.

8. See Perry 1926, 126 for a very similar methodological strategy: "It follows that there can be no conclusive proof of a general definition of value, short of its success in facilitating the solution of all questions of value."

9. H. Sidgwick, 1907, bk. I, chap. IX, sec. 4; G. E. Moore, *Principia Ethica,* sec. 50.

10. A very incisive articulation of this idea can be found in the influential work of R. B. Perry: value (in the "generic," metaethical sense) is relational, related to human interests: "The fact that M takes an interest in *a* consists in a relation of *a* to M; but this fact itself is not relative to M's judgment about it, or to the judgment of any other subject. The judgments about such facts may be as universal or as absolute, as true or false, as any logic or theory of knowledge can possibly require" (Perry 1926, 38). I should add that the person-affecting thesis is compatible with the view—like Perry's (p. 52)—treating desire as prior to its

object, as well as the view—like Raz's—treating the object as prior and seeking to explain what makes it worthy of being desired. In other words, the *direction* of the relation of value and evaluator is not an issue for the person-regarding view. Value can exist independently of the act of valuation (and in that respect is not similar to Berkeleyan "sense data"), but it must affect *someone, somehow*.

11. Joseph Raz argues for "a humanistic principle," according to which "the explanation and justification of the goodness or badness of anything derives ultimately from its contribution, actual or possible, to human life and its quality" (Raz 1986, 194). This appears to be a person-affecting principle, especially as Raz adds that the humanistic principle is not committed to the idea that every life has intrinsic value (ibid.). However, I am not sure whether Raz would be willing to go all the way with many of the implications of a person-affecting view.

12. The third concept in the Platonic triad, beauty, seems to lie somewhere between truth and goodness. Raz correctly sees no contradiction between the humanistic principle and the intrinsic value of works of art (pp. 200–201). However there are many philosophers who would resist the person-affecting concept of value in aesthetics, although they would go along with it in ethics. Intuitively I can better see the plausibility of an impersonalist understanding of the concepts of "harmony" or "variety" than of any moral value; yet, so many aesthetic values have to do with human perception and the way a human mind is "affected" by certain experiences that the analogy of beauty and truth becomes less attractive. However, the nature of aesthetic value lies beyond the scope of our discussion.

13. On this I agree with James Griffin, who rejects a mentalistic analysis of value. Desires (and even more so volitions, I should add) cannot be exhaustively analyzed in experiential terms. His notion of accomplishment, as the typical nonmentalistic kind of human value, is again fully compatible with a person-regarding view, and indeed intuitively we consider accomplishment as something typically achieved by "volitional" beings, and hardly attributable to "the world." Griffin does not explicitly address the problem of impersonalism, but from his understanding of utility in terms of well-being, and the desire-centered analysis of value, one may surmise that he would adhere to a person-affecting approach. See Griffin 1986, pt. 1, particularly pp. 64–68, and, what might be the closest to my view, p. 157.

14. A philosophical example of that fallacy is Callicott 1984, 299ff.

15. Animals are a controversial case because it is not clear whether they have interests, or "volitions" of some kind. If we decide they have, then for our purposes of identifying the carriers of value they should be regarded as "persons." But it is hard to see how trees can have standing, as claimed by some radical environmental theorists.

16. Sumner 1986 is also an example for many ecologists' confusion between the anthropocentrism of subjectivism and that of the person-affecting conception. In a convincing critical response in the same volume, Morris treats plants and inanimate objects as *indirect* moral objects, deriving their standing from the way they affect human beings (the direct moral objects). I would add to the list of indirect objects potential (future) human beings.

17. But as this meta-ethical analysis does not tell us which volitions constitute the *right* values, normative value theory has to articulate criteria for distinguishing between the valuable and the valueless. For genethics there is the particular problem of formulating criteria for the *formation* of volitions, as we will see in chapter 6. If the volitions of future people are not given, then it might be that these genesis problems could only be solved in terms of *our* volitions.

18. One should again be cautious however not to confuse person-affectingness and emotivism. Hobbes, for instance, says that good and evil "are ever used with relation to the person that useth them." Although the person-affecting thesis agrees with Hobbes that nothing is simply and absolutely good or evil in the sense of being "taken from the nature of the objects themselves," I do not wish to deny "any common rule of good and evil," as long as these values relate to the volitions of *some* persons (See *Leviathan*, pt. 1, ch. 6). The same distinction between restricted volitionism, which is a version of emotivism, and volitionism as person-affectingness applies to Hume.

CHAPTER 4: EXISTENCE

1. Bayles 1980 is definitely the most comprehensive essay on futurity problems that is written from a generocentric point of view (see especially chap. 2 and the three appendices). I follow Bayles in many issues, such as the distinction between actual and potential people, the person-affecting framework, the flaws of contractarian or utilitarian solutions to genesis problems, the interdependence of population policies and intergenerational distribution of resources. However, being specifically concerned with questions of population, Bayles deals only sparingly with the other two dimensions of genethics: existence and identity.

2. I intentionally avoid the abortion issue, which is sometimes debated in terms of the moral standing of "potential" people, for this is *not* the notion of potentiality I am suggesting to use here. Whether "a wonder kitten" (which by using a wonder drug will eventually become a person) is a nonperson still deserving of moral concern (e.g., not to be aborted) is a metaphysical problem which—as George Sher rightly points out—cannot be decided on formal, logical grounds (such as Hare's version of the Golden Rule) *alone* (Sher 1976/1977, 188–190). The notion of potentiality used in the abortion debate is based on views regarding the properties that a being will eventually have and which will make "it" a human being (Hare 1974/1975, 209–210). Such a concept of potentiality assumes that a being actually exists, although it does not yet have the full properties of a moral subject; our concept of potentiality is defined here through the dependence of this existence on our choice. For a deep and detailed discussion of the notion of potentiality in the context of both abortion and procreation, see Tooley 1983, chap. 6. My use of the term "potential" is closer to what Tooley calls "possible," but his solution to genethical paradoxes is similar to the one suggested here in its person-affecting nature (see Tooley 1983, chap. 7).

3. Part of Mary Warren's failure to account within a person-affecting conception for the wrongness of conceiving a miserable child, a failure elegantly

analyzed by Anglin, is due to her confusion between a metaphysical concept of potentiality and a volitional one (of the type suggested here). She defines a potential person as "an entity which is not now a person but which is capable of developing into a person, given certain biologically and/or technologically possible conditions." Once the ambiguity is removed and a volitional definition adopted, the full consequences of a symmetry between the creation of happy people and the avoidance of creating unhappy ones can be drawn, without being exposed to Anglin's correct criticism (see Warren 1977, 275ff.; and Anglin 1978).

4. One might follow Govier's idea of treating future actual people as less real than present actual people, because the former's existence is merely probable (Govier 1979, 109). But such ontological distinctions of degrees of reality are controversial and in any case superfluous from the point of view of deciding moral considerability, which is a yes-or-no issue.

5. Again, I avoid the abortion debate, and, as in the case of wrongful life, I wish to remain on the theoretically (and morally) safe side by referring to the preconceptive period as that in which persons might be considered potential. For Platonists believing in the preconceptive existence of an identifiable soul even this might be considered not early enough for the demarcation of actuality. But then, if the soul is eternal, it seems that it must be treated as always and necessarily actual.

6. A diametrically opposite view is presented by Stearns 1972, 621. Stearns, motivated by anti-Narvesonian impersonalism, lays on us duties of beneficence toward children whom we have contracted (i.e., chosen) to produce, but exempts us from any duty toward people whose future existence we can predict but over which we have no control.

7. Delattre draws the analogy between saving for the future without knowing for sure the number and identity of future people and trying to save people from a house on fire without knowing whether there actually are any people in the house and who they are. In both cases the very possibility that there are human beings having certain needs lays upon us moral responsibility. Their "actual" existence is not a condition of such responsibility (Delattre 1971/1972). This is an attempt to ground obligations to future generations without granting rights to nonexisting people (p. 257). But the attempt is based on epistemological considerations (the lack of certainty regarding the existence of people in the future or in the burning house) rather than on the logical distinction between actual and potential people. The analogy (and indeed the responsibility) applies, therefore, only to what we called future actual people.

8. See Parfit 1984, 351–356, who refers to the problem as that of "nonidentity", and Kavka 1982, 93–95, who dubs it as "the paradox of future individuals." The same challenge is raised by Adams 1979, 57, who claims that any economic and energy policy affects the patterns of marriage and family planning and hence the particular identity of future people. See also Schwartz 1978, 3–7, who refers to the problem as that of "the Disappearing Beneficiaries."

9. In the whole discussion of the actual-potential distinction, and particularly in the counterargument to Parfit's reliance on strong identity I follow an original and forceful article by Trudy Govier. Govier not only adheres to an

actual-potential distinction, but convincingly distinguishes between the future (probable) existence of *some* (unidentifiable) people, and *specific* people (having full personal identity). See Govier 1979, particularly 110–111. However, I part company with her concerning the asymmetry issue, which will be discussed below. For a similar solution to the paradox of future individuals in terms of a distinction between the actual existence of people of a certain kind and the actual existence of specific people, see Jones 1976, 40.

10. In the course of the discussion of equality of opportunity Bernard Williams raises the same question, arguing that there must be a limit to the degree of abstraction of the identity of individual persons from the social and environmental conditions in which they "happen" to live. But he concedes that even the individual's deepest "characteristics could be *pre-arranged* by interference with the genetic material" (Williams 1973, 246), creating "dizzying consequences." Genethics is concerned exactly with these dizzying consequences, whereas ethics is concerned with the treatment of actual people, who are always individuated by *some* properties.

11. The whole notion of potentiality thus assumes free will. In a deterministic picture of an inevitable future the person denoted by such definite descriptions is necessarily a unique individual, even though its identity is not *known* to us in the present (see Burgess 1978). The first person born in London in January 2015 is, therefore, fully potential only if we can choose to create a state of affairs in which there is no such being. But it is a partly actual person if there will be such a person, though we do not know whether it will be male or female, black or white, and so forth.

12. Peter Singer, too, assigns moral standing to inevitably existing people in the future despite their having no determinate particular identity. However, Singer is solely concerned with the number of those inevitable people, whereas I believe that their personal traits might sometimes affect our decision whether to treat them as actual or potential (i.e., the way the distinction is relativized should be more explicitly articulated). Singer proposes a principle according to which we should not add to the population of inevitably existing future people if a subgroup of the expanded world with the same number of the inevitable persons will have a lower average quality of life. But, having given up the requirement of identifiability of inevitable people, how would Singer *identify* that subgroup? It seems that defining what we call the group of actual future people only in terms of number is not a sufficiently rich way of referring to *them*, and once genesis problems involve different numbers (as Singer's subgroup), the whole group of possible future unidentifiable persons becomes potential. See Singer 1976, 88 and 99 n. 9. For a more detailed discussion of Singer's view, see below, chap. 5.

13. There is a longstanding debate on the moral status of past (dead) people and the nature of our obligations toward them. I do not have any particular view concerning the extent of our obligations to past people, but I would certainly wish to include them in the group of *actual* people; for their existence is obviously not dependent on our decision and their identity is fully fixed. So they are at least candidates for moral concern. In relation to *potential* people I reach the conclusion opposite to that of Kavka, who argues that future potential

people deserve the same concern as present people, whereas past people deserve less (Kavka 1978, 188–189). But note that with respect to those express wishes of past people that would certainly have been different today had the person still existed, and different in a way that would have been dependent on *us,* these past people are better viewed as potential. This is a form of what might be called "retroactive paternalism."

14. This sci-fi example has its real-life counterparts. In February 1990 an American woman decided to conceive a child as a last chance of finding a bone-marrow donor for the child's ailing sister. Her decision raised a heated public debate as to the ethical legitimacy of such a decision. Similar cases in medical ethics concern the creation of human embryos as a source for brain cells proven to be the only known therapy in Alzheimer and Parkinson diseases. The compromise solution of allowing the use of cells from naturally aborted embryos while prohibiting the intentional conception of children for that kind of use is psychologically understandable and maybe pragmatically justifiable, but it seems to me logically and ethically inconsistent.

15. Kavka ultimately derives the undesirability of the existence of restricted lives from the idea of the dignity of persons. But as we have already seen in chapter 2, this is an idea that is particularly difficult to reconcile with impersonalism, for it is a typically person-affecting value or principle. See Kavka 1982, 105–106. See also Bayles 1975/1976, 301–302. Bayles tries to justify a legal prohibition on the creation of lives of a quality below a certain level; but it is not clear whether his justification is social in nature, that is, pertaining to the welfare of actual beings, or in terms of the good of the potential persons.

16. See Woodward 1985/1986, 815. Woodward tries to justify the existence of nonconsequentialist reasons for the moral wrongness of such a premature pregnancy. But although his general argument for the validity of nonconsequentialist reasoning in morality is cogent, he fallaciously conflates cases of promises and discrimination of actual people and genesis decisions regarding potential people. Woodward's analogy between promises and procreation (p. 825–826) fails to take seriously the difference between harming an actual person by making a promise to him (and creating an expectation on his part) which is known to be impossible to fulfill, and deciding to conceive a child whose future rights would not be respected. (The same criticism can be directed at McMahan's similar analogy in McMahan 1981/1982, 125.) Even if there are "deontological" constraints on the fourteen-year-old girl, these are typically "parentocentric," self-regarding, or at least not regarding any individual child; anyway they do not create any rights on the part of the potential child (not to be born). In that respect Woodward fails to overcome Parfit's nonidentity problem, which is the main project of his paper.

It is also a highly doubtful strategy to prohibit "the creation of rights and obligations that would probably or inevitably be violated" (p. 821), since this would entail a total prohibition on the creation of new persons. For as there cannot be any human being who would be exempt from all pain and suffering, so there cannot be any human being who would never be a victim of any act of deception, harm, discrimination, and immoral treatment. Woodward's prohibition on the creation of situations in which rights would be violated can be grounded only in impersonal terms (the minimization of right-violation in the world); but this contradicts his attempt to salvage person-affectingness from Parfit's critique. For exactly the same reasons, MacLean's attempt to distinguish between harming and wronging as a way to justify in nonconsequentialist terms a prohibition on the creation of handicapped children cannot overcome the problem of the absence of an individuated subject who is the wronged party. See MacLean 1983, 196.

17. It is thus a fallacious analogy that Kavka presents between the (potential) slave child and a person getting hold of the only source of water in a village and demanding an exceedingly high price for it from his actually existing fellow-inhabitants, for *pace* Kavka, existence is "a benefit" only to actual human beings, and thus no procedure for providing it "for some group of potential recipients" can be classified as extortion. Nor does Kavka's characterization of life as something that people "would pay practically any price" to have make sense in the case of potential people. (See Kavka, 1982, 106–108.) Equally problematic is Kavka's condemnation of the argument justifying the conception of a slave child by referring to the *post hoc* (extorted) consent of the child to the "deal" (Kavka 1982, 110). Again, potential people cannot be seen as partners to any contract, and *ipso facto* to any *unfair* contract. To be a victim of extortion one has to be able to say that one could have got a better deal, which is impossible to show in the slave-child case.

18. Narveson's analogy was invented in response to Sumner's critique of the inconsistency of the asymmetry argument (Sumner 1978, 108–109). I share Sumner's critique of the inconsistency, though I reject the fully impersonal, total-utilitarian point of view from which it is derived. Sumner wants all potential people to be counted in genesis considerations; I wish to allow only actual people to be counted; Narveson takes the middle, inconsistent, way: counting potential persons when they are expected to suffer, but only actual people when the potential ones are expected to be happy. The same inconsistency appears in Narveson's second conclusion (p. 55): "new additions ought to be made if the benefit to all, *excluding* the newcomer, would exceed the cost to all, *including* him or her." Why should the inclusion criteria be dependent on the difference between benefit and cost? For a similar critique, see McMahan 1981/1982, 101.

19. And see the discussion of the double-edged force of some arguments for asymmetry, including Narveson's, in chapter 2 above. There are many other philosophers who adopt some form of the asymmetry argument (e.g., Govier 1979, 111ff.; Warren 1978, 282–283) who argue that it is wrong to create people whom one knows are going to be unhappy, although it is morally neutral to create happy people; see Bennett 1978, 62–63, who follows Narveson's asymmetry arguments. Bennett offers the following rule to account for the asymmetry: "The question whether an action A is morally obligatory depends only upon the utilities of people who would exist if A were not performed." Thus, it is obligatory to *avoid* conceiving a defective child; for failure to do so would be a disutility for the child. But, as we have already argued in chapter 2, it is hard to see how being born defective is itself a disutility in person-regarding terms. Michael Tooley argues for asymmetry in terms of the analogy to promising: producing a miserable child is

morally wrong like making a promise that I know in advance that I will not be able to fulfill. But there is nothing wrong in refraining from making promises that can be honored or begetting children to whom I will be able to exercise my parental duties (Tooley 1983, chap. 7).

20. I agree, though, with Hanser's critique of Parfit in the second part of his article. Parfit at least implies that by causing someone to exist with a life worth living one benefits him or her. Since I object to this proposition as being inconsistent with a genuine person-affecting conception, I take Hanser's point that no amount of benefit allegedly involved in bringing someone into this world can outweigh (and hence justify) the suffering of the subject once born into the world. However, Hanser, like so many others, tends to support the asymmetry principle on the basis of the priority of avoiding suffering over the creation of happiness; this is a separate (normative) issue, to be raised only *after* the logical assignability of utility of whatever sort is settled (which is the issue here).

21. A similar critique of Hare's equal treatment of abortion and contraception is proposed by Hutchinson, but on a slightly different basis. According to Hutchinson, abortion consists in wronging an actual being, whereas contraception is only preventing the actualization of a possible happy life. Hutchinson's view is that actual lives (like those of fetuses) have priority over the lives of potential beings (which also have some value). Only through a Williams-type argument, defending the integrity of individuals, can the prevention of the procreation of happy children be justified. This view can be maintained only because Hutchinson believes in the existence of moral reasons that are not person-affecting (Hutchinson 1982, 66ff.). The view presented here does not have to appeal to "Williams-type defenses" for acting against the utility principle in matters of procreation, because it denies impersonalism altogether.

22. This good might be considered less weighty than the parallel misery, as Negative Utilitarians maintain, and thus greater amounts of it would be required to outweigh the misery added to the world; but it would still be considered an intrinsic good. Negative Utilitarianism is, in that respect, irrelevant to the logical issue of symmetry; it relates only to the manner in which different sorts of utility are weighted in the utility calculus. And see Leslie 1983 and 1989 for a similar argument connecting symmetry and impersonalism. Leslie's general point is that the existence of a large number of happy people justifies the existence of some small number of unhappy ones.

23. In my book on supererogation I argued that supererogatory acts are "continuous" with nonobligatory morally valuable acts, that is to say they have the same kind of moral quality or value. Consequently, if procreation is value-neutral, it cannot be supererogatory. See Heyd 1982, 130ff. See also on the subject of supererogation and future generations Sikora 1979, particularly 465–466; and Anglin 1977, 752.

24. The value of life and the disvalue of misery can, of course, be treated as objective by person-affecting conceptions no less than by impersonalism; misery, for instance, is bad for its subject, indeed for any subject, independent of the person's subjective perception of it.

25. J. Narveson has pointed out to me that the impersonalist might be

satisfied with the very existence of humanity without being concerned with the number of living humans. Many environmentalists are content with the preservation of a threatened species through a policy in which a high percentage of the species' individual members are turned into hamburgers or fur coats.

26. An interesting version of the impersonal conception can be found in *Mishnah,* "Sanhedrin" (chap. 4, sec. 5): with regards to Cain, who slew his [childless] brother, it is said "the *bloods* of thy brother cry" (not "the *blood* of thy brother cries"), since the reference is both to Cain's blood *and* to the blood of his posterity. "Therefore, but a single man was created in the world, to teach that if any man has caused a single soul to perish from Israel scripture imputes to him as though he had caused a whole world to perish" (and the text proceeds to claim the same for saving souls).

27. Note that in his recent book, Nozick tends to the cosmic conception of value and offers a bold Platonic theory of value based on degrees of reality: the more reality, the better. Accordingly, he interprets the divine motives for the creation of the world (and humanity) in totally *non*volitional terms (that is excluding self-interest or needs from the account). See Nozick 1989, 224–225. Nevertheless, Nozick seems still to be bound by some person-affecting inclinations, as he oscillates between the principle of the impersonal value of the existence of (happy) children and the intrinsic value of the existence of humanity on the one hand and the constraints of avoiding Parfit's Repugnant Conclusion and the procreation of slave children on the other (see pp. 228–229).

28. This view is further discussed in Bloch and Heyd 1981. Another thought-experiment that might shed some light on our problem is the challenging Humean question: "Ask yourself, ask any of your acquaintance whether they would live over again the last ten or twenty years of their life." Can the imaginary "replay" of a human life be considered a good? Well, it depends. First, on the identity of the subject living the original life with that living the "replayed" life. Secondly, on the worthiness of the original life. Thus, I am inclined to reject my own former view that if life is worth living, then it is also worth *re*-living, unless the notion is strictly interpreted in person-affecting terms, namely, as a benefit *to* the subject of the double life. See Heyd 1983, esp. 25–27.

29. Is there a philosophically interesting distinction between gratitude (toward persons) and gratefulness (toward states of affairs) as some philosophers hold? Even if there is, it hardly overcomes the logical problems of attributing value to coming to be, since the difference in the objects of both attitudes notwithstanding, the subject in both cases alike must be an actual person whose situation was somehow ameliorated. Filial gratitude cannot similarly be derived from the allegedly supererogatory nature of the parents' choice to create the child. Even if there was some pain involved in the process of creating the child, the child was not the beneficiary of this pain, which for that reason cannot be understood as a "sacrifice." See also Jecker 1989, 74.

30. Elsewhere, Parfit refers to our psychologically deep asymmetrical intuitions as founded on "a bias" toward the future, thus admitting a form of asymmetry *in attitude* to the two forms of nonexistence, although from a "timeless" point of view the symmetry still remains (Parfit 1984, 175).

31. Palle Yourgrau believes, against Nagel, that inexistence before and after

life are ontologically symmetrical and that the only difference between the two is psychological and epistemological (not knowing in advance the identity of the not-yet-conceived person). Yourgrau's suggestion however is based on a mysterious distinction between being and existence (both the dead and the unconceived have being, although they do not exist anymore, or yet, respectively). See Yourgrau 1987, 84–101. Another defense of the symmetry of the two kinds of inexistence is offered by Rosenbaum 1989/1990, who also deals with the possibility that if the two kinds of inexistence are indeed symmetrical, the conclusion can be the opposite to the consolatory one offered by Lucretius, namely that we should fear both death *and* prenatal inexistence (p. 368). We will return to Rosenbaum's argument in chapter 6.

32. There are philosophers who say that although a handicapped child is wronged by its parents when they decide to bring it into the world, society does not interfere because of the value of parents' privacy and autonomy. But this argument does not hold water. For *after* the child is born, society is believed to have the right to intervene in the way the parents treat it in a much more extensive way than in the preconceptive stage of the parents' decision. This may serve as an indication of the logical distinction between the attitude toward potential beings and the treatment of actual beings on the lines suggested here. Otherwise, why is it a legal crime for parents intentionally to cause a handicap in their existing children, whereas it is not a crime to conceive a child while suffering from rubella? The hesitancy of the state to interfere in the mother's treatment of her fetus is a sign of the uncertainty we feel with regard to the fetus' status: is it closer to a potential being or to an actual one? and in what respects and aspects of its life?

It should also be noted that the more privacy the parents are granted in their procreative choices, the more responsibility might be laid upon them for the outcome of their choices. Precisely because a planned handicapped child is an actual person for society, society might have the right to condition noninterference with its creation by laying responsibility on the parents for the child's upbringing. For otherwise it is society that would become responsible for the extra costs involved in taking care of the child. Anyway, this is an intragenerational case of responsibility distribution rather than a genethical one. It is forcefully argued in O'Neill and Ruddick 1979, 25–38. I may add that taking the actual-potential distinction seriously entails an ethical (and maybe legal) distinction between the possibly legitimate interference of the state in the allocation of babies for adoption and the conceptually absurd attempt to regulate artificial insemination. The state has an interest in guaranteeing the actual baby the best parents possible, but it cannot prohibit a woman's trying to conceive by artificial means on the grounds of the "interests of the child" (e.g., to be born into a certain kind of family).

33. For an excellent analysis of the analogy between the genesis problems of parents and God's creation of the world, see Adams 1972, 317–332. Adams takes a person-affecting approach to the subject, but assumes that God is constrained in his creation by his obligation to the species as a whole, which he himself wants to enjoy a certain quality of life (pp. 330–332). This assumption makes it irrational rather than morally wrong for God to create miserable

human beings, inconsistent with his own original intention rather than bad in itself.

34. In the fairly extensive philosophical literature on genesis problems the closest to my generocentric thesis is MacLean 1983. MacLean goes all the way with the implications of Parfit's nonidentity problem and is willing to reach the conclusion that our duty to create a "good world" rather than a bad one should be understood as based solely on *our* ideals and interests. However, MacLean sees the generocentric interest in the continuation of humanity, the conservation of nature, and the transmission of knowledge and culture as a *moral* value (p. 193), since it is the way we give meaning to our lives, an expression of an "extra-phenomenal value." MacLean, I believe, is correct in his analysis of the extraphenomenal interest we have in posterity, but that hardly makes it an obligation, or a moral duty, to *create* posterity, let alone "to create the best world possible" (p. 193), which smacks of impersonalism. Even if there is a self-regarding moral duty to invest our life with meaning, it is a duty only on the assumption that we actually live, (or decide to go on living). The question of the existence of future people (which has been the concern of this chapter) precedes that of the way they should be treated, or the sort of environment we leave to them.

CHAPTER 5: NUMBERS

1. In the often quoted "Tragedy of The Commons," Garrett Hardin elegantly presents the problem of population as a counter-example to the "invisible hand" argument: the satisfaction of individual interests (in procreation) leads to a public disaster (Hardin 1968, 1244). The only way to avoid catastrophe is, Hardin says, political. That includes the legal restriction and regulation of the right of individuals to procreate freely. A similar point is made in Miller and Sartorius 1979: the fact that in many cases individuals do not stand to gain anything by reducing the number of their children makes it necessary to control population trends by governmental policies rather than by an appeal to self-interest or benevolence.

2. I am indebted to Jan Narveson for suggesting the market alternative, although I am more skeptical than he is regarding its morality and efficiency in regulating population trends.

3. See Foot 1978. Note, however, that Foot's classical article deals with the doctrine of "double effect," in which the relevant distinction is between killing and letting die, or between negative and positive duties. Our arguments against asymmetry in chapter 4 make these distinctions irrelevant to genethics. At least from the point of view of the handicapped child there is no difference whether it was just "allowed" to be born in defect or intentionally created so as to suffer from that defect.

4. See Taurek 1976/1977, 300–307, who argues against aggregation in the context of saving lives, and Parfit 1977/1978, who criticizes Taurek's person-affecting approach and its inconsistent application. Parfit argues for the additive nature of utilities both on the intra- and interpersonal levels. Sanders 1988 follows Parfit's generally impersonal view in his proposal to see death not only

as a loss *to* people but also as a loss *of* people (meaning a loss to the world). The fact that rights are less susceptible to aggregation than welfare or "utility" supports our suggestion in chapter 2 that right-based moralities are less likely candidates than their goal-based rivals for handling genethical problems.

5. Some medical ethicists draw a distinction between the duties of the doctor to the individual patient and the duties of society to the "aggregate" overall promotion of health. I believe that this is a plausible distinction (especially as elaborated in the analysis of what Guido Calabresi has dubbed "tragic choices"); yet this is irrelevant to the issue of impersonalism, since society's duty is also—in my view—restricted to the (overall) health of *actual* people, that is, the notion of public health should not be stretched into the really impersonal domain of potential beings.

6. See, for example, Hanser 1990, 55. Hanser raises this issue in his attempt to deny—*contra* Parfit—that nonidentity is problematic, or that person-affecting considerations play a role beside the impersonal ones in deciding genesis problems. Note also that some sort of interpersonal, quantitative comparison must be allowed in order to account for the simple preference of, for example, giving a piece of cake to the person who might enjoy it most.

7. See Griffin 1986, 94–95 and chap. 7, regarding the issue of the extension of intra- to interpersonal considerations in weighting welfare. Griffin's claim that intrapersonal comparisons are sometimes no less difficult than their interpersonal counterparts because of significant changes in personality and character will prove to be highly relevant to our discussion in the next chapter.

8. Of course, one could qualify the average version and allow the procreation of a slightly less happy generation if that were the only way to promote *in the long run* the average happiness of humanity. But how long? And is not this a sacrifice of people's well-being for the sake of the greater well-being of other people, which is objectionable in the same way as the analogous sacrifice of actual people within a generation is objectionable? One could also qualify the average principle by applying it only in cases where the very continuation of the human race is not guaranteed. Thus, it would be justified to bring into the world children less happy than their parents if that were the only way to ensure the continued existence of future generations. The Malthusian warning, then, does not refer to optimum population size, but rather to the duty to refrain from the creation of *that* number of people which would lead to the ultimate destruction of the whole species. But then we are back with the problem of justifying the overriding value of the *existence* of humanity.

9. Note that Parfit, who believes in the benefit involved in the very fact of being born, might find it extremely difficult to *calculate* both average and total utilities involved in various population policies, since as we have shown in chapter 4, even those who (falsely) believe that birth as such is a benefit do not even have a clue as to the *relative weight* of being born in the overall utility of an individual's life. Anyway, our person-affecting approach to value denies any value to coming into existence.

10. Think of the simple case in which both P and N are 1. If we do nothing, John will exist "anyway." If we decide to bring Mary to life, it will be Bob who will inevitably exist ("instead of" John). Now, Singer's principle allows us to

beget Mary as long as either Bob *or* Mary are at least as well off as John. This implies that it is not wrong to have Mary if she is better off than John even though Bob is miserable! Now, if Bob *and* John refer to a person who is at least relatively actual (e.g., to Mary's parents), then the implication sounds definitely immoral (sacrificing the welfare of an actual person in the name of overall utility). And if John and Bob can only be identified as being "one person," then it seems that Mary's parents can go ahead in their procreative plans on a purely parentocentric basis and ignore the requirement not to reduce any abstract (impersonal) standard of living.

For a critique of Singer's solution from a similar point of view (arguing that Singer does not take identity seriously enough), see Parfit 1976*a*.

11. Attfield convincingly criticizes Parfit for his distinction between life that has only a "personal" value (viz., for its subject, who does not regret being alive, although his life is of a very low quality, *barely* worth living) and life that is intrinsically good (worth living). Parfit says that the addition of the latter to the world is morally good, whereas there is no such good (and obligation) in creating life of the former kind. Either any addition of a life with positive value is of (impersonal) moral value, or the addition of worthwhile life can never be thought of as a moral improvement. See Attfield 1987, 166.

12. Hurka's attempt to block the Mere Addition Paradox by an analogy with a collection of paintings is hardly convincing. It is true that there is a sense in which a collection of one hundred superb paintings is better than a collection of the same paintings *plus* two hundred mediocre ones. But we have already shown (in chapter 4) that the value of "collections" of people is "reflexive" in a way that cannot be said of paintings. Brian Barry suggests an argument that is of the same structure as Hurka's: it is worse to kill *n* people thus eliminating a whole culture, than to kill *n* people who belong to different cultures that will all continue after their deaths (Barry 1983, 28–29).

13. The partiality in favor of one's own population size is reflected in the inconsistent asymmetry between our preference of our own world to a much larger (Z-world) which has a greater total but lower average utility, and our unwillingness to treat as superior a world much smaller than our own with a higher average though smaller total utility. See Ng 1989, 242ff., for an elegant critique of the idea of a Repugnant Conclusion. Ng believes that in deciding the number of future people we should follow a total utilitarian guideline as long as their number does not affect us. When it does affect us, we may favor our own interests over those of future people (even when that would mean not opting for the greatest total utility). Ng comes close to a generocentric view, but still gives weight to impersonal considerations in subscribing to total utilitarianism as a generally valid guiding principle. Accordingly, Ng solves Parfit's problems by simply *accepting* the Repugnant Conclusion (p. 242), thus securing the impersonal value of both the continued existence of humanity and its overall highest welfare.

14. This can easily be illustrated by the parallel case of the number of siblings in a nuclear family. The preferences of only children and those of children in larger families differ regarding the desirable or optimal number of children in a family. An only child might be brought up to like his or her status as an only child,

whereas the child in a large family might become dependent on the existence of siblings for his or her welfare. The addition of another child can often change the preferences of a first (only) child in what Jon Elster would call an "adaptive" way. The same applies to the differences in preferences regarding population size and density between New Yorkers and Nebraskans, and theoretically to the differences between our judgments and those of the inhabitants of a demographically smaller (or larger) planet.

15. Adams's view typically reflects that generocentric bias, claiming that a world of a few tens of thousands would call for population increases, but our world, of 4 (sic) billion cannot be improved by adding people, even if their addition is not burdensome to us. However, I am not clear why the reason for Adams's claim, namely using those people as "vessels for additional happiness," does not apply equally to a world of a few tens of thousands. Adams gives no reason for his preference of the current population size. See Adams 1989, 474.

16. For further discussion of the shift in "adaptive preferences," typical to many genesis problems of identity, see chapter 6.

17. P. Gould and W. Kolb, *Dictionary of the Social Sciences*, 1964.

18. P. Ehrlich and R. L. Harriman, *How To Be A Survivor* (New York: Baltimore Books, 1971), 12.

19. Sidgwick offers an impersonal version of an optimum based on the multiplication of average happiness and the number of people enjoying it (Sidgwick 1907, 415–416). His suggestion, in my view, is inconsistent with the person-affecting theory of value expressed in his debate with Moore (see above, chapter 3). For a staunch support of the total, classical version of utilitarianism in the context of fixing optimum population size, see Sumner 1978, 91–111. I tend to agree with Sumner that the classical principle, unlike its average or Rawlsian rivals, can offer a fixed optimal number, but I cannot accept the impersonal ethics in which it is embedded.

20. Dasgupta 1988. A similar version of this article appears elsewhere (Dasgupta 1987). See also Dasgupta 1974 for a similarly person-affecting approach.

21. Dasgupta also challenges the very repugnance of the Repugnant Conclusion as being based on an unrealistic and misleading portrayal of the Z-world by Parfit (p. 117). This criticism is in line with my above argument against the RC as based on a present-state bias.

22. Michael Bayles suggests the "equivalent principle": "a duty not to render it substantially unlikely that future generations can have an indefinitely sustainable quality of life as high as it has, an equivalent quality of life" (Bayles 1980, 21). This principle, however, ignores the genethical aspect and takes the number of future people as given. Bayles himself says that it is derived from the principle of beneficence "to presently existing people," which is exactly the extension that cannot be justified when applied to potential people. Bayles then suggests that the quality of life be first determined and the "population characteristics" adjusted to it (p. 22). But this is also an untenable proposal, since generocentrism claims that the value of a particular quality of life is itself "person-regarding" and hence cannot serve to determine the number of created people.

23. Inequality is less troublesome in the intergenerational sphere than within a generation, because it then involves less envy, less competition, less injury to self-esteem. Nevertheless Parfit strongly argues against any social discount of future generations (Parfit 1983, 31–37). But Parfit's mostly convincing arguments do not address the actual-potential distinction (taking future people as all actual), and hence do not undermine my tentative notion of a discount. It is true that as long as much of the rate of growth in the world is due—as it still is today—to uncoordinated, natural, "inevitable" processes, future people should be considered by us as *actual*, even beyond the next generation or two, and the only arguments for discounting them are the (partly false) epistemological appeals to ignorance of their needs. Distant location in time should not serve as a basis for discrimination. But take family planning, in which both we and our own children can be taken as making decisions regarding *potential* people: here it is not ignorance of the procreative preferences of our offspring but rather the fact that we have some control over these preferences that makes them less weighty in our present choices. This is a different concept of a discount.

24. For an excellent treatment of these and other related topics, which we cannot discuss in any detail in the present essay, see Bayles 1980, particularly chaps. 5 and 6.

25. For a comprehensive discussion of these matters, see Bayles 1979. Bayles argues correctly that the right to procreate "does not constitute an insuperable moral objection to population control" (p. 21), and that the ultimate justification of such control lies in the fact that a limited population growth rate is a public good that can only be achieved for all by political means (p. 17).

26. Again, the market cannot be relied upon here. The number of children produced by the parents' generation is optimal if it is the outcome of free voluntary choices and exchanges. But that fact that all the parents are fully satisfied with the number of offspring is by no means (logically or empirically) connected to the satisfaction of the children. They might, for example, wish to have had more fellow-beings and resent the fact that for egoistic reasons their parents avoided larger families.

27. This is not always sufficiently realized by those who deal with the question of licensing parents, such as Lafollette 1979/1980, 184–185, 193–195. On this issue I fully agree with Jones 1976, 38–39.

28. For an opposite view, restricting the right to reproduce on the basis of the moral standing of the potential child "who is not consulted," see Chadwick 1987, 6. Ruth Chadwick argues that the natural right to reproduce cannot exhaust the moral considerations of reproduction and believes in the coherence of suits for wrongful life. Others deny the natural right of parenthood on the basis of self-determination involving the hypothetical consent of the child, for such a consent can make sense only after the child's birth (Floyd and Pomerantz 1981, 137–138). I agree with the view that there is no "relational right to have children," but I leave open the question whether or not there is a parentocentric right to parenthood.

Onora O'Neill offers an excellent analysis of the tension between private and public interests in the context of procreation, but intentionally limits her discussion to the *means* of regulating population growth. She also consciously avoids the case of wrongful life. However, although I can see why O'Neill believes that deciding to conceive a child creates parental responsibilities and duties, it is not clear why from the point of view of the child it makes a difference whether the conception was intentional or unintended. I cannot pursue that complex issue here, but it seems that parental obligations and duties, not being a matter of agreement between parents and children, must relate to the distribution of responsibility between actual people, that is, between (usually) biological procreators and society. See O'Neill 1979, 29ff.

CHAPTER 6: IDENTITY

1. In Rorty's own formulation, the fourth is the issue of "what sorts of characteristics identify a person as *essentially* the person she is, such that if those characteristics were changed, she would be a significantly different person, though she might still be differentiated and re-identified as the same" (Rorty 1976, 2). Thus, a person might undergo a radical change of character in which she would not see *herself* as "the same person" anymore, although her finger-prints would still serve as a means of reidentifying her as metaphysically (or legally) the same person.

2. The question of the essential nature of the human species is also of interest in genethical theory, although it does not have the first-person character-istic of the evolution of an individual's identity. We will see, however, that the process of a gradual change in the identity of the human race initiated by human beings resembles the decision regarding the change in identity of an individual (whether taken by another individual, such as the parents, or by the individuals themselves in the course of their lives). But even here, we are interested in the ethics of evolutionary change from the internal point of view, namely as a choice of the human race regarding *its* future identity, rather than in the abstract metaphysical definition of what is "real" human nature, its "objective essence."

3. Ruth Chadwick cautions that a decision to beget a child "is not simply a question of self-determination or of using one's own body as one wishes," for "it produces a new person who is not consulted" (Chadwick 1987, 6). Yet, from a consistently person-affecting view no consultation regarding either the exis-tence or the identity of a child is conceptually or hypothetically possible, and hence the fact that the child is not consulted does not make the parents' decision either paternalistic or constrained by the standing of the child.

4. Parfit 1973, Parfit 1984, chap. 15. See also Zemach 1987/1988, 227ff. Zemach, who suggested a nonessentialist view of personal identity long before Parfit (see Zemach 1987/1988, 209 n.), shares Parfit's impersonalism as well as his belief in the relative insignificance of personal identity for ethics, but in even more radical form. Both Parfit and Zemach find utilitarianism the only possible ethical theory consistent with impersonalism, both in the sense of the alternative to person affectingness and the alternative to essentialist theories of personal identity. For a powerful critique of Parfit's atomistic view of personal identity, see Korsgaard 1989. Korsgaard develops a Kantian view of personal identity in terms of the unity of agency as an alternative to Parfit's conception that is based on Humean sequences of experiences. Personal identity is shown to be a *practi-*

cal necessity. This accords well with my Aristotelian claim (see below, chap. 8) that the intentional structure of action points to the importance of *personal* survival, without being committed to any particular definition of the precise borderlines of "the person."

5. The idea of the gradual formation of personal identity (under the metaphor of a branching tree) should not be confused with Parfit's notion of personal identity as based on mere psychological continuity (Parfit 1984, 207). Although there is of course an element of continuity in the former, the stem (or the branches that have turned into stems) constitutes the essential nature of the person. The view proposed here might be described as gradual essentialism. Even if from a third-person point of view there is no essential core of human traits which constitutes one's identity, from the first-person point of view there is a set of such traits, without which persons cannot think of themselves as being the same person.

6. Through psychotherapy or conversion we can partly undo the work of the parents who forged our identity in early childhood, but so far it seems completely fantastical that we could as adults change our genetic makeup.

7. A notable exception is Glover, who elaborates the analogy between genetical and educational means of determining the type of persons we create. See particularly Glover 1979, 87, and 1984, chap. 3, which is a most comprehensive and sensitive discussion of the ethics of genesis formation, although not from a person-affecting view, and not as part of a general genethical view.

8. There is a deep psychological threat in the blurring of borderlines, especially those defining the human as distinct from the nonhuman. Glover correctly emphasizes that the fear (particularly relevant to genethics) of not being able to decide the *moral* status of a certain creature is a widespread cause of opposition to radical tampering with human nature (Glover 1984, chap. 2). This, I believe, in general stands behind much of the human tendency to avoid facing genethical dilemmas.

9. Glover correctly observes that the distinction between negative and positive in this context presupposes a concept of a "defect," about which we are far from being clear (Glover 1984, chap. 2). We might add that the asymmetry in common attitudes to negative and positive genetic intervention is hard to justify, as Negative Utilitarianism in general is a problematic theory. From a generocentric point of view it seems that other things being equal (risk, knowledge of the consequences, relation to the core of already determined traits) there are no grounds for such asymmetry.

10. Pinocchio, Collodi's famous marionette, is potentially human in the metaphysical sense when at the beginning of the story he exists in (or as) a piece of wood, but he is actual in the sense that his human traits are already fixed in him, which is exactly the ground for his plea to be saved from the carpenter's hatchet. The combination of Geppetto's genesis power in carving a humanlike marionette out of a piece of wood and this marionette's gradual coming to fully human life is a beautiful metaphor for identity formation by both genetic engineering and education as we wish to describe it.

11. Approaching the formation of identity (genetic identity in particular) as a one-time event rather than as a gradual process leads to paradoxes such as

treating any genetic intervention as amounting to murder! (Karin-Frank 1987, 225–226). This approach also denies the analogy between education and genetic engineering, claiming that the latter is a violent attack on a person's autonomy (Karin-Frank 1987, 221ff.). But we shall later see that a concentric view can coherently deal with the distinction between relevant stages of evolving identity and the corresponding degree of autonomy and the way in which it constrains intervention—both educational and genetic.

12. Note that if the aggressive nature is part of the identity of the future person, the justification for the removal of its genetic cause cannot appeal to the person's own interest but only to the welfare (security) of other (actual) coexisting or neighboring beings.

13. See particularly Jones 1976, 35, who holds the apparently inconsistent view that parents have obligations to secure both the "detachable" and the "undetachable" (identity-fixing) properties of their children, although the children have no corresponding rights. Nor do future people have a right to be created through a *random* natural process rather than through a controlled and artificially engineered technique (Glover 1979, 87).

14. An interesting case is the hypothetical "meddling with the sexual orientation of children" (Crocker 1979). Should we give a three-year old child a medication that would guarantee his or her heterosexual inclination later in life? On the one hand, sexual orientation is fairly close to the core of the child's identity, and hence is potential for us, the parents. This implies that we are free to choose sexual orientation for our children before it is naturally formed. On the other hand, this freedom might be curtailed by hardships imposed by social norms (or by other existing traits of the individual) involved in having a particular sexual tendency. The indeterminacy of the case reflects the uncertainty we feel toward the status of sexual orientation in the "identity tree" as well as our hesitancy regarding the way we want society to treat various tendencies. Crocker's solution, namely giving the pill because that is what the child would have chosen, is hardly plausible, since a person without a sexual orientation cannot choose one—unless this choice is based on other (prior) traits and interests (such as conforming to the majority practice, believing in certain religious prohibitions, etc.).

15. Cloning might be a limiting case on the other side of the spectrum: it is the creation of a human being which leaves no room for variation, which is an exact replica of what we are. Why do we shudder at the idea of having exact copies of ourselves almost as fervently as we do at the idea of having offspring completely different from us (nonhuman)? What is the value of that middle ground between the absolute conservatism of cloning and the radical anarchism of wild genetic engineering? Ruth Chadwick rightly denies the adequacy of the arguments against cloning based on its "unnaturalness," on its being based on human *hubris,* and on the right of children to be born genetically unique (i.e., with no other identical copies roaming around in the world). See Chadwick 1982, 201–209. See also chapter 8.

16. As in population policies, the distributive considerations involved in the regulation of procreation (e.g., forced sterilization of the mentally deranged) must face the problem of balancing the value of the welfare of future *actual*

people with the value of privacy and the right to parenthood. This balancing may be achieved by means of a social contract mechanism. But note that prohibiting the "genetically unfit" from procreating altogether is harsher than limiting the *number* of children.

17. Jon Elster has noted that by mastering evolution, humanity has gained the power to maximize not only its own biological utility by adapting itself to the environment, but also that of future generations by manipulating their genetic traits: from local maximizers humans have become global maximizers, being able to forgo certain short-term advantages for the sake of long-term rewards. This is the creative mastering of the evolutionary process itself. (Elster 1979, chap. 1). But, if the generocentric perspective is adopted, then the idea of global maximization becomes problematic and cannot be viewed as just an extension of the local concept. In Elster's words, global maximization cannot be accounted for in functional terms but must refer to intentional attitudes. See Macklin 1979, where a case is made for genetic intervention in individual cases but not as a general eugenic policy. However, I do not understand why Macklin views genetic betterment as "dehumanizing." It seems to be dehumanizing only in the neutral descriptive sense of potentially leading to traits other than those now associated with humanity.

18. Detaching the genetic determination of persons' identities from the natural process of conception, pregnancy, and birth raises interesting philosophical questions, as provocatively noted by Rosenbaum 1989, 363, n. 31. For example, an individual might say in the future: "I wish I was born 50 years later." Nevertheless, despite the crucial role of genetic makeup in the constitution of our identity, the parents, home, and historical and cultural background into which we are born also play an important part in our identity, and hence would always make such expressions of regret not fully coherent.

19. It is equally problematic whether or not the state should regulate the ways in which children are reared, such as in the issue of whether homosexual or lesbian couples should be allowed to adopt a child. Such adoptions would definitely change the traditional concept of a family, but if the family setup is itself a basic identity-forming factor, then it cannot be asked whether such changes are in the interest of the child.

20. Recall the story of Pinocchio, which was mentioned in the first section of this chapter. At the beginning, there is only a vaguely human voice coming out of a chunk of wood, imposing only the minimal (negative) duty of not hurting the "creature" mysteriously hidden in it. The carpenter's responsibility consists merely in the cautious use of the hatchet; Geppeto, who receives the piece of wood from the carpenter, can use it to carve a marionette to *his* liking. But gradually the marionette develops a life of its own, and a "moral" relationship is created between it and its creator. This implies more and more duties of respect for the individual character of the marionette-boy, which has acquired certain irreversible traits.

21. Glover believes that autonomy is a supreme educational value and may be promoted even by genetic engineering, but he seems to base his view on the impersonal value of autonomy rather than on the "real" interests of the child

(its core identity), and accordingly believes in prohibiting the creation of "happy slaves" by either genetic or educational means. See Glover 1984, chap. 12.

22. Analogously, Dewey's principle of "expanded options," according to which education must primarily seek the development of the richest repertory of options for choice, is criticized by Bereiter for being too value-neutral and potentially legitimizing the upbringing of a child to be, for example, dishonest. Bereiter argues that "child care should be concerned with increasing the quality of children's immediate experience" and boldly gives a generocentric answer to the question "by whose standard?": "Inevitably, by the standard of people who have control" (Bereiter 1973, 14, 23–24).

23. I fully share Ruddick's denial of a sharp dichotomy of the parents as either gardeners or guardians (O'Neill and Ruddick 1979, 125–128). As Ruddick aptly puts it, the interests of the child, which are the focus of education, are a mixture of the parents' will and the child's needs (or in my terms, the generocentric formation of new branches and the constraints of the given stem). I would only add that there is a hierarchy in the exercise of these two functions: the more evolved the products of our gardening, the wider our responsibility as guardians and custodians. The idea of education as a genesis process cannot accept theories of education that see the role of the parents *solely* as that of custodians.

24. The emphasis on the issue of paternalism in the philosophy of education is directly linked (either as a cause or as an effect) to the relative neglect of discussion of education as a genesis process. Most philosophers of education (like Mill) regard the *incompetence* of the child as the starting point for the justification of paternalistic adult intervention in the child's life. But incompetence typically presupposes a set of actual rights and interests that a child can be said to have although it is not capable (yet) of exercising them by itself. Our concern is with the creation of these very rights and interests rather than the question of the stage at which the parental rights should be transmitted to the child. And see Bereiter 1973, 10, who admits that for a child to be able to exercise autonomy we have to shape his personality, and that only gradually and at the age of adolescence can he become the subject of "educational rights." See also Aviram 1990. Aviram discusses my view (p. 220 and n. 28) as part of his radical argument for the liberation of children. I am indebted to Aviram for directing my attention to some of the issues in the philosophy of education that proved relevant to my project.

25. There are, of course, those extreme cases in which a child is removed by the state from its parents' home. Such a drastic move is justified in terms of the actual interests and rights of the child (not to be abused). The justification of compulsory school education runs on similar lines of protecting the child's right to become equipped with what would be good for *it*. Here the state is not acting only on the basis of its coordinative role.

26. Again, much of the literature in the philosophy of education focuses on the distribution of the right to educate between state and parents through the lens of children's rights, that is, who can better protect these rights and develop the actual in-built interests of the child. The genethical perspective in education

is concerned with the distributive problem as a genesis issue on a par with that of numbers, that is, the distribution among state and families of the power and right to decide the number of future people.

27. For the tension between the social interests of creating citizens of a certain type and parental freedom to determine the child's character (e.g., in the often discussed case of the Amish), see Henley 1979, 254–264. Henley lists the various sources of the authority to educate, including the autonomy of the parents to decide their children's values, but does not specifically refer to the genesis aspects underlying this parental autonomy.

28. Cases of international adoption procedures or the fostering of Jewish children in Polish convents during World War II are interesting borderline cases. Many people have the strong intuition that the original, biological identity of the child includes also the national or religious identity of its natural parents, that is, that these belong to the core identity. Therefore, although the child is too young to be conscious of this identity, those who rear it have to respect this "inborn" aspect of its life and not to force on it the nationality or religion of its foster parents. I tend, however, to think that these intuitions are based on the biological facts of the way the child looks (in the case of adoption) or on a certain duty toward the natural parents assumed to have an interest in their child being brought up in their religion (in the case of the Jewish child saved by nuns).

29. I absolutely agree with Robert Adams that one's actual past is partly constitutive of what one is, of one's identity, and hence that although we often judge our life as worse than it could have been, we become so attached to the commitments and projects undertaken in its course that we do not wish to have had a different life. Adams is one of the few philosophers who explicitly refer to the gradational aspects of identity formation, for example in claiming that "the earlier a possible life branches off from one's actual life . . . the weaker the self-interest relation between them," and boldly implies that Helen Keller cannot regret her early-acquired handicap (Adams 1979, 60–61).

30. Parfit's famous case of the Russian nobleman illuminates this point from a slightly different angle. The idealistic socialist young Russian judges the predicted change in his moral profile as so drastic that from his present point of view it will not be "him" anymore. He can therefore ask his wife now not to cooperate with the requests of the "corrupt" later self who will refuse to give land to the peasants. But Parfit avoids the problem of the first-person identity of the future self, namely whether the older Russian will view himself as a different person from his younger counterpart. The retrospective view of personal identity may be different from the prospective view. Commitments and categorical desires can serve as a basis for defining our personal identity projected into the future, but be condescendingly laughed off as irrelevant in a backward looking self-identification. See Parfit 1984, 327–328.

31. Elster 1982, 233. Elster's claim that, like Nozick, he is "engaged in a polemic against end-state principles in ethical theory" (p. 238) epitomizes his skepticism regarding any attempt to solve all problems of rational choice on an *impersonal* level of ordinal or cardinal principles of utilitarianism. See Glover 1984, chap. 12. Glover does not explain why genetic and educational manipula-

tion for the enhancement of autonomy is permitted, whereas the "adjustment" of human desires for the sake of increase in overall satisfaction is prohibited.

32. One implication of a person-affecting view of identity and adaptation is that when an identity change occurs under compulsion, the fact that the life of the "new" person is "happier" cannot justify the loss of the identity or integrity of the former person; this is so not because of the superior value of identity over satisfaction, but because more satisfaction can logically be of value only on the basis of the continuity of identity. It should be noted that Elster is concerned with adaptive *preferences* rather than "adaptive identities," that is, in judging the desirability of particular adaptive preferences he presupposes the identity of a person and hence can make such judgments in terms of, for instance, the autonomy of a particular individual. See Elster 1982, 233–234. Furthermore, the context of education often involves the external creation of preferences, defined by Elster as "manipulation," rather than adaptive preference formation.

CHAPTER 7: EMPIRICAL CONSTRAINTS

1. As part of the empirical constraints on genethical choices it is worth noting the well-known fact that a higher standard of living is not only a reason for restraint in family planning and in population policies, but also a means for achieving this restraint. This serves as a powerful motive, and hope, for success in avoiding the population bomb, although it requires more concerted international effort on part of the richer world in aiding the poorer countries than the present one.

2. Laslett 1979. Laslett also notes that the overlap of generations makes the concept of generation ambiguous and vague and hence hardly a subject of rights or duties. According to Gauthier, generational overlap is the condition for intergenerational cooperation—and hence for the applicability of moral principles of saving and conservation. The overlap also secures the applicability of Gauthier's principle of "mutual unconcern" and frees intergenerational principles from their dependence on affective assumptions such as Rawls's motivational assumption (Gauthier 1986, 298–305).

3. Martin Golding argues that the fact that we know so little about the values of people in the distant future entails that we cannot know what to want for them, and hence that we had better concentrate on caring for the more immediate generations, whose welfare we have more rational tools to ensure (Golding 1972, 98). Again, despite the untenability of discounting the welfare of future people, there is a strong pragmatic reason to act on some form of a principle of social discount in planning for the future.

4. Routley, too, confuses person-affectingness with anthropocentrism. He thus claims that if only human beings are of intrinsic value then expansive population policies (ignoring the costs to the environment) become morally required (Routley 1984, 333). But a person-affecting view does not reach that antiecological conclusion, because it does not hold that the very existence of people is a good *per se* which should be promoted. On the contrary, this is the view of impersonalism. Person-affectingness is equally opposed to assigning

value both to Nature and to Mankind as such. It only argues that whereas nature can have value for people, people cannot have value for nature.

5. I refer to the famous *Gaia* hypothesis of James Lovelock, according to which biological and physical nature together form an organic system (Lovelock 1987, 152). Inanimate nature is dependent on the existence of life, and undermining life would mean harming the whole organism by destroying the homeostasis that holds the whole world together. Now even if such a wild hypothesis is proven, it has little ethical import, since even Lovelock does not ascribe volitions (in his words "sentience") to Gaia. With Aldo Leopold, who thought that nature not only has life and metabolism but also soul and consciousness it would be more difficult to argue ... See also Goodpaster 1978 who adopts a radical view granting moral status to any living entity including trees, while ignoring the distinction between needs and interests.

6. See, for instance, Scherer and Attig 1983, intro. The view proposed there is that a new ethics would be derived from a nontraditional metaphysics in which human beings are not conceived as separate entities at war with the natural world, but rather as part of nature, living in harmony with it.

7. "For we have come to a point where, if we limit our use and abuse of the environment, it is in our self-interest to do so" (De George 1979, 104). De George also hopes that in the absence of specific obligations to distant generations, the obligations we have to the immediate ones would, by transitivity, secure the interests of further generations.

8. However, even this claim may be questioned by the supposition that what nature really "wants" is that each organism pursue its own interests. I owe this point to Jan Narveson.

9. The idea of stewardship is seen by John Passmore as sufficient to deal with the ethics of man's relation to nature, and for that reason there is no need for a new ethic in the revolutionary sense first suggested by Aldo Leopold in the 1940s (Passmore 1974, 3–5). Passmore does not deal directly with the relationship between ecological and genesis problems, and hence it remains an open question whether he would be willing to endorse generocentrism, but he convincingly argues for the coherence of a nondespotic interpretation of the biblical idea of man's dominion over nature.

10. Although Hardin does not refer to the distinction between the deep and the shallow versions of ecological concern, it seems that he is closer to the shallow; for his argument is basically drawn in game-theoretic terms, and he mentions von Neumann and Morgenstern's proof that there is no unique solution to a two-variable problem (the optimum balance between the number of people and the quality of the environment). It is therefore the *irrationality* of uncontrolled population growth which calls for political restriction of procreation rather than the independent value of nature. For a critical discussion of the idea of optimum population size in empirical terms (economic and psychological) and in terms of the moral costs involved in its achievement, see Passmore 1974, 134–140.

11. For a good survey of the arguments for a new, "nonanthropocentric" ethics, although not in the context of genesis problems, see Callicott 1984.

Again we must note the recurring risk of fallaciously conflating person-affectingness with anthropocentrism (selfishness, instrumental value for humans). However, toward the end of the article, Callicott introduces a Humean approach as a solution, an approach that concedes that ethics depends on human valuers and on their feelings without claiming that the objects of these feelings must be other human beings; see especially, pp. 303–305. Tom Regan also believes that nonhuman (even inanimate) beings have moral standing because they are held by human beings to have intrinsic value. But generocentrism argues that this is a typically person-affecting ascription of value and hence cannot establish an impersonal environmental ethics as attempted by Regan (1981).

CHAPTER 8: SELF-TRANSCENDENCE AND VICARIOUS IMMORTALITY

1. In Nagel 1986, chap. 11, one can find a deep discussion of self-transcendence, the eternal human struggle to reconcile the subjective and the objective perspectives about the meaning of life, the impossible boot-strapping involved in this attempt. However, Nagel ignores genesis behavior as a unique form of engaging in that struggle. See also Partridge 1981, 204ff., where self-transcendence is presented as the basic need that explains our care for future generations in a similar way to that presented here.

2. For a good formulation of the relationship between meaning in life and integration of disparate moments by transcending the limits of an individual life, see Nozick 1981, particularly 594–600.

3. See Heyd 1983. There are many reasons that make such a prolongation of life hardly attractive. Recall Williams's Makropulos case, which highlights "the tedium of immortality."

4. The analogy between the commitment to a transgenerational project and the commitment to a personal project within an individual biography is suggested by Adams. But Adams views this commitment to the future of humanity in ethical (even religious) terms of a duty of loyalty and respect, which are typically impersonal (Adams 1989, 472–473). For a similar view, which could be interpreted in person-affecting terms, see Kavka 1978, 197. Kavka argues that a long life of gradual progress and accomplishment is superior to a life of rapid consumption and intense satisfaction on both individual and species levels.

5. In recent years MacIntyre has been a prominent advocate of an anti-individualistic ethical theory in which human values and norms can be understood only in their communal and historical setting. His emphasis on the concept of virtue is of course natural: traits of character, unlike actions, are dispositional and projective, that is, relate to a whole biography. See A. MacIntyre, *After Virtue* (Notre Dame: University of Notre Dame Press, 1981), esp. chap. 15.

6. Generations, unlike nations and families, do not have a particular identity. Their role in the first-person identity of an individual seems therefore to be weaker and more remote than that of family and nationality. However, the continuation of families and nations is intimately connected to the existence of

future generations. In that respect, our personal interest in the family and community to which we belong is the mediating motive for having descendants in general.

7. See MacLean 1983, 190ff. We have a moral interest in the welfare of posterity, but that does not mean that the person-affecting framework must be abandoned. The duty to create a better world is a self-regarding duty in the sense that it serves as a source of meaning for our own lives.

8. See Partridge 1981, 204–205. Partridge speaks specifically of obligations to future generations as stemming from the idea of self-transcendence. This idea consists of taking seriously the endurance of something that is *not* oneself, implying that the existence of a future is a necessary part of the meaning of the present. I agree with Partridge's view that human beings live on the memories of the past and with projects for the future (which is also Nietzsche's conception of human self-transcendence in his essay "Of the Use and Disadvantage of History for Life"); but this only explains why they want to have children, not why they have a duty to continue humanity. In the view proposed here, self-transcendence is itself a person-affecting value and hence cannot give rise to ethical obligations to create new people.

9. Some philosophers who follow Narveson's person-affecting view of utilitarian morality still insist on assigning value to the continuation of the species in terms of the unfinished project of *homo sapiens*. Thus, Jonathan Bennett believes that the continuation of the human race is not a moral obligation, indeed not a moral issue at all. Yet he sees it as an unprincipled (though not unstructured) personal preference, implying that the discontinuation of "this great biological and spiritual adventure" would be "a great shame—a pity, *too bad*" (Bennett 1978, 66). But Bennett's "pro-humanity stance" does not rest on the argument from the structure of meaningful human life as outlined above, but more specifically on the value of past endeavor and the shame of leaving it unfinished. The problem is that Bennett does not show why the person-affecting conception applies only to moral value and not to other sorts of values and preferences. Brian Barry also maneuvers between a person-affecting restriction on moral judgments and strong convictions regarding the "cosmic impertinence" of taking risks with the continuation of humanity. Barry admits that such a move outside the framework of ethical principles relating to human interests creates "great intellectual discomfort," but nevertheless sticks to the impersonal idea of human custody over the planet and the need for a "new ethic" (Barry 1977, 284). Again, I find this approach problematical, and I believe that the widely shared pro-humanity convictions can be better accounted for in terms of a notion of the meaningful life of actual people than in the vague terms of cosmic impertinence.

10. This double aspect of human self-transcendence is concisely formulated by Kant: "[Man] has a character which he himself creates, insofar as he is capable of perfecting himself according to the ends he himself adapts. . . . as such he first *preserves* himself and his species; secondly, he trains instructs and *educates* his species." See Kant, *Anthropology,* trans. M. Gregor (The Hague: Nijhoff, 1974) 183.

11. Annette Baier uses the language of morals when she speaks of the duty we have toward past generations not to discontinue the enterprise in which they have invested so much. It is as if we must get their permission to commit collective suicide. The view adopted here, however, denies such moral duties toward our ancestors, as we never *chose* to be born, to become members of that "cross-generational community." Furthermore, we might feel alienated from, or even opposed to, the content of the project started by our predecessors. See Baier 1981, 177–178.

12. In assigning value to the propagation of the species, Kant is speaking of what we referred to as the "replicative" dimension of human self-transcendence. But as we have already seen in chapter 2, Kant is also aware of the trans-generational aspect of the human enterprise as the condition of the moral biography of the individual. Finally, on the line of our threefold classification in this chapter, we find in Kant an attempt to interpret self-transcendence in metaphysical terms of the most general relation between man and the nonhuman world (nature, God). This is the subject of most of the discussion in the *Third Critique*.

13. For a different approach to theodicy, see Nozick 1989, chap. 19. Nozick offers various explanations for the proposition that God created the world to begin with together with the fact that there is evil in it. From the person-affecting viewpoint adopted here it seems that the reasons why, in Nozick's own opinion all these explanations fail, lie in the impersonalistic approach to the question. There is indeed no satisfactory answer to the question why an imperfect, finite, and partly evil world should be created, unless one is willing (which Nozick is not) to speak in "theocentric" terms ("good for God"). Nozick correctly draws the analogy between creating universes and creating new people (p. 229), but suggests a solution that is equally unconvincing in both cases, namely the desirability of creating an entity if it enjoys a certain minimum level of positive value ("a certain substantial level above zero"). For on what basis is this threshold decided? It is only toward the end of the discussion that Nozick proposes the answer in terms of God's *image* (which is the closest to our approach), but unsurprisingly immediately becomes concerned that this solution is "too humanocentric" (p. 235), namely, person-affecting!

14. Jonas argues that although there is no answer to the question why there *is* a world, there is an answer to the question why there *ought* to be a world (p. p. 49): "The capacity of value (worth) is itself a value, the value of all values." The mere openness to the difference between worth and worthlessness is, according to Jonas, ground for the absolute preferability of existence to nothingness. But Jonas admits that this is an "ontological axiom" and confesses that he does not know whether it is an analytic or a synthetic principle (p. 80). The flaw in Jonas's impersonalism lies in the ambiguity of the status of "the value of all values": on the one hand, the existence of the condition of all values (i.e., there being something, the existence of humanity) is considered a metaphysical principle that lies beyond ethics (p. 44); on the other hand, it is specifically referred to as a "value," and its realization as an "ought." Jonas is led to a rigid form of impersonalism through his correct critique of the theological (Leibnizian) solution to the problem of creation: God must also have had a reason, independent

of his brute will, to create the world (pp. 47–48). Furthermore, my argument is the opposite of Jonas's: even if there were an answer to the question why the world is, it would not make sense to ask why it ought to be. The metaphysical necessity of the existence of the universe does not provide an ethical explanation to it.

15. For a different view, see Nozick 1981, chap. 2 *passim*. Nozick claims that the question why there is something rather than nothing makes perfect sense, although it admits only of "strange" answers. This is not the place to argue with Nozick's elaborate (impersonalistic) approach, but much of it is indeed "strange": for example the claim that existence and inexistence can be compared in terms of their probabilities, or which of the two is more "natural" as a state (as if existence and nonexistence are predicates of states or possible states of affairs).

Bibliography

Adams, R. M. 1972. "Must God Create the Best?" *Philosophical Review* 81: 317–332.

———. 1979. "Existence, Self-Interest, and the Problem of Evil." *Nous* 13: 53–65.

———. 1989. "Should Ethics Be More Impersonal?" *Philosophical Review* 98:439–484.

Anglin, B. 1977. "The Repugnant Conclusion." *Canadian Journal of Philosophy* 7:745–754.

Anglin, W. 1978. "In Defense of the Potentiality Principle." In R. I. Sikora and B. Barry (eds.), *Obligations to Future Generations*, 31–37. Philadelphia: Temple University Press.

Attfield, R. 1983. *The Ethics of Environmental Concern.* New York: Columbia University Press.

———. 1987. *A Theory of Value and Obligation.* London: Croom Helm.

Aviram, A. 1990. "The Subjection of Children." *Journal of the Philosophy of Education* 24:213–234.

Baier, A. 1981. "The Rights of Past and Future Persons." In E. Partridge (ed.), *Responsibilities to Future Generations: Environmental Ethics*, 171–183. Buffalo: Prometheus Books.

Barry, B. 1977. "Justice Between Generations." In P. M. S. Hacker and J. Raz (eds.), *Law, Morality, and Society*, 268–284. Oxford: Clarendon Press.

———. 1978. "Circumstances of Justice and Future Generations." In R. I. Sikora and B. Barry (eds.), *Obligations to Future Generations*, 204–248. Philadelphia: Temple University Press.

———. 1983. "Intergenerational Justice in Energy Policy." In D. MacLean and P. G. Brown (eds.), *Energy and the Future*, 15–30. Totowa, N.J.: Rowman and Littlefield.

265

Bayles, M. 1975/1976. "Harm to the Unconceived." *Philosophy and Public Affairs* 5:292–304.

———. 1979. "Limits to a Right to Procreate." In O. O'Neill and W. Ruddick (eds.), *Having Children*, 13–24. New York: Oxford University Press.

———. 1980. *Morality and Population Policy*. Alabama: University of Alabama Press.

Bennett, J. 1978. "On Maximizing Happiness." In R. I. Sikora and B. Barry (eds.), *Obligations to Future Generations*, 61–73. Philadelphia: Temple University Press.

Bereiter, C. 1973. *Must We Educate?*. Englewood Cliffs, N.J.: Prentice-Hall.

Bickham, S. 1981. "Future Generations and Contemporary Ethical Theory." *Journal of Value Inquiry* 15:169–177.

Bloch, S., and Heyd, D. 1981. "The Ethics of Suicide." In S. Bloch and P. Chodoff (eds.), *Psychiatric Ethics*, 185–202. Oxford: Oxford University Press.

Bond, E. J. 1988. " 'Good' and 'Good for': A Reply to Hurka." *Mind* 97:279–280.

Burgess, J. P. 1978. "The Unreal Future." *Theoria* 44:157–174.

Burke, E. 1968. *Reflections on the Revolution in France*. Harmondsworth: Penguin.

Callicott, J. Baird. 1984. "Non-Anthropocentric Value Theory and Environmental Ethics." *American Philosophical Quarterly* 21:299–309.

Chadwick, R. 1982. "Cloning." *Philosophy* 57:201–209.

———. (ed.) 1987. *Ethics, Reproduction and Genetic Control*. London: Croom Helm.

Cohen, J. 1989. "*Be Fertile and Multiply, Fill the Earth and Master It*". Ithaca: Cornell University Press.

Crocker, L. 1979. "Meddling with the Sexual Orientation of Children." In O. O'Neill and W. Ruddick (eds.), *Having Children*, 145–154. New York: Oxford University Press.

Daniels, N. 1979*a*. "Wide Reflective Equilibrium and Theory Acceptance in Ethics." *Journal of Philosophy* 76:256–282.

———. 1979*b*. "Moral Theory and the Plasticity of Persons." *Monist* 62:265–287.

———. 1980. "Reflective Equilibrium and Archimedean Points." *Canadian Journal of Philosophy* 10:83–103.

Dasgupta, P. 1969. "On the Concept of Optimum Population." *Review of Economic Studies* 36:295–318.

———. 1974. "On Optimum Population Size." In A. Mitra (ed.), *Economic Theory and Planning*, 109–133. Calcutta: Oxford University Press.

———. 1987. "The Ethical Foundations of Population Policies." In D. Gale Johnson and Ronald D. Lee (eds.), *Population Growth and Economic Development*, 631–659. Madison: University of Wisconsin Press.

———. 1988. "Lives and Well-Being." *Social Choice and Welfare* 5:103–126.

De George, R. T. 1979. "The Environment, Rights, and Future Generations." In K. E. Goodpaster and K. M. Sayre (eds.), *Ethics and Problems of the 21st Century*, 93–105. Notre Dame: University of Notre Dame Press.

Delattre, E. 1971/1972. "Rights, Responsibilities, and Future Persons." *Ethics* 82:254–258.

Dworkin, R. M. 1973. "The Original Position." *University of Chicago Law Review* 40:500–533.

———. 1977. "Justice and Rights." In R. M. Dworkin, *Taking Rights Seriously*, 150–183. Cambridge, Mass.: Harvard University Press.

Elster, J. 1979. *Ulysses and the Sirens*. Cambridge: Cambridge University Press.

———. 1982. "Sour Grapes." In A. Sen and B. Williams (eds.), *Utilitarianism and Beyond*, 219–238. Cambridge: Cambridge University Press.

English, J. 1977. "Justice Between Generations." *Philosophical Studies* 31:91–104.

Feinberg, J. 1980. "Is There a Right To Be Born?" In J. Feinberg (ed.), *Rights, Justice, and the Bounds of Liberty*, 207–220. Princeton: Princeton University Press.

———. 1984. *Harm to Others*. New York: Oxford University Press.

Floyd, S. L., and Pomerantz, D. 1981. "Is There a Natural Right to Have Children?" In A. Arthur (ed.), *Morality and Moral Controversies*, 131–138. Englewood Cliffs, N.J.: Prentice-Hall.

Foot, P. 1978. "The Problem of Abortion and the Doctrine of the Double Effect." In P. Foot (ed.), *Virtues and Vices*, 19–32. Oxford: Basil Blackwell.

Frondizi, R. 1971. *What Is Value?* La Salle, Ill.: Open Court.

Galston, W. A. 1980. *Justice and the Human Good*. Chicago: University of Chicago Press.

Gauthier, D. 1986. *Morals by Agreement*. Oxford: Clarendon Press.

George, R. 1987. "Who Should Bear the Cost of Children?" *Public Affairs Quarterly* 1:1–42.

Glover, J. 1979. "How Should We Decide What Sort of World Is Best?" In K. E. Goodpaster and K. M. Sayre (eds.), *Ethics and Problems of the 21st Century*, 79–92. Notre Dame: University of Notre Dame Press.

———. 1984. *What Sort of People Should There Be?* Harmondsworth: Penguin.

Golding, M. P. 1972. "Obligations to Future Generations." *Monist* 56:85–99.

Goodpaster, K. E. 1978. "On Being Morally Considerable." *Journal of Philosophy* 75:308–325.

Govier, T. 1979. "What Should We Do About Future People?" *American Philosophical Quarterly* 16:105–113.

Griffin, J. 1986. *Well-Being*. Oxford: Clarendon Press.

Gutmann, A. 1987. *Democratic Education*. Princeton: Princeton University Press.

Hanser, M. 1990. "Harming Future People." *Philosophy and Public Affairs* 19:47–70.

Hardin, G. 1968. "The Tragedy of the Commons." *Science* 162:1243–1248.

———. 1981. "Who Cares for Posterity?" In E. Partridge (ed.), *Responsibilities to Future Generations: Environmental Ethics*, 221–234. Buffalo: Prometheus Books.

Hare, R. M. 1974/1975. "Abortion and the Golden Rule." *Philosophy and Public Affairs* 4:201–222.

Henley, K. 1979. "The Authority to Educate." In O. O'Neill and W. Ruddick (eds.), *Having Children*, 254–264. New York: Oxford University Press.

Heyd, D. 1982. *Supererogation: Its Status in Ethical Theory*. Cambridge: Cambridge University Press.

———. 1983. "Is Life Worth Reliving?" *Mind* 92:21–37.

———. 1986. "Are 'Wrongful Life' Claims Philosophically Valid?" *Israel Law Review* 21:574–590.

———. 1988. "Procreation and Value: Can Ethics Deal With Futurity Problems?" *Philosophia* 18:151–170.

Hoffman, L. W., and Hoffman, M. L. 1973. "The Value of Children to Parents." In J. T. Fawcett (ed.), *Psychological Perspectives on Population*, 19–76. New York: Basic Books.

Hubin, D. Clayton. 1976/1977. "Justice and Future Generations." *Philosophy and Public Affairs* 6:70–83.

Hurka, T. 1983. "Value and Population Size." *Ethics* 93:496–507.

———. 1987. " 'Good' and 'Good For'." *Mind* 96:71–3.

Hutchinson, D. S. 1982. "Utilitarianism and Children." *Canadian Journal of Philosophy* 12:61–73.

James, W. 1949. "The Moral Philosopher and the Moral Life." In W. James, *Essays on Faith and Morals*, 184–215. New York: Longman's.

Jecker, N. 1987a. "Reproductive Risk Taking and the Nonidentity Problem." *Social Theory and Practice* 13:219–235.

———. 1987b. "The Ascription of Rights in Wrongful Life Suits." *Law and Philosophy* 6:149–165.

———. 1989. "Are Filial Duties Unfounded?" *American Philosophical Quarterly* 26:73–80.

Jonas, H. 1984. *The Imperative of Responsibility*. Chicago: The University of Chicago Press.

Jones, H. 1976. "Genetic Endowment and Obligations to Future Generations." *Social Theory and Practice* 4:29–46.

Kant, I. 1928. *Critique of Judgment* (trans. J. C. Meredith). Oxford: Clarendon Press.

———. 1934. *Religion Within the Limits of Reason Alone* (trans. T. M. Greene and H. H. Hudson). Chicago: Chicago University Press.

———. 1963a. "Idea for a Universal History from a Cosmopolitan Point of View." In *On History* (trans. L. W. Beck). Indianapolis: Bobbs-Merrill.

———. 1963b. *Lectures on Ethics* (trans. L. Infield). New York: Harper and Row.

Karin-Frank, S. 1987. "Genetic Engineering and the Autonomous Individual." In J. D. G. Evans (ed.), *Moral Philosophy and Contemporary Problems*, 213–229. Cambridge: Cambridge University Press.

Kavka, G. S. 1978. "The Futurity Problem." In R. I. Sikora and B. Barry (eds.), *Obligations to Future Generations*, 180–203. Philadelphia: Temple University Press.

———. 1982. "The Paradox of Future Individuals." *Philosophy and Public Affairs* 11:93–112.

Korsgaard, C. M. 1983. "Two Distinctions in Goodness." *Philosophical Review* 92:169–195.

———. 1989. "Personal Identity and the Unity of Agency: A Kantian Response to Parfit." *Philosophy and Public Affairs* 18:101–132.

Lafollette, H. 1980. "Licensing Parents." *Philosophy and Public Affairs* 9: 182–197.

Laslett, P. 1979. "The Conversation Between Generations." In P. Laslett and J. Fishkin (eds.), *Politics and Society* (fifth series), 36–56. New Haven: Yale University Press.

Leslie, J. 1983. "Why Not Let Life Become Extinct?" *Philosophy* 58:329–338.

———. 1989. "The Need to Generate Happy People." *Philosophia* 19:29–33.

Lovejoy, A. O. 1936. *The Great Chain of Being.* Cambridge, Mass.: Harvard University Press.

Lovelock, J. 1987. *Gaia: A New Look at Life on Earth.* London: Oxford University Press.

Mackie, J. L. 1978. "Can There Be a Right-Based Moral Theory?" *Midwest Studies in Philosophy* 3:350–359.

Macklin, R. 1979. "Parents and Genetic Counselors: Moral Issues." In O. O'Neill and W. Ruddick (eds.), *Having Children,* 80–95. New York: Oxford University Press.

MacLean, D. 1983. "A Moral Requirement of Energy Policies." In D. MacLean and P. G. Brown (eds.), *Energy and the Future,* 180–197. Totowa, N.J.: Rowman and Littlefield.

McMahan, J. 1981/1982. "Problems of Population Theory." *Ethics* 92:96–127.

Miller, F., and Sartorius, R. 1978/1979. "Population Policy and Public Goods." *Philosophy and Public Affairs* 8:148–174.

Naess, A. 1973. "The Shallow and the Deep Long-Range Ecology Movement: A Summary." *Inquiry* 16:95–100.

Nagel, T. 1986. *The View from Nowhere.* New York: Oxford University Press.

Narveson, J. 1967. "Utilitarianism and New Generations." *Mind* 76:62–72.

———. 1973. "Moral Problems of Population." *Monist* 57:62–86.

———. 1978. "Future People and Us." In R. I. Sikora and B. Barry (eds.), *Obligations to Future Generations,* 38–60. Philadelphia: Temple University Press.

Ng, Yew-Kwang. 1989. "What Should We Do about Future Generations?" *Economics and Philosophy* 5:235–253.

Nielsen, K. 1973. "The Enforcement of Morality and Future Generations." *Philosophia* 3:443–448.

———. 1982. "Grounding Rights and the Method of Reflective Equilibrium." *Inquiry* 25:277–306.

Nozick, R. 1981. *Philosophical Explanations.* Cambridge, Mass.: Harvard University Press.

———. 1989. *The Examined Life.* New York: Simon and Schuster.

O'Neill, O., and Ruddick, W. (eds.). 1979. *Having Children.* New York: Oxford University Press.

Parfit, D. 1973. "Later Selves and Moral Principles." In A. Montefiore (ed.), *Philosophy and Personal Relations*, 137–169. London: Routledge.

———. 1976a. "On Doing the Best for Our Children." In M. D. Bayles (ed.), *Ethics and Population*, 100–115. Cambridge, Mass.: Schenkman.

———. 1976b. "Rights, Interests, and Possible People." In S. Gorovitz (ed.), *Moral Problems in Medicine*, 369–375. Englewood Cliffs, N.J.: Prentice-Hall.

———. 1977/1978. "Innumerate Ethics." *Philosophy and Public Affairs* 7: 285–301.

———. 1982. "Future Generations: Further Problems." *Philosophy and Public Affairs* 11:113–172.

———. 1983. "Energy Policy and the Further Future." In D. MacLean and P. G. Brown (eds.), *Energy and the Future*, 31–37; 166–179. Totowa, N.J.: Rowman and Littlefield.

———. 1984. *Reasons and Persons*. Oxford: Clarendon Press.

———. 1986. "Overpopulation and the Quality of Life." In P. Singer (ed.), *Applied Ethics*, 145–164. Oxford: Oxford University Press.

Partridge, E. (ed.). 1981. *Responsibilities to Future Generations: Environmental Ethics*. Buffalo: Prometheus Books.

Passmore, J. 1974. *Man's Responsibility for Nature*. London: Duckworth.

Perry, R. B. 1926. *General Theory of Value*. New York: Longman's.

Rawls, J. 1971. *A Theory of Justice*. Cambridge, Mass.: Harvard University Press.

Raz, J. 1982. "The Claims of Reflective Equilibrium." *Inquiry* 25:307–330.

———. 1986. *The Morality of Freedom*. Oxford: Clarendon Press.

Regan, T. 1981. "The Nature and Possibility of an Environmental Ethic." *Environmental Ethics* 3:19–34.

Richards, D. A. J. 1983. "Contractarian Theory, Intergenerational Justice, and Energy Policy." In D. MacLean and P. G. Brown (eds.), *Energy and the Future*, 131–150. Totowa, N.J.: Rowman and Littlefield.

Rorty, A. O. (ed.). 1976. *The Identities of Persons*. Berkeley, Los Angeles, London: University of California Press.

Rosenbaum, S. E. 1989/1990. "The Symmetry Argument: Lucretius against the Fear of Death." *Philosophical and Phenomenological Research* 50:353–373.

Roupas, T. G. 1977/1978. "The Value of Life." *Philosophy and Public Affairs* 7:154–183.

Routley, R. 1984. "People vs. the Land: The Ethics of the Population Case." In R. Birrell et al. (eds.), *Populate and Perish?*, 325–351. Sydney: Fontana.

Routley, R., and Routley, V. 1978. "Nuclear Energy and Obligations to the Future." *Inquiry* 21:133–179.

Sanders, J. T. 1988. "Why the Numbers Should Sometimes Count." *Philosophy and Public Affairs* 17:3–14.

Scherer, D., and Attig, T. 1983. *Ethics and the Environment*. Englewood Cliffs, N.J.: Prentice-Hall.

Schwartz, T. 1978. "Obligations to Posterity." In R. I. Sikora and B. Barry (eds.), *Obligations to Future Generations*, 3–13. Philadelphia: Temple University Press.

Sher, G. 1976/1977. "Hare, Abortion, and the Golden Rule." *Philosophy and Public Affairs* 6:185–190.

Sidgwick, H. 1907. *The Methods of Ethics.* London: Macmillan.

Sikora, R. I. 1978. "Is It Wrong to Prevent the Existence of Future Generations?" In R. I. Sikora and B. Barry (eds.), *Obligations to Future Generations,* 112–166. Philadelphia: Temple University Press.

———. 1979. "Utilitarianism, Supererogation and Future Generations." *Canadian Journal of Philosophy* 9:461–466.

Singer, P. 1976. "A Utilitarian Population Principle." In M. Bayles (ed.), *Ethics and Population,* 81–99. Cambridge, Mass.: Schenkman.

———. 1981. *The Expanding Circle.* New York: Farrar, Strauss, and Giroux.

Singer, S. Fred (ed.). 1971. *Is There an Optimum Level of Population?* New York: McGraw-Hill.

Smart, J. J. C. 1961. *Outline of a System of Utilitarian Ethics.* Melbourne: Melbourne University Press.

Smart, R. N. 1958. "Negative Utilitarianism." *Mind* 67:542–543.

Sprigge, T. L. S. 1968. "Professor Narveson's Utilitarianism." *Inquiry* 11: 332–346.

Stearns, J. B. 1972. "Ecology and the Indefinite Unborn." *Monist* 56:612–625.

Sterba, J. P. 1980. "Abortion, Distant Peoples, and Future Generations." *Journal of Philosophy* 77:424–440.

Sumner, L. W. 1978. "Classical Utilitarianism and the Population Optimum." In R. I. Sikora and B. Barry (eds.), *Obligations to Future Generations,* 91–111. Philadelphia: Temple University Press.

———. 1986. "Subjectivity and Moral Standing." In W. Sumner et al. (eds.), *Values and Moral Standing,* 1–15. Bowling Green Studies in Applied Philosophy, vol. VIII.

Surber, J. P. 1977. "Obligations to Future Generations." *Journal of Value Inquiry* 11:104–116.

Taurek, J. M. 1976/1977. "Should the Numbers Count?" *Philosophy and Public Affairs* 6:293–316.

Tedeschi, G. 1966. "On Tort Liability for 'Wrongful Life'." *Israel Law Review* 1:513–538.

Tooley, M. 1983. *Abortion and Infanticide.* Oxford: Clarendon Press.

Vetter, H. 1971. "Utilitarianism and New Generations." *Mind* 80:301–302.

Warren, M. A. 1977. "Do Potential People Have Moral Rights?" *Canadian Journal of Philosophy* 7:275–289.

Williams, B. 1973. *Problems of the Self.* Cambridge: Cambridge University Press.

Woodward, J. 1985/1986. "The Non-Identity Problem." *Ethics* 96:804–831.

Yourgrau, P. 1987. "The Dead." *Journal of Philosophy* 84:84–101.

Yovel, Y. 1980. *Kant and the Philosophy of History.* Princeton: Princeton University Press.

Zemach, E. M. 1987/1988. "Looking Out for Number One." *Philosophy and Phenomenological Research* 48:209–233.

Index